VOLUME 571

SEPTEMBER 2000

THE ANNALS

of The American Academy *of* Political
and Social Science

ALAN W. HESTON, *Editor*
NEIL A. WEINER, *Assistant Editor*

FEMINIST VIEWS OF
THE SOCIAL SCIENCES

Special Editor of this Volume
CHRISTINE L. WILLIAMS
University of Texas
Austin

 Sage Publications, Inc. *THOUSAND OAKS LONDON NEW DELHI*

The American Academy of Political and Social Science

3937 Chestnut Street   Philadelphia, Pennsylvania 19104

Origin and Purpose. The Academy was organized December 14, 1889, to promote the progress of political and social science, especially through publications and meetings. The Academy does not take sides in controverted questions, but seeks to gather and present reliable information to assist the public in forming an intelligent and accurate judgment.

Meetings. The Academy occasionally holds a meeting in the spring extending over two days.

Publications. THE ANNALS of the American Academy of Political and Social Science is the bi-monthly publication of The Academy. Each issue contains articles on some prominent social or political problem, written at the invitation of the editors. Also, monographs are published from time to time, numbers of which are distributed to pertinent professional organizations. These volumes constitute important reference works on the topics with which they deal, and they are extensively cited by authorities throughout the United States and abroad. The papers presented at the meetings of The Academy are included in THE ANNALS.

Membership. Each member of The Academy receives THE ANNALS and may attend the meetings of The Academy. Membership is open only to individuals. Annual dues: $61.00 for the regular paperbound edition (clothbound, $90.00). Add $12.00 per year for membership outside the U.S.A. Members may also purchase single issues of THE ANNALS for $14.00 each (clothbound, $19.00). Add $2.00 for shipping and handling on all prepaid orders.

Subscriptions. THE ANNALS of the American Academy of Political and Social Science (ISSN 0002-7162) is published six times annually—in January, March, May, July, September, and November. Institutions may subscribe to THE ANNALS at the annual rate: $327.00 (clothbound, $372.00). Add $12.00 per year for subscriptions outside the U.S.A. Institutional rates for single issues: $59.00 each (clothbound, $66.00).

Periodicals postage paid at Thousand Oaks, California, and at additional mailing offices.

Single issues of THE ANNALS may be obtained by individuals who are not members of The Academy for $20.00 each (clothbound, $31.00). Add $2.00 for shipping and handling on all prepaid orders. Single issues of THE ANNALS have proven to be excellent supplementary texts for classroom use. Direct inquiries regarding adoptions to THE ANNALS c/o Sage Publications (address below).

All correspondence concerning membership in The Academy, dues renewals, inquiries about membership status, and/or purchase of single issues of THE ANNALS should be sent to THE ANNALS c/o Sage Publications, Inc., 2455 Teller Road, Thousand Oaks, CA 91320. Telephone: (805) 499-0721; FAX/Order line: (805) 499-0871. *Please note that orders under $30 must be prepaid.* Sage affiliates in London and India will assist institutional subscribers abroad with regard to orders, claims, and inquiries for both subscriptions and single issues.

Printed on recycled, acid-free paper

THE ANNALS
© 2000 by The American Academy *of* Political *and* Social Science

Editorial Office: 3937 Chestnut Street, Philadelphia, PA 19104.

For information about membership* (individuals only) and subscriptions (institutions), address:

SAGE PUBLICATIONS, INC.
2455 Teller Road
Thousand Oaks, CA 91320

Sage Production Staff: MARIA NOTARANGELO, KATE PETERSON, DORIS HUS, and ROSE TYLAK

From India and South Asia, *write to:*		*From Europe, the Middle East,* *and Africa, write to:*
SAGE PUBLICATIONS INDIA Pvt. Ltd		SAGE PUBLICATIONS LTD
P.O. Box 4215		6 Bonhill Street
New Delhi 110 048		London EC2A 4PU
INDIA		UNITED KINGDOM

*Please note that members of The Academy receive THE ANNALS with their membership.
International Standard Serial Number ISSN 0002-7162
International Standard Book Number ISBN 0-7619-2274-1 (Vol. 571, 2000 paper)
International Standard Book Number ISBN 0-7619-2273-3 (Vol. 571, 2000 cloth)
Manufactured in the United States of America. First printing, September 2000.

The articles appearing in the ANNALS are abstracted or indexed in *Academic Abstracts, Academic Search, America: History and Life, Asia Pacific Database, Book Review Index, CAB Abstracts Database, Central Asia: Abstracts & Index, Communication Abstracts, Corporate ResourceNET, Criminal Justice Abstracts, Current Citations Express, Current Contents: Social & Behavioral Sciences, e-JEL, EconLit, Expanded Academic Index, Guide to Social Science & Religion in Periodical Literature, Health Business FullTEXT, HealthSTAR FullTEXT, Historical Abstracts, International Bibliography of the Social Sciences, International Political Science Abstracts, ISI Basic Social Sciences Index, Journal of Economic Literature on CD, LEXIS-NEXIS, MasterFILE FullTEXT, Middle East: Abstracts & Index, North Africa: Abstracts & Index, PAIS International, Periodical Abstracts, Political Science Abstracts, Sage Public Administration Abstracts, Social Science Source, Social Sciences Citation Index, Social Sciences Index Full Text, Social Services Abstracts, Social Work Abstracts, Sociological Abstracts, Southeast Asia: Abstracts & Index, Standard Periodical Directory (SPD), TOPICsearch, Wilson OmniFile V,* and *Wilson Social Sciences Index/Abstracts,* and are available on microfilm from University Microfilms, Ann Arbor, Michigan.

Information about membership rates, institutional subscriptions, and back issue prices may be found on the facing page.

Advertising. Current rates and specifications may be obtained by writing to THE ANNALS Advertising and Promotion Manager at the Thousand Oaks office (address above).

Claims. Claims for undelivered copies must be made no later than six months following month of publication. The publisher will supply missing copies when losses have been sustained in transit and when the reserve stock will permit.

Change of Address. Six weeks advance notice must be given when notifying of change of address to ensure proper identification. Please specify name of journal. **POSTMASTER:** Send address changes to: THE ANNALS of the American Academy of Political and Social Science, c/o Sage Publications, Inc., 2455 Teller Road, Thousand Oaks, CA 91320.

THE ANNALS

of The American Academy of Political
and Social Science

ALAN W. HESTON, *Editor*
NEIL A. WEINER, *Assistant Editor*

--- FORTHCOMING ---

See page 2 for information on Academy membership and
purchase of single volumes of **The Annals.**

CONTENTS

BOOK DEPARTMENT CONTENTS

INTERNATIONAL RELATIONS AND POLITICS

AFRICA, ASIA, AND LATIN AMERICA

EUROPE

UNITED STATES

PREFACE

Among the many achievements of the feminist movement of the 1970s was the unprecedented influx of women into academia. The social sciences were a major beneficiary of this effort. Over the last 25 years, women have entered the social sciences in huge numbers. Among these new entrants are many feminists who have introduced novel ways of understanding and studying the social world. Although the impact of feminism varies widely, every one of the social science disciplines has been touched by the feminist movement. From anthropology to geography to sociology, feminist scholars have reached the highest rungs of their disciplines: feminists are now chairs of major departments, holders of endowed professorships, and even presidents of professional associations. Several social science journals are now devoted exclusively to feminist theory and research. In some fields, graduate students are third-generation feminists; they can be overheard reflecting on the influences of their feminist "grandmothers." Feminism is so strong in a few areas that it has inspired backlashes, with prominent academics expending a great deal of time and energy trying to debunk feminist perspectives.

This special issue of *The Annals* reports on this revolution in progress. I invited several leading and up-and-coming feminist researchers to reflect on the most significant insights and contributions of feminism to their fields of study. About half of the authors discuss the impact of feminism on their academic disciplines, including anthropology, archaeology, criminology, geography, political science, and psychology. The others discuss feminism's influence on specific social science topics, including studies of the mass media, work, migration, sexuality, and family. These somewhat idiosyncratic choices, based largely on my personal interests and background in sociology, led me to an unanticipated observation: it seems that feminism has had the strongest impact on fields that are open to interdisciplinary research. Where reigning paradigms are strong and the range of accepted methodologies is limited, feminist perspectives tend to be marginalized. On the other hand, fields that are theoretically eclectic and interdisciplinary appear to be the most welcoming to feminist influence.

This is but one of several general impressions I garnered from the insightful articles that are collected in this volume. In this introduction, I will draw out two more specific themes that emerged from my reading of these works: first, the relationship between feminist scholarship and feminist activism; and, second, the ongoing controversies and future directions of feminist social science. Since this entire volume is devoted to feminism, I will begin by defining what feminism means to social scientists.

It was surprising to me that few of the authors attempted to define feminism themselves. This may be a sign of the successful incorporation of feminist perspectives into the canon of social science. Perhaps feminism is taken for granted now; perhaps everyone already knows what it means. Alternatively, the absence of a definition might reflect the authors' reluctance to speak for a movement that is characterized by multivocal, richly textured, and dynamic debates. In many ways, feminism is a movement that refuses to be pinned down, even by its proponents.

In general, feminist social scientists are referring to two things when we use the term "feminism." First and foremost, we refer to the social movement begun in the 1970s to demand equal rights, respect, and opportunities for women throughout society. This feminist movement is sometimes referred to as the "second wave" in acknowledgment of the first U.S. feminist movement, devoted to gaining women's suffrage in the late nineteenth and early twentieth centuries. Many women academics today see themselves as beneficiaries of the second wave because it successfully challenged several of the barriers to women in male-dominated careers.

"Feminism" is also used to describe a general approach to understanding the status of women in society. In lieu of theories that consider all differences between men and women either as biological or as socially necessary, feminists maintain that gender differences reflect unequal power arrangements in society, in particular, a social system in which men and masculine qualities are more highly valued and privileged than women and femininity. The various social science disciplines specify different mechanisms in the reproduction of this inequality. For instance, psychologists tend to look at the development and attribution of personality characteristics; geographers examine the allocation and control of space; criminologists focus on how gender shapes social definitions of deviance. Although there is a wide range of theoretical sophistication among the different specialties, all feminist social scientists share the goals of understanding the sources of this inequality and advocating changes to empower women.

FEMINIST ACTIVISM

These two meanings of feminism are linked in the works of many feminist social scientists. Several of the articles in the present collection draw connections between feminist activism and feminist research in the academy. Many of the authors point to how social science research has been used to further the interests of women in society. In criminology, for example, feminist research on violence against women has been used to rally public support for funding battered women's shelters and domestic abuse hotlines in many communities. Feminist psychologists practically invented the term "sexual harassment"; their research on the topic demonstrated its pervasiveness and its serious consequences for working women, resulting in greater organizational and legal attention to the problem. Feminist economists and other scholars who study work have successfully documented the contours of the wage gap, providing strong support for public policies such as affirmative action and pay equity.

In some fields, feminist research has been directly influenced by feminist activism. This is true in psychology, where feminist consciousness-raising sessions inspired changes in therapeutic practice. Feminist critiques of the mass media were fueled in part by feminist protests against the stereotypical depictions of women on television and in advertising. These critiques in turn have resulted in demands for better representation of women in the culture industry. In anthropology, feminist field-workers have been known to reshape their interests and commitments according to the concerns of the women they study. Some feminist archaeologists are partnering with descendant peoples in order to preserve the latter's cultural heritage.

These links to activism have made feminist social scientists into pariahs in some fields, especially in those that place a high value on objectivity, neutrality, and the other trappings of positive science. Feminists have found that having an applied, activist agenda can undermine their professional status and scientific credibility. As geographers Lynn Staeheli and Patricia Martin put it, practice takes a beating in academia. Such applied research is rarely published in the top journals. Political scientists Gretchen Ritter and Nicole Mellow note that explicitly feminist work in their field appears only in specialty journals that reach narrow audiences; the top journals rarely publish research on gender unless the focus is on documenting differences in men's and women's political behavior—an approach that often fails to challenge conventional understandings of politics. Archaeologist Kelley Hays-Gilpin recalls learning, as a graduate student in the 1970s, that the key to success was to think and act like a man. She laments that even today many in her profession resist calling themselves feminist out of concern that their research will be labeled unscientific.

Some have responded to this generic suspicion toward feminist activism in the academy with stealthiness. It is not uncommon for feminists in the social sciences to eschew the label entirely, with consequences that are not entirely bad. Psychologist Judith Worell claims that feminist psychology has been most successful at infiltrating the mainstream canon when it has not been labeled as such. According to Judith Auerbach, who directs a social science research division of the federal government, by avoiding the term "feminism" and by pitching their ideas to appeal to the paternalism of lawmakers, social scientists have been able to secure funding for feminist research that has directly influenced public policy.

In addition to concerns about politics and activism, there are many other reasons why pockets in the academy remain hostile to explicitly feminist work. Among the factors identified by the authors in this collection are the continued overrepresentation of men in top positions, the prioritizing of areas of inquiry that ignore gender, and the hegemony of certain research methodologies (especially the exclusive use of statistical procedures) that make it difficult to recognize alternative standpoints. Overcoming these barriers will be a major challenge facing feminist social science in the future.

CONTROVERSIES IN FEMINIST SOCIAL SCIENCE

This collection is entitled "Feminist Views of the Social Sciences" to emphasize that not all feminists see the social world in the same way. Part of what draws scholars to feminist research is the dynamic and often intense debates that have characterized the endeavor from the start. Although it is common to hear references to "the feminist perspective" as if it were one thing, every one of the fields represented here contains a variety of feminist perspectives, which sometimes clash in unanticipated ways.

Several of the authors in this collection identify a tension between their goal to research and advocate on behalf of women, and their capacity to faithfully reflect the viewpoints and interests of other women. Academic women researchers occupy a rather privileged position in society; often our interests are at odds with those of the women we study and supposedly try to help. This tension is addressed most poignantly by anthropologist Ravina Aggarwal, who discusses some of the overtly racist practices of previous generations of feminist anthropologists and the uneasy relationships between contemporary anthropologists and the members of the cultures they study. She tells one story of a feminist anthropologist who was castigated by a respondent when presented with the book that resulted from her fieldwork: "Your book has no importance," she was told. Insights garnered through feminist social science research do not necessarily address or reflect the interests of the studied population. In fact, some anthropologists and geographers today have concluded that all fieldwork is an expression of unilateral Western hegemony.

This tension between feminist researchers and our intended constituency is also discussed in the article on family studies by sociologist Maxine Baca Zinn. She argues that early feminist critiques of the family as a hotbed of patriarchal oppression resulted in a largely unintended devaluation of the social support that many women, especially women of color, derived from their family lives. Instead of having their consciousness raised, some women responded to this critique by abandoning feminism, which they perceived as undermining their struggle against racism and other forms of social oppression.

In some cases, the authors lament not that feminist social science research is ignored or deemed irrelevant but that it is misappropriated in ways that bolster existing gender stereotypes. Hays-Gilpin points to the popularization of ancient goddess worship as an example. Although this topic has enormous popular appeal to feminists outside the academy, feminist scholars believe that it is based on inaccurate and incomplete understandings of the archaeological record. Similarly, Worell reports that popular psychology books on male-female relationships often exaggerate scholarly claims and may result in a greater reification of gender differences. Even other scholars are sometimes guilty of this misappropriation. Staeheli and Martin point out that feminists in a variety of disciplines have begun to use several terms from geography, including "space," "mapping," and "boundaries"—but without the careful, nuanced meanings attached to these terms by geographers.

Of course, no scholar can control all uses and interpretations of her research. But this may be an especially difficult problem for feminists because our work is often misrepresented or cast in unflattering light by the popular media, as Lynn Chancer describes. She notes that the press often pits factions of feminists against each other when it reports on issues like pornography and prostitution, undermining efforts to communicate across acrimonious divides. Feminist social scientists clearly need to do a better job of communicating our theories and research to others if we are to be at all effective at accomplishing our activist goals.

Several of the articles suggest possible avenues for such improvement. Auerbach, for example, calls for feminist scholars to avoid jargon and to translate their research problems and issues into more accessible language. Several others endorse interdisciplinary and collaborative research. Existing disciplinary boundaries tend to balkanize the social world into discrete analytical categories that bear little resemblance to people's lived experience in the social world. As Pierrette Hondagneu-Sotelo and Craig Watkins and Rana Emerson point out, some of the most pressing social issues today—the mass migration and displacement of populations, the effects of economic globalization, the widening of the gap between rich and poor—cannot be fully understood from the vantage point of a single discipline, especially not one that was constituted at the last turn of the century, when the social world was vastly different. It is hoped that projects such as this special issue of *The Annals* will enhance the dialogue between disciplines and inspire more fruitful cross-disciplinary collaboration.

Even within a single field, researchers too often have to make choices that result in prioritizing certain forms of social organization and ignoring others, resulting in inadequate and incomplete understandings of the social world. Scholars of work and of crime, for example, often are forced to choose between studying gender and studying race, class, or other forms of social domination, when, in fact, all of these operate together in the social world. Dana Britton attributes these divisions in criminology in part to outmoded methodological procedures used in the collection of official statistics. Feminists have been at the forefront of methodological innovation in a variety of fields—most notably, anthropology—but more work is needed. Garnering greater recognition for these efforts is an ongoing challenge that feminists scholars will continue to face in the future.

Finally, enhancing the relevance and the accessibility of feminist scholarship will require a renewed commitment to mentoring the future generations of feminist researchers. The academy is still too white, too male, and too middle class. If we are to continue to produce meaningful research, the doors to the academy must be pushed open more widely to include nontraditional students in our graduate programs. We should endeavor to incorporate more varied curricula and advanced technologies in our pedagogy that are capable of reaching out to those whose interests have been underrepresented in social science research. Archaeology and geography present innovative models that other disciplines might follow. Just as the feminist movement of the 1970s revolutionized the social sciences, the third wave of feminism, in the new millennium, brings hope for more exciting and invigorating changes ahead.

ACKNOWLEDGMENTS

In the best style of feminist social science, this collection represents a truly collaborative effort. Its successful completion depended most on the diligence and care of the authors, who always responded with goodwill and grace to my myriad requests. Among the many lessons they taught me is that feminism is thriving all over the social sciences, and for that I feel renewed and grateful. I also thank the scholars to whom I turned for insider reviews of the articles: Rebecca Bigler, Meenakshi Gigi Durham, Nancy Jurik, Irene Padavic, Patricia Richards, Debra Umberson, Kamala Visweswaran, Jennifer Wolch, and Alison Wylie.

CHRISTINE L. WILLIAMS

ANNALS, *AAPSS*, **571**, September 2000

Traversing Lines of Control: Feminist Anthropology Today

By RAVINA AGGARWAL

ABSTRACT: Feminist anthropology has been a forerunner in debates about power differentials between those observing and those being observed. This article explores how theoretical interventions made by third-wave feminists have led to revisions of the canon, particularly in the understandings of methodology (fieldwork), subject matter (culture), and ethnographic writing. It also highlights some of the problems of placing gender at the center of experience, over differences based on race, class, or sexual orientation. While some feminists have pointed to the impossibility of an ethical feminist anthropology, others have suggested that interdisciplinary ideas and linkages outside academia can lead to greater participation in public policymaking and social struggles that affect the lives of women being studied.

Ravina Aggarwal teaches creative ethnography, critiques of travel, and political and feminist anthropology at Smith College. Having worked in Ladakh, India, for several years, she is committed to socially conscious research and educational reform and has just translated a book of short stories from Urdu called About That Forsaken Paradise. *Currently, she is working on the completion of her book,* Ibex Hunters and Turquoise Trails: Hybridity and Marginality on the Borders of Ladakh, India.

NOTE: The author is grateful to Frederique Apffel-Marglin, Kamala Visweswaran, Christopher Wheeler, and Christine Williams for their suggestions.

A few weeks ago, I attended a lecture in the Ladakh Himalayas in North India about the impact of globalization on the traditional culture of the region. Addressing an audience primarily comprising Western tourists, the speaker, a famous European environmentalist, remarked, "Unlike anthropologists who look to criticize minute details of a culture, we are looking at the overall positive aspects of it." She went on to discuss the importance of the indigenous women's alliance that she had initiated. News had just arrived that a civilian woman tending to her fields had been killed in the cross-border shelling across the Line of Control that divides the territories of India from Pakistan. Infractions and violations of this disputed line have led the two countries to war several times and have claimed many lives. The alliance to which the speaker alluded had become one of the most visible women's organizations in the district. It listed, among its accomplishments, the relief assistance that it had provided to women displaced by the war.

I had been working on issues of gender as an anthropologist in this area for over 10 years, so the comment made earlier lingered in my mind. Implicit in the speaker's categorization was a clear demarcation between the goals and objectives of activism and those of anthropology. The former, she had implied, were committed to seeking positive depictions of women in marginalized cultures and finding concrete ways of redressing the material conditions of women's lives in a world where the distribution of power and resources was glaringly unequal. She characterized the latter as an analytical approach that specialized in the trade of cultural knowledge but failed to comprehend the larger picture or put this knowledge to social use.

There was considerable validity in her portrayal of anthropology as cultural deconstruction. Through the years, anthropology had carved a separate domain for itself with fieldwork and participant observation as its foremost methods, and culture, especially the culture of non-Western societies, as its core subject matter. During the 1980s, however, it could no longer profess sole propriety of the culture concept. Cultural studies and literary criticism programs were claiming to be far more radical and relevant approaches, demystifying the supposed neutrality of texts and mindful of social divisions based on race, gender, and class. Responding to these challenges, anthropology witnessed the advent of a new postmodern "reflexivity" that sought to deconstruct universalistic and absolute assertions of scientific truth. It aimed to solve the "crisis in representation" by recognizing "partial truths" (Clifford 1986) and cultural fragments and by acknowledging the embeddedness of both the ethnographer and the cultures being studied in colonial and global networks of power. Through textual reform and greater collaborative efforts, ethnography, the written product of fieldwork, was to engage with the world as a form of cultural critique.

Under these circumstances, when the objective authority and neutrality of ethnographies were being contested, a new gap was opened for writings from those communities that had hitherto been marginalized. Feminist anthropologists, who had been relegated to the outskirts of the profession, took this opportunity to draw attention to lineages of feminists who had been neglected within the discipline and to further explore new genres for writing texts that were publicly accessible and politically conscious. By the end of the century, the number of writings by feminist anthropologists soared, and more and more women were admitted into academic anthropology.

At the same time, there were feminist anthropologists, activists, and public policymakers outside the domains of academia who were dealing with the complexities of responsible cultural representation to combat social injustice. Could writing more personal and reflexive ethnographies effect a more egalitarian practice for anthropology? A cautionary note was forwarded by Nancy Hartsock (1987), who argued that postmodernism's celebration of decentralization and indeterminacy just at the moment when feminists, ethnic minorities, and other historically disenfranchised people were claiming a center was just another way for dominant groups to retain power. While anthropology may have been a forerunner in the business of cultural translation, transporting rare anecdotes for consumption across formerly impenetrable borders, suggested Ruth Behar (1993), it did not necessarily alter relations of power.

When women in several parts of the world are threatened by new forms of imperialism, deterritorialization, violence, and economic exploitation, what is to be gained from feminist anthropological research? This article traces some of the theoretical debates and revisionary interpretations of canonical history that have shaped third-wave, or contemporary, feminist anthropology in the United States. It goes on to examine the tensions in the relations between feminism and anthropology and shows how feminist redefinitions of conventional classifications of fieldwork, culture, and self and other have substantially altered the methodological and epistemological trajectories of anthropology. The section that follows engages with discussions of form and writing evoked by postmodernism's concerns with knowledge, power, and the position of the observer. Feminist anthropologists have argued that, due to their multiple and ambiguous strands of identification, women in the past used life histories, ethnographic novels, and other experimental genres to compose texts that dissolved barriers based on race, class, and gender. The article describes the scope and limitations of these claims and provides a survey of new styles of feminist ethnographies. Finally, the last segment returns to questions of social relevance, political accountability, and activism, laying out some of the advocacy struggles in which feminist anthropologists are participating, for, as Deborah Gordon (1995) advises, "When academic research and publication are under intense public scrutiny, we need to articulate why and how feminist research matters" (375).

FEMINIST ANTHROPOLOGY IN CONTESTED FIELDS

Ever since the phrase "feminist anthropology" first replaced "anthropology of women" in the late seventies, it has made its way into course catalogues, journals, and advertisements for anthropology positions. In 1988, the Association of Feminist Anthropology was launched as a subdivision of the American Anthropological Association to serve as a platform for extending mentorship, professional links, and publication and conference support and for improving the visibility of women in the field. Yet for almost as long as this term has been used in anthropological literature, controversies have abounded as to whether a feminist anthropology can exist at all and, if so, what form it must assume.

Three major temporal periods, or waves, in the history of feminist anthropology have been identified by Kamala Visweswaran (1997). The first wave is rooted in suffragist movements of the Progressive Era and is marked by its efforts to record women's roles in culture. During the first phase of this period, extending from 1880 to 1920, sex and gender were collapsed into a single empirical category, and biology was thought to determine social roles. Feminists asserted that women could improve public governance by introducing into it their natural domestic abilities of compassion and care. In the second phase, which spanned from 1920 to 1960, a separation was made between biological sex and socially constructed gender roles. Margaret Mead and Ruth Benedict were among the leading figures of this time, which beheld the publication of several life histories of and ethnographies on women.

With the second wave of feminism in the United States, gender emerged as the foundational lens of feminist analysis and not just as another ingredient in the holistic descriptions of cultures. Texts like Simone de Beauvoir's *Second Sex* ([1952] 1953) and Betty Friedan's *Feminine Mystique* (1963) inspired anthropological collections like *Women, Culture and Society*, edited by Michelle Rosaldo and Louise Lamphere (1974), and *Toward an Anthropology of Women*, edited by Rayna Rapp (1975). The notion of universal sisterhood prevailed whereby it was assumed that women all over the world shared similar experiences. It was believed that an anthropology done by women on women would erase the prejudices of masculinist science and that the shift from analytical ethnographies to experience-based narratives would signify more authentic discourses on women.

In later years, however, a growing dissatisfaction emerged with the tendency in anthropological projects concerned with the discovery of women to cast other women in "the image of ourselves undressed" (Rosaldo 1980, 392). "Betrayal" was inherent in the ethnographic process, argued Judith Stacey (1988), and discordances between the expectations, methods, and even writings of feminism (which is dedicated to narrowing the distance between women) and those of ethnography (which is predicated on their separation) permitted at best a "partially feminist ethnography." Correspondingly, in an earlier article, Marilyn Strathern (1987) had described the relationship between feminism and anthropology as "awkward." Anthropology presumed a clear distinction between a "Western" self studying a "non-Western other." According to Strathern, feminism mocked the pretensions of compatibility and mutuality in anthropology's notion of self by exposing the patriarchal dominance within the discipline, which subjected all women to being other. Anthropology, on the other hand, mocked feminism's illusions of empathically identifying with the subjection of the other by pointing to feminists' common origin within a Western scientific paradigm.

As Kamala Visweswaran (1997, 595) counsels, it is vital to read the "strategies of disidentification" in women's writings and not merely rely on "moments of gender identification." Thus, during the Progressive Era, cutting-edge feminists had argued for suffrage by referring to the rights enjoyed by Native American women. Western women, unlike their Native American counterparts, had been denied the right to vote or inherit property equally even though they were supposed to hail from a "civilized" society at the apex of the evolutionary ladder (Visweswaran 1997). Feminist anthropologists making this argument nevertheless did not oppose the subjugation and racism that Native Americans and other culturally oppressed people

suffered. For example, Elsie Clews Parsons, who had funded the anthropological research of several women and financed the *Journal of American Folklore*, supported eugenic remedies of birth control for poor women. Alice Fletcher, who meticulously documented the music and rituals of Native American societies, was instrumental in the passage of the Omaha Act of 1882 and the Dawes Severalty Act of 1887, which would even further deprive these groups of land (Lurie 1966; Visweswaran 1997).

Similarly, second-wave women's liberation struggles became identified with the civil rights movements of the sixties so that their divergent purposes and perspectives were frequently obscured. Popular life histories such as Marjorie Shostak's *Nisa: The Life and Words of a !Kung Woman* (1981), which aimed to convey an African woman's rites of passage in her own words, still catered to white, middle-class preoccupations with sexual freedom and consciousness raising and downplayed factors like racism, slavery, and the consolidation of family networks that Afro-American feminists had rallied for (Gordon 1991).

Consequently, third-wave feminism (from 1980 onward) has been demarcated by critiques against the assumptions of universal sisterhood. Feminists of color and of different sexual orientations have argued that sex, and not just gender, is a social construct. They have challenged the centralization of gender as a constant construct, with race, class, and sexuality thrown in as mere variables. Further, through its revolt against simplistic distinctions between anthropological observers and the subjects of their inquiry, third-wave feminist ethnography has not only charted its own course but also shaped the heart of anthropological epistemology and its central tenets of culture and fieldwork.

Fieldwork has been anthropology's paramount mode of research. Ethnographies derived their authoritative stance from their ability to convey intimate knowledge of other cultures with a scientific expertise that was thought to be distinguishable from the subjective genre of travelogues. That the experience of fieldwork is different for women has been well documented in several volumes (Golde 1970; Warren 1988; Bell, Caplan, and Karim 1992). Of late, however, feminists have associated fieldwork with unilateral Western hegemony. Fieldwork, writes Visweswaran (1994), propagates a doctrine of difference and distance by separating the notion of home as the ultimate domain of intellectual activity from the image of the field as a transformative but temporary space, generally confined to remote or peripheral locales. For example, Margaret Mead, who was responsible for drawing attention to the study of adolescent girls, sexual temperaments, maternal behaviors, and roles of women in general, supported fieldwork in small-scale societies like Samoa because she felt their lack of complexity qualified them as natural laboratories for anthropology. Such a dichotomy has led to the treatment of non-Western cultures as blank texts devoid of history or temporality. A similar attitude continues to be transmitted through study-abroad programs, which rarely require the same amount of rigor and preparation for trips to Third World countries as they may for trips to European ones.

Visweswaran (1994) invites anthropologists to substitute homework for fieldwork rather than abandoning research abroad or romanticizing home as a place without restrictions. After all, the domestic sphere is often the starting place of gender discrimination. At home, Western women, too, were denied equal access to education, work, and travel by patriarchal norms. Their journeys into exterior fields were accomplished with considerable cost and hardship at home, but, paradoxically, they availed themselves of the privileges offered by their white, middle-class status to sustain them in the field. The homework method proffered by Visweswaran calls for detailed and difficult analyses of the positions of power occupied by the anthropologist and the culture she comes from. It also suggests a return to basic archival and library reading to foster a deeper consideration of historical forces of colonialism, nationalism, and globalization. This approach takes feminist anthropology away from just a reliance on participant observation or personal testimonies, which were crucial to second-wave feminism. Homework becomes a task of taking more seriously the knowledge, humanity, and history of cultures being studied.

Criticisms of the legacy of fieldwork have also been voiced by postcolonial writers who maintain that anthropology has created artificial field areas in order to forward its own agenda, attributing exotic, abstract essences and characteristics to places and then naturalizing them so that the residents of those places come to be regarded as static, immobile "natives" (Appadurai 1988). As a corrective to the dangers of generalization that the concept of culture has generated, Lila Abu-Lughod (1991) makes a case for "writing against culture" and for grounding ethnography in the particular contingencies of women's lived experience instead. She argues that with the transnational movement of immigrants and travelers, anthropology is increasingly being practiced by those with refracted, "halfie" identities who are forcing it to reconsider seemingly clear-cut disjunctions between self and other (Abu-Lughod 1990). That feminist rapport cannot be presupposed due to the existence of a common nationality, race, or sexual orientation has also been discussed by Narayan (1993), Page (1988), and Lewin (1995, 322-35). In the wake of these appraisals, feminists have campaigned for the creation of new anthropological locations by exploring their own locatedness in dominant sites.

By locating the body as a historically and socially constructed arena, feminists have condemned both biological determinism and the hierarchical split between mind and matter posited by modern rationalist science. They have lobbied for the erasure of negative values assigned by science to bodily characteristics that are considered female (Martin 1987); others have argued that emotions that are often given a feminine connotation are not inert psychological states but products of culture (Lutz 1990). Still others have contended that the performance of motherhood and other kinship roles is linked to ways in which women's bodies are controlled by colonialism and industrial capitalism (Scheper-Hughes 1992). These interpretations of the body can prove useful for administering gender-sensitive public health policies and countering misogynist and homophobic opinions that make power differentials seem normal.

Feminist anthropologists argue that cultural agents do not merely reproduce but also resist forms of domination in everyday acts. This has been a meaningful revision to standard depictions of women as apolitical, private, and incapable of public policymaking (Abu-Lughod 1991). Moreover, the renewed attention to homework has contributed to deliberations on alternate forms of kinship (Trawick 1990; Weston 1991), reproductive rights (Ginsberg 1989; Strathern 1992), and state sponsorship of discriminatory procedures in military organizations (Enloe 1990). Writing against culture has opened avenues for tying local practices to transnational movements (Tsing 1993), for exposing the plight and resistance maneuvers of women laborers in multinational corporations (Ong 1987), and for highlighting the inequities of travel and global capitalism (Enloe 1990).

Feminist anthropology has come a long way since the Women's Anthropological Society was first started in 1885 as a corollary to the Anthropological Society of Washington, which had only men among its members (Lurie 1966, 35-39). But the place of women in society and the cultural framing of sex and gender relations continue to be disputed in modern times. The question remains as to whether third-wave feminism can prove truly representative and beneficial and improve the lives of all women equally. Moreover, in spite of their conflicting positions as both marginal and central figures in the discipline of anthropology, there remains little doubt that feminist anthropologists are now at the forefront of radical and innovative anthropology.

"AN ANTHROPOLOGY WITHOUT EXILES": (RE)FORMING THE BOUNDARIES OF FEMINIST WRITING

The landmark anthology *Writing Culture* (1986), now regarded as a classic of postmodern anthropology, did not include feminist anthropologists. One of its editors, James Clifford, writes in the introduction, "We were confronted by what seemed to us an obvious—important and regrettable—fact. Feminism had not contributed to the theoretical analysis of texts. . . . [it had] not produced either unconventional forms of writing or a developed reflection of textuality as such" (20-21).

Not surprisingly, this omission from what was hailed as new and revolutionary was strongly protested by feminist anthropologists. It generated investigations into the literary and experimental motifs in women's writings and exposed the sexist practices of inclusion and exclusion within the discipline. Lila Abu-Lughod (1990) suggested that if indeed women did tend to write ethnographies in reserved and conservative styles that could not be considered experimental and postmodern, it might be attributed to the pressures they faced in the academy to prove themselves as scientists. Mascia-Lees, Sharpe, and Cohen (1989) contended that Clifford had himself used a feminist ethnography, Shostak's *Nisa: The Life and Words of a !Kung Woman*, to substantiate his proposal that allegory was the linking factor between traditional and new ethnography. They alleged that his statements displayed a masculine propensity "to write about feminists rather than inviting them to write for themselves" (13).

Historically, women writers had been pioneers of experimental forms, but their work had been classified as bounded by their female subjectivity and deemed incapable of transcendence or innovation. Thus Margaret Mead endeavored to make anthropology a household topic of discussion by writing for popular journals like *Redbook* and *Nation*, but her *Coming of Age in Samoa*, which questioned the universal applicability of developmental psychology, was seldom cited as a leading example of anthropological theory. Women of color such as Zora Neale Hurston and Ella Deloria, who were creatively blurring distinctions between ethnography, autobiography, and fictional prose to redress representations of minority communities by dominant groups, could not achieve the status of legitimacy in a discipline that was committed to distinguishing those observing from those being observed.

The academy has not been a favorable place for women. Even the highly acclaimed Ruth Benedict, whose *Patterns of Culture* was a best-seller, was denied a university position for several years. Women who accompanied their anthropologist husbands to the field rarely made advances in their academic careers despite the appropriation of their labor in ethnographic production. Some like Elizabeth Fernea and Edith Turner produced more experiential but less valued memoirs as opposed to the more scientific ethnographies of their husbands, an asymmetrical trend that Barbara Tedlock (1995) terms "representational segmentation."

In later years, too, with the further professionalization of the field, women ethnographers were compelled to confront their positionality both at home and abroad. The trials they faced were sometimes reflected in their ethnographies, preempting the confessional and reflexive genres that would follow. An example of such writing is the ethnographic novel *Return to Laughter* (1964), in which the author, Laura Bohannon (under the pseudonym Elenore Smith Bowen), elaborated on her fieldwork experience among the Tiv of Nigeria. This fictional technique allowed the reader to glimpse the colonial heritage of anthropology. It also demonstrated the potentially transformative role that cross-cultural research can play; this is seen when Bohannon questions the principles and premises of her own society as standards by which to measure

others. Even though she accepts an invitation to enter Tiv female ritual space as a symbolic senior woman, it is the male world of politics that she most craves to comprehend. Bohannon's anecdotes about the dilemmas of identity and belonging are notable theoretical interventions, showing that solidarity between women cannot be taken for granted.

The new postmodern movement rebelled against the claims of ethnographic monographs to authority, objectivity, and transparency. But it neglected to acknowledge that women writers, tied in complex relations of power, had already been deploying personal narratives, life stories, life histories, biographies, and other unorthodox forms of scholarly writing. In an attempt to give greater credence to the words of female subjects, the life history method had been embraced by a surge of ethnographies of women in the 1930s (Landes 1938; Underhill [1936] 1979), and it continues to find popularity in feminist writing today (Behar 1993; Brown 1991; Shostak 1981), spawning some of the most widely read ethnographic accounts over the years. Contemporary feminists like Lila Abu-Lughod (1991) have woven together nuanced, contingent, and evocative narratives to articulate the tension and ambivalence in the placement of women in society. Some feminists (such as Visweswaran [1994]) have advocated "autoethnographies" to situate and clarify the position of the investigating feminist author, while others (Narayan 1994; Kondo 1995) have used autobiographical plays and novels to return the gaze and unveil the discriminatory politics and practices of academic institutions.

Not all feminists, however, have chosen reflexive genres to express themselves. For instance, Erika Friedl's *Women of Deh Koh* (1989), which is presented with the stated objective of writing stories of women and not about them, attempts to draw the readers into the experience and meaning of life in an Iranian village, away from the stereotypical representations about the tedium and toil of people who live in isolated mountainous communities and away from the depictions of rural women as subordinate, oppressed, and ignorant, with little or no control over their lives. Her collection of 12 short stories, based on several years of fieldwork, are presented from the point of view of the women she encountered. The voice of the ethnographer does not impose upon the text, although it is hinted at. In one of the most powerful examples of ethnographic writing, a narrative entitled "Mamlaus Is Telling a Story," the author's presence is made manifest as one of the listeners and even one of the fabricators of cultural stories. Friedl skillfully crafts conventional plot props—a stormy night, a social gathering around a warm kitchen fire, and talk of dervishes and demons—to negotiate lines between history and legend, to recount and debate local and national political histories, and to probe the conventions of morality and justice. Truth and lies are both prevalent in the composition of reality, the tale suggests, and words from the mouths of women are passed on

to others in Iran, to be further carried and read by those of us who live in other parts of the world.

Even as ethnographies in the 1980s and 1990s were being restructured and were reaching out beyond conventional doctrinal terrains to convey with vivid sensuality the experiences of fieldwork and to stave off charges of being dull and boring, commentaries by literary critics and works of feminist literature were trickling in through once resistant disciplinary borders. Maxine Hong Kingston's *Woman Warrior* (1976), Zora Neale Hurston's *Their Eyes Were Watching God* (1937), and *This Bridge Called My Back* (1981), edited by Cherrie Moraga and Gloria Anzaldua, were being absorbed in anthropology courses. Outlining and defining feminist ethnography in 1988, Kamala Visweswaran observed that "experimental ethnography has been strangely reluctant to embrace other forms of writing, like the novel, short story, diary, or autobiography" and asked, "At a time when literary critics read such texts as expressive culture, why can't anthropologists?" (39).

Accordingly, a decade after *Writing Culture* heralded the onset of a new ethnographic focus, the publication of *Women Writing Culture*, edited by Ruth Behar and Deborah Gordon (1995), paved the way for a distinct literary and political path for anthropology. While *Writing Culture* was often accused of remaining at the level of ideological manual, espousing experimental writing in theory rather than truly embracing it, *Women Writing Culture* consciously strove to show that theory and experimental writing need not be mutually exclusive. Beautifully composed articles on the contributions of feminist ancestors were juxtaposed with fictional narratives that dramatized the marginalization of women in the contemporary academy. Voices of radical border poets were carried from Israel to converse with an insightful unraveling of the masculine roots of Western travel and discovery. An essay exploring lesbian identity was accompanied by a collaborative piece on Afro-American and Chinese American discourses that hoped to foster parallel community building. Reacting against earlier omissions of women's writings, *Women Writing Culture* celebrated the breadth and diversity possible in feminist anthropology today. "If there is a single thing, a common land that all of us are seeking," declared Ruth Behar (1995), "it is an anthropology without exiles" (8).

FEMINIST ANTHROPOLOGY
AT THE CROSSROADS OF
ACADEMIA AND ACTIVISM

The cover of *Writing Culture* iconoclastically foregrounds the male anthropologist composing ethnographic fields with his typewriter, belying any supposition that ethnography is an exact replica of an external reality. The cover of *Women Writing Culture* displays a single anthropologist, too, this time a woman, the cynosure of watchful eyes. But this picture of the observer being observed does not extol the individuality of the ethnographer; rather, the eyes are suggestive of the intersection of the individual with a collective identity that does not merely look back with curiosity or resistance but also "looks out for" other women (Behar 1995, 2).

This proposition of "looking out for" and working with others is important for negotiating a feminist practice that is not just about form. Aspirations of postmodern ethnography to inspire balanced dialogues between writers and their subjects must not be restricted to moments when texts are being fashioned but additionally must entail a practical and methodological format conducive to dialogue as well (Page 1988). Perhaps also, as Elizabeth Enslin (1994) has suggested, rather than salvaging ethnography by searching for new experimental trends in writing, we must accept the risk that participation in an equitable and socially accountable academic practice may sometimes take us beyond the realms of writing. Instead of merely seeking more effective ways to represent people, the test of a politically sensitive anthropological approach may more effectively be measured by "whether we can be accountable to people's own struggles for self-representation and self-determination," writes Visweswaran (1988, 39).

The ground-level techniques of anthropological inquiry may deem it especially suited to pursue such collaborative work. Hosting conferences can sometimes transform fortress-like university campuses and bring professionals and activists face to face. At a conference entitled "Frontline Feminisms," held in 1997 at the University of California, Riverside, artists, activists, and academic feminists, with a high representation of anthropologists, came together to confront the violence and degradation induced by repressive governments, dispossession, homelessness, and the proliferation of nuclear weapons. The panelists comprised those reading testimonials, those working on direct mobilization, and those keeping records about atrocities and resistances. Although there were differences in positions and outlooks and cases with deep paradoxes, rarely did anyone claim to be a dispassionate analyst.

Planning for community literacy can open another path for activism. Since a vast majority of feminist ethnographers are educators who spend hours preparing for and philosophizing about the techniques of teaching, it might turn out that the continuity in transferring their pedagogical skills to such programs might reduce the dissonance that fieldwork produces between what we know from the field and what we do at home. As Enslin (1994) puts it, "I am attempting to negotiate not just a six-month or one-year period of 'fieldwork' in western Chitwan, but a lifetime of social and political practice" (557). Enslin writes about her involvement in the literacy project initiated by the Nari Jagaran Samiti in Nepal, where her in-laws lived and where she worked as an anthropologist. On presenting a leading activist of this organization with a copy of her dissertation, she was told, "Your book has no importance. After all, what is writing? You looked, you saw, and based on that, you wrote a book. But that book won't do anything if not accompanied by work, by practice.

Right?" (541). Stricken by that remark, Enslin was moved to lend her abilities to an effort that she did not inaugurate or pilot but one that was already being steered by women she studied and that she could no longer ethically ignore.

Another example of a community literacy undertaking is provided by Deborah Gordon's description of the El Barrio Project in East Harlem (1995, 373-89). The program was for mothers in the economically distressed Puerto Rican community, which had registered high rates of school dropouts. Conducted in conjunction with Hunter College, it was administered by a staff that included oral historians from the Hunter faculty. The strength of this venture lay in the manner in which feminist understandings of identity and meaning, and methods of interactive learning and reflexive studies of classroom behavior, were employed to promote a "critical" over a "functional literacy" so that the women could ward off damaging stereotypes about themselves, take advantage of social services, and improve their employment prospects.

Feminist ethnographers have also been vocal in condemning acts of violence against women. They have opposed acts of aggression that occur not only on battlefields elsewhere or on the twilight frontiers of inner cities but also closer to home, on university campuses that can be hotbeds of perilous masculine rites (Sanday 1992).

Academic institutions can provide a space for the airing of activist agendas, but they can also endanger the activist process by reducing it to just another spectacle or discursive ritual. Commodification and appropriation of these knowledges can jeopardize their autonomy. The trajectory of acquiring tenure and the paucity of resources and models that facilitate interconnections with public projects make it difficult to break the seclusion of the ivory towers of academia. Disillusioned with developmental economics and professional affiliations, the members of the grassroots Andean organization PRATEC, described by Frederique Apffel-Marglin (Apffel-Marglin with PRATEC 1998), have sought cultural affirmation and territorial repossession for peasants by deprofessionalizing themselves and offering workshops and channels of communication that are integrated with local ways of learning and living. Apffel-Marglin reconciles her feminist practice with her own partial location in the academic universe by creating centers of "mutual learning," forging liaisons with community groups, and encouraging students to embark upon internships with neighborhood community projects for credit.

Conversely, precautions must be taken to avoid being swept away by the romance of activism, expecting it to be instantly collaborative, rewarding, or redemptive. Venturing beyond disciplinary and professional lines of control can signal to others an infringement on spaces and rights. Nonacademic enterprises that work at grassroots levels, too, are beleaguered by their dependence on external sources of funding and the charisma of individual personalities, arrangements that are often more appealing to Western trends than popular needs, hierarchies, and essentialisms.

Under such circumstances, it is not the substitution of theoretical dialogues that will automatically generate a committed feminism. Theories that acknowledge their locations in particular histories of control and in particular struggles can lead to better collective conversations and engagements (Enslin 1994). So also writing need not necessarily be individualistic as has been forcefully demonstrated by the Jamaican group Sistren (Sistren with Ford-Smith 1987); "writing with" rather than "writing about" cultures can be one way of using anthropological expertise for the direct benefit of the cultures we work in (Apffel-Marglin with PRATEC 1998). In a similar vein, Karen McCarthy Brown, author of the award-winning biographical ethnography *Mama Lola: A Vodou Priestess in Brooklyn* (1991), has taken her anthropological expertise to another frontier, enabling minority and diasporic students in the Newark, New Jersey, area to gather oral histories of religious practices in their communities and better cope with the vicissitudes of urban living at a time when anti-immigrant sentiment looms large. I hope that my own efforts at collaboratively translating heterodox literatures that represent diverse perspectives that continue to survive in Ladakh despite nationalist and fundamentalist quests to silence them will prove useful for channeling information to postwar healing efforts.

Practical accountability and awareness of being multiply positioned requires us to adopt various strategies of action and state our allegiances to different audiences in different homes. Perhaps an abandonment of anthropology might be inimical to certain types of feminist activism, but for a thriving feminist anthropology, however partial and transformed, the challenge lies in striking a balance between teaching, theory, creative writing, and participatory advocacy.

References

Abu-Lughod, Lila. 1990. Can There Be a Feminist Ethnography? *Women and Performance: A Journal of Feminist Theory* 5(1):7-27.

————. 1991. *Writing Women's Worlds: Bedouin Stories.* Berkeley: University of California Press.

Apffel-Marglin, Frederique with PRATEC. 1998. *The Spirit of Regeneration: Andean Culture Confronting Western Notions of Development.* London: Zed Books.

Appadurai, Arjun. 1988. Introduction: Place and Voice in Anthropological Theory. *Cultural Anthropology* 3: 16-20.

Beauvoir, Simone de. [1952] 1953. *The Second Sex.* Trans. and ed. H. M. Parshley. New York: Knopf.

Behar, Ruth. 1993. *Translated Woman: Crossing the Border with Esperanza's Story.* Boston: Beacon Press.

————. 1995. Introduction: Out of Exile. In *Women Writing Culture,* ed. Ruth Behar and Deborah Gordon. Berkeley: University of California Press.

Behar, Ruth and Deborah Gordon, eds. 1995. *Women Writing Culture.* Berkeley: University of California Press.

Bell, Diane, Pat Caplan, and Wazir Jahan Karim, eds. 1992. *Gendered Fields: Women, Men and Ethnography.* London: Routledge.

Bowen, Elenore Smith. 1964. *Return to Laughter.* New York: Doubleday.

Brown, Karen McCarthy. 1991. *Mama Lola: A Vodou Priestess in Brooklyn.* Berkeley: University of California Press.

Clifford, James. 1986 Introduction: Partial Truths. In *Writing Culture: The Poetics and Politics of Ethnography,* ed. James Clifford and George Marcus. Berkeley: University of California Press.

Enloe, Cynthia. 1990. *Bananas, Beaches and Bases: Making Feminist Sense of International Politics.* Berkeley: University of California Press.

Enslin, Elizabeth. 1994. Beyond Writing: Feminist Practice and the Limits of Ethnography. *Cultural Anthropology* 9(4):537-68.

Friedan, Betty. 1963. *The Feminine Mystique.* New York: Norton.

Friedl, Erika. 1989. *Women of Deh Koh: Lives in an Iranian Village.* New York: Penguin Books.

Ginsberg, Faye. 1989. *Contested Lives: The Abortion Debate in an American Community.* Berkeley: University of California Press.

Golde, Peggy, ed. 1970. *Women in the Field: Anthropological Experiences.* Berkeley: University of California Press.

Gordon, Deborah. 1991. Engendering the Ethnographic Imagination. Ph.D. diss., University of California, Santa Cruz.

————. 1995. Border Work: Feminist Ethnography and the Dissemination of Literacy. In *Women Writing Culture,* ed. Ruth Behar and Deborah Gordon. Berkeley: University of California Press.

Hartsock, Nancy. 1987. Rethinking Modernism: Minority vs. Majority Theories. *Cultural Critique* 7(Fall): 187-206.

Hurston, Zora Neal. 1937. *Their Eyes Were Watching God: A Novel*. Philadelphia: J. B. Lippincott.

Kingston, Maxine Hong. 1976. *The Woman Warrior: Memoir of a Girlhood Among Ghosts*. New York: Knopf.

Kondo, Dorinne. 1995. Bad Girls: Theater, Women of Color, and the Politics of Representation. In *Women Writing Culture*, ed. Ruth Behar and Deborah Gordon. Berkeley: University of California Press.

Landes, Ruth. 1938. *The Ojibwa Woman*. New York: Columbia University Press.

Lewin, Ellen. 1995. Writing Lesbian Ethnography. In *Women Writing Culture*, ed. Ruth Behar and Deborah Gordon. Berkeley: University of California Press.

Lurie, Nancy. 1966. Women in Early American Anthropology. In *Pioneers of American Anthropology*, ed. June Helm. Seattle: University of Washington Press.

Lutz, Catherine. 1990. Engendered Emotion: Gender, Power, and the Rhetoric of Emotional Control in American Discourse. In *Language and the Politics of Emotion*, ed. Lila Abu-Lughod and Catherine Lutz. New York: Cambridge University Press.

Martin, Emily. 1987. *The Woman in the Body: A Cultural Analysis of Reproduction*. Boston: Beacon Press.

Mascia-Lees, Frances, Patricia Sharpe, and Colleen Cohen. 1989. The Postmodern Turn in Anthropology: Cautions from a Feminist Perspective. *Signs* 15(1):7-33.

Moraga, Cherrie and Gloria Anzaldua. 1981. *This Bridge Called My Back: Writings by Radical Women of Color*. Watertown, MA: Persephone Press.

Narayan, Kirin. 1993. How Native Is a "Native" Anthropologist? *American Anthropologist* 95(3):671-86.

———. 1994. *Love, Stars and All That*. New York: Pocket Books.

Ong, Aihwa. 1987. *Spirits of Resistance and Capitalist Discipline: Factory Women in Malaysia*. Albany: State University of New York Press.

Page, Helan. 1988. Dialogical Principles of Interactive Learning in the Ethnographic Relationship. *Journal of Anthropological Research* 44(2): 163-81.

Rapp, Rayna, ed. 1975. *Toward an Anthropology of Women*. New York: Monthly Review Press.

Rosaldo, Michelle. 1980. The Use and Abuse of Anthropology: Reflections on Feminism and Cross-Cultural Understandings. *Signs* 5(Spring):389-417.

Rosaldo, Michelle and Louise Lamphere, eds. 1974. *Women, Culture and Society*. Stanford: Stanford University Press.

Sanday, Peggy. 1992. *Fraternity Gang Rape: Sex, Brotherhood, and Privilege on Campus*. New York: New York University Press.

Scheper-Hughes, Nancy. 1992. *Death Without Weeping*. Berkeley: University of California Press.

Shostak, Marjorie. 1981. *Nisa: The Life and Words of a !Kung Woman*. Cambridge, MA: Harvard University Press.

Sistren with Honor Ford-Smith. 1987. *Lionheart Gal: Lifestories of Jamaican Women*. Toronto: Sister Vision.

Stacey, Judith. 1988. Can There Be a Feminist Ethnography? *Women's Studies International Forum* 11(1):21-27.

Strathern, Marilyn. 1987. An Awkward Relationship: The Case of Feminism and Anthropology. *Signs* 12(2):276-92.

———. 1992. *After Nature: English Kinship in the Late Twentieth Century*. New York: Cambridge University Press.

Tedlock, Barbara. 1995. Works and Wives: On the Sexual Division of Textual Labor. In *Women Writing Culture*, ed. Ruth Behar and Deborah Gordon. Berkeley: University of California Press.

Trawick, Margaret. 1990. *Notes on Love in a Tamil Family*. Berkeley: University of California Press.

Tsing, Anna Lowenhaupt. 1993. *In the Realm of the Diamond Queen: Marginality in an Out-of-the-Way Place*. Princeton, NJ: Princeton University Press.

Underhill, Ruth. [1936] 1979. *Papago Woman*. Prospect Heights, IL: Waveland.

Visweswaran, Kamala. 1988. Defining Feminist Ethnography. *Inscriptions* 3-4:27-44.

———. 1994. *Fictions of Feminist Ethnography*. Minneapolis: University of Minnesota Press.

———. 1997. Histories of Feminist Ethnography. *Annual Review of Anthropology* 26:591-621.

Warren, Carol. 1988. *Gender Issues in Field Research*. Newbury Park, CA: Sage.

Weston, Kath. 1991. *Families We Choose: Lesbians, Gays, Kinship*. New York: Columbia University Press.

ANNALS, *AAPSS*, **571**, September 2000

Feminism and Federally Funded Social Science: Notes from Inside

By JUDITH D. AUERBACH

ABSTRACT: In order for feminist social science research to influence the transformation of society toward more equitable gender arrangements, it must both be undertaken and be applied in the policy arena. For these to happen, feminist social scientists must be active players in the research policy and funding enterprise, particularly at the federal level. The discussion of how feminist social science has had an impact, and can have an even greater one, both on and through federally funded research is framed in two larger contexts: the broader federal science and technology (S&T) enterprise and the impact of feminism on society generally. A selective review of developments in both the representation of women in S&T and attention to issues of gender in the content of scientific research demonstrates that, although much progress has been made, much remains to be done. Some strategies for furthering the feminist project through the federal research enterprise are offered.

Judith D. Auerbach is the behavioral and social science coordinator and prevention science coordinator in the Office of AIDS Research, National Institutes of Health. In 1998, she served as assistant director for social and behavioral sciences in the White House Office of Science and Technology Policy. She is a past president of Sociologists for Women in Society. She continues to publish and present in the areas of science policy, HIV/AIDS, women's health, and gender. She received her doctorate in sociology from the University of California, Berkeley.

GIVEN its emergence in the context of the late-twentieth-century women's movement, contemporary feminist scholarship has always been connected to feminist action. The goal of much feminist social science is not just to advance knowledge but also to apply that knowledge to progressive social change. By highlighting the ways in which sex and gender operate as major organizing principles—in particular, how they confer unequal power and status to males and females and the consequences thereof—feminist scholars aim to inform the transformation of society toward more equitable arrangements.

This transformation can occur only if (1) feminist social science research is undertaken, which generally requires funding support, and (2) that research is applied in the policy arena. For both of these to happen, feminist social scientists must be active players in the research policy and funding enterprise, particularly at the federal level. This is not an easy task for a number of reasons, including the historical marginalization of feminist scholarship (in part because of its political linkages) and the relative dearth of influential feminist social scientists in the highest echelons of science policymaking and the scientific establishment. Even still, there has been notable progress in this regard.

In this article, I identify some of the ways in which feminist social science has had an impact—and can have an even greater one—both on and through federally funded research, by placing the discussion in two larger contexts. The first is that of the broader federal science and technology (S&T) enterprise and the place of the social sciences within it, as many of the issues of feminist scholarship are actually issues of the status of the social sciences generally. The second context is that of feminism generally, as much of the success or failure of feminist social science reflects the impact of the feminist movement on social and political life in America. For this discussion, I refer to two dimensions of the feminist project: claims for gender equity (for example, through more proportional representation of women in S&T) and greater attention to gender and "women's" issues in the content of scientific research. This is by no means a comprehensive review of either of these dimensions, rather a reflection based on experience inside the federal science policy apparatus.

I begin with an anecdote. A few years ago, during the annual meeting of the American Sociological Association, I served as moderator on a panel entitled something like "The Social Dimensions of AIDS." In the course of the discussion following paper presentations, someone made the point that the kind of HIV/AIDS research she and other sociologists conducted typically does not receive funding from federal agencies, such as the National Institutes of Health (NIH). This person's research focused on theory development, specifically around gay and lesbian sexuality, gender identity, and social status, or what has become known as "queer theory." The link with HIV/AIDS is in understanding how the gay and lesbian community became both vulnerable to HIV/AIDS and mobilized around combating it. When she asked me how she could get such research funded by NIH, I suggested she "lose the 'queer.'" This was not meant to be glib or rude (although it did produce much chuckling). Rather, it was said to make the point that in a highly politicized funding environment—as the federal agencies often find themselves to be—sometimes the titles and terms used to characterize research proposals can determine their success or failure. If influential members of Congress who determine the budgets of federal research agencies are uncomfortable with, or hostile to, certain kinds of research, they will be sure to preclude it from funding, as they have done in recent times with much social science research in general (during the Reagan administration), fetal tissue transplantation research, research that can be interpreted as promoting homosexuality, and research on needle exchanges for preventing transmission of infectious diseases between injecting drug users.

Did I mean that this person should not consider submitting a grant proposal in her area? Not at all. Rather, I was suggesting that a change of phrase might make the difference between receiving funding and not (the scientific merit of the project notwithstanding). For many scholars, this is an unpalatable suggestion, as they believe that the power of words lies in the particular words themselves; to be told that those are not the ones that can be used seems like an intellectual and political betrayal.

The tension between conducting the research that social scientists believe is important to conduct—especially where it is linked to desirable social change—and compromising somewhat to make that research fundable is one of the first challenges feminist social scientists might face in attempting to break into the federal science arena. But an even more basic one is acquiring an understanding of how federal science policy, including priority-setting and funding decisions, is made. This is not part of the average graduate degree program in most social science disciplines, so following is a brief primer, provided as context for the remainder of the article.

FEDERAL S&T FUNDING: THE BUDGET PROCESS

Any assessment of federal science priorities and funding must begin with an understanding of the annual budget process. The U.S. federal government is the largest funder of research in the world. In FY1999, total spending for S&T (characterized in the budget as "research and development," or "R&D") was about $79.3 billion. Of this total, approximately $33.0 billion was devoted to research (as opposed to technology or product development); of the sum devoted to research, about $1.5 billion, or 4.5 percent, could be considered social and behavioral sciences (NSF 1999a). Although there are only a few federal agencies whose specific mission is to support S&T, such as NIH, the National Science Foundation (NSF), and the National Aeronautics and Space Administration, most federal agencies do have some sort of research program that supports it. Social and behavioral research is funded not only by NIH and NSF but also by the Departments of Agriculture, Commerce, Defense, Education, Energy, Health and Human Services, Housing and Urban Development, Interior, Justice, Labor, State, and Transportation and by a host of independent agencies, such as the Environmental Protection Agency, the National Endowment for the Humanities, the Smithsonian Institution, and the U.S. Institute for Peace.

The science budgets of these agencies, like all other federal programs, are a function of politics, in particular, the relationships between the president and his or her administration, Congress, and constituency groups. Every year, as the budget is developed and the congressional appropriations process plays out, these interests compete, conflict, and negotiate until the final allocations are determined.

For example, when this article was first being drafted, we were in the midst of the FY2000 appropriations process. The president's budget (which comes out each February) requested about a 2.7 percent increase over FY1999 for NIH. This compares to a nearly 15 percent increase Congress appropriated for FY1999. Early in the process, as happens every year, the congressional appropriators considered whether to meet, exceed, or reduce the president's request, and they took testimony from interested parties. The director of NIH, as well as the directors of its constituent institutes (for example, the National Institute of Mental Health, the National Institute of Child Health and Human Development, the National Cancer Institute, and so forth), appeared before the appropriations committees to defend the president's budget (even though most would have preferred greater increases, they were part of the administration and had to defend its budget). Constituency groups also appeared before the committees to opine about whether the president's request was sufficient or not to address the research of particular interest to them (usually they said it was not). In the case of NIH, there are two main constituency groups. The first are the so-called disease groups, representatives of people afflicted with certain diseases or disorders for which NIH is conducting research on prevention, care, or cures. Sometimes famous people speak for these groups to give their causes more visibility: for example, the actor Michael J. Fox recently has become a spokesperson for Parkinson's disease and lobbied for increased funds for the NIH institutes that support research in that area (Garnett 1999), as did Christopher Reeve for spinal cord injury research.

The second type of constituency group for NIH is the biomedical and behavioral (including social) researchers who apply to and receive grants from NIH to conduct scientific studies on diseases, disorders, and other health-related conditions. They are usually represented by their professional associations, a number of which are invited to testify annually during the congressional appropriations hearings. For example, the Consortium of Social Science Associations, as the umbrella organization of the professional societies in the behavioral and social sciences, periodically testifies on their behalf and advocates for increased funds for social and behavioral research programs within the NIH institutes (for example, programs on child development, the demography of aging, social network factors in disease transmission and prevention, and so on). Similarly, the Association of American Medical Colleges testifies on behalf of academic medical centers that conduct health research and train the next generation of clinical researchers and practitioners; it advocates for increased funds for the NIH programs that support such research and training.

Constituency groups are not the only ones with particular funding interests. Within the president's overall budget request, the administration itself identifies some specific scientific initiatives and priorities, for example, developing a preventive vaccine against HIV. Members of Congress also have their own particular interests, usually related to diseases or disorders afflicting themselves or family members, for example, prostate cancer, breast cancer, Alzheimer's disease, and Parkinson's disease (Zitner 1999). The determination of which of these interests succeeds and what levels of funding prevail for what programs is part of an elaborate dance in which the congressional appropriators have the last bow (notwithstanding a presidential veto of the whole appropriations bill, which happens periodically). In addition to setting funding levels, the appropriations committees—with the help and at the prodding of advocacy groups— also write reports that articulate their recommendations (sometimes in the form of demands) about particular programs or areas of emphasis. The agencies receiving funds are obliged to address this report language. In recent years, such report language has instructed NIH to increase its attention to, and support for, among other things, research on women's health and on the behavioral aspects of diseases and disorders.

This complicated process just crudely described for one subagency (NIH is part of the Department of Health and Human Services) takes place not only in the larger context of all S&T funding but also in the context of other, non-S&T national funding priorities. Moreover, for the past few years, all funding priorities have operated in the context of the balanced-budget agreement struck by Congress and the president in 1997, which caps all federal spending at certain levels. What this fundamentally means is a zero-sum game. S&T is only one facet of the capped federal budget, and the health sciences are only one facet of S&T. Thus the budget of NIH competes not only with other programs within its same appropriation bill (Health and Human Services, Education, and Labor) but also, theoretically, with all other discretionary budget items, including other science agency budgets, such as that of NSF. Whether issues of concern to feminist social scientists are part of this overall budget process is a function of whether they are on the radar of people who make federal S&T policy, members of Congress, the administration, or the constituency groups that lobby on behalf of both voters and campaign contributors.

FEDERAL S&T
FUNDING: CONTENT

The process of S&T funding is not divorced from its content. As noted earlier, decisions about increased or decreased dollars for any particular science agency or research program reflect the priorities of Congress and/or the administration. Moreover, within S&T, there exists a hierarchy of disciplines, determined both by national policy priorities and by the culture of science. For example, for much of the mid- to late twentieth century, political concerns about the encroachment of communism and the Soviet empire in particular meant that the greatest S&T emphasis in funding was on weapons-based research, and physics was the most valued area of science. With the collapse of the Soviet Union, and a diminution of the sense of direct military threat to the United States, that emphasis has waned in relative terms. By the end of the twentieth century, as different national priorities have emerged based on economic, political, and demographic trends, other areas of science have ascended the S&T hierarchy. Most notable among these are the health sciences, as evidenced by the precipitously increased budget of NIH, and information technology, the subject of a new, multiagency programmatic

initiative at the White House. The health sciences hold the promise of new technologies and products to improve health and longevity (which, of course, are of interest to the massive, and aging, baby-boom cohort) and have spawned new industries in biotechnology and genetic engineering that contribute to a booming economy. Information technologies are behind the current transformation of industrial society from one based on manufacturing material products to one based on processing information, and they also contribute to the booming economies of the United States and other highly developed nations.

Within general areas of science, there are also hierarchies, and in the U.S. system, these tend not to favor the behavioral and social sciences. For example, in the health sciences, although NIH supports a great deal of behavioral and social research, it is generally thought of and referred to as a "biomedical" science institution. Its structure and culture clearly favor the biological sciences over the clinical, behavioral, and social sciences. There is a historical current of antipathy for the behavioral and social sciences within the NIH institutional structure, as many biomedical scientists do not perceive behavioral and social research to be of the same caliber as their own sciences. Finally, even within the behavioral and social sciences at NIH, there is a hierarchy of disciplines. Psychology is more favored than sociology or anthropology, for example, perhaps because its content and methods— especially experimental psychology— generally are closer to those of the biological sciences and perhaps because it is linked to an organ system, the brain.

In addition to these hierarchies of scientific discipline and methodologies, there are also differential expectations about outcomes. Although basic research in the biological sciences is valorized at NIH, behavioral research and social research usually are expected to have direct application. Indeed, the term "basic research" is used in NIH to connote fundamental biological sciences but not fundamental behavioral and social research. The common tripartite description of NIH's program is "basic, clinical, and behavioral" research. Thus, although the expansion of basic knowledge in an area of virology or immunology (for example, how HIV particles bind with certain cell receptors) is celebrated as a primary objective of NIH funding, a similar expansion of basic knowledge in an area of sociology or anthropology (for example, how gender norms in a given culture confer vulnerability to infectious diseases on women and girls) is not or, at least, was not until very recently. (I will come back to this a bit later on.)

This leads to another important point about the relationship between the content of research and federal S&T funding, which will not be surprising to feminist (or probably any) social scientists. It is that, to the extent that research is perceived to be threatening to those making decisions about S&T policy, it will not be supported easily. Any research that is perceived to be inherently political is suspect to federal funders. Feminist scholarship, with its focus on gender arrangements, addresses a fundamental issue in the lives of policymakers and decision makers. Like Marxist scholarship, it challenges core beliefs about social arrangements that might lead to demands for social change. This makes policymakers, like most people, quite uncomfortable, especially if they are enjoying the privileges of existing gender arrangements. (A favorite Washington anecdote refers to the fact that the U.S. Congress is the last group in America in which the traditional arrangements of employed husband/father and homemaker wife/mother still predominate.)

IMPACT OF FEMINISM ON THE S&T AGENDA AND FUNDING

The second context in which to examine the impact of feminism on federally funded social science research is that of the impact of feminism on S&T more generally. Although difficult to demonstrate in a causal way, the impact of political feminism (as distinguished from feminist scholarship per se) has perhaps been most significant in the realm of gender equity claims, specifically for greater representation of women in the S&T enterprise. Efforts to enhance the education, training, and employment of more girls and women in science and technology have increased significantly in the last couple of decades. These have required breaking down longstanding stereotypes and deeply held beliefs about gender differences and preferences, namely, that girls and women are less suited to science than boys and men because they lack technical capacity. In great part based on rigorous feminist scholarship, legal and policy changes in the late twentieth century, especially affirmative action, have provided the institutional grounding for challenging the barriers formed from these stereotypes.

As a result of a host of concerted efforts on the part of schools, universities, scientific societies, and women's advocacy groups, the participation rates of women in S&T education and careers have grown precipitously, although they still lag far behind those of men in many scientific disciplines. For example, women now are earning close to 50 percent of the bachelor's degrees in science and engineering (S&E), up from 38 percent in the early 1980s. However, most of these are in the social sciences; women earned only 33 percent of the bachelor's degrees in physical sciences and mathematical and computer sciences and 17 percent in engineering in 1995. Similarly, women now are earning about 31 percent of doctoral degrees in S&E, with most still in the social sciences. For example, while women earned more doctorates than did men in psychology (the only S&E field for which this is the case), they earned only 10 percent of the doctorates in engineering in 1995. With respect to postgraduate employment, women composed slightly more than 22 percent of the S&E labor force and 22 percent of the doctoral scientists and engineers in 1995. Again, most of these women were social and psychological scientists rather than physicists and engineers (NSF 1999b).

In addition to increased representation in academia and industry, women also are more represented now in positions of power and authority in government, where S&T policy and funding decisions are made. Women as members of Congress and the cabinet, as staff within federal agencies, and as scientific peer reviewers all have an influence on the shaping of the federal S&T agenda. This influence could be seen most clearly in, inter alia, the rise of women's health research as a major item in the federal biomedical science agenda. As described in more detail elsewhere, this is the result of very determined action by women's health activists (including feminist scholars), a number of congresswomen, the existence of a female director of NIH, and the emergence of sophisticated women-focused (if not explicitly feminist) lobbying and public affairs firms (Auerbach and Figert 1995; Narrigan et al. 1997). Although it had its origins in the women's health movement that had been in existence for decades, the more recent policy action probably required the confluence of the following factors. It began with a Public Health Service Task Force on Women's Health Issues, which issued its report in 1985 and was cochaired by Dr. Ruth Kirschstein, the first and still one of the only female directors of an NIH institute. (Currently, Dr. Kirschstein is acting director of NIH, and women are directors of only 2 of the 25 NIH institutes and centers.) Key recommendations of that report, which were subsequently picked up by the Congressional Caucus on Women's Issues—headed at the time by Representatives Patricia Schroeder (D-Colo.) and Olympia Snowe (R-Me.)—were greater attention to women's health issues and greater efforts to include women in NIH-supported clinical trials. Soon after, a number of other actions ensued, key among them being the creation of the Office of Research on Women's Health at NIH in 1990 (although it did not receive statutory authority until 1993) and the development of the Women's Health Initiative. The latter is a major longitudinal study of women's health that was introduced by Dr. Bernadine Healy, the first (and so far only) woman director of NIH, within two weeks of her confirmation in April 1991. These and other actions have resulted in much greater attention being paid to diseases and disorders that disproportionately affect women and in greater participation of women in clinical trials.

At the staffing level, the proportion of women in senior scientific administration positions with direct involvement in developing the NIH institutes' extramural programs increased from about one-third to one-half between 1990 and 1999 (NIH Human Resource Program Support 1999).

All of this, of course, takes place in a context in which women in the aggregate have more education, have more income, and participate politically more than ever before. It is not hubris to say that the impact of the feminist movement on American

political and social life in general is at the root of any particular advances in the S&T arena.

IMPACT OF FEMINIST
SCHOLARSHIP

In addition to greater representation of women in S&T, feminism is also responsible for affecting the content of S&T. To some degree, feminist scholarship has infiltrated the federal S&T enterprise, although it has done so in a somewhat diluted form. This is clearest in the ways in which the concept of gender has made its way into the common lexicon, for both good and bad, as noted elsewhere (Auerbach 1999). Although the use of the term "gender" in scientific research signifies some recognition of the social and cultural dimensions of biological sex, in many situations, "gender" has merely become a proxy for "sex" because it is perceived as a more "politically correct" term. One place in which this is most apparent is in the *NIH Guidelines on the Inclusion of Women and Minorities as Subjects in Clinical Research* (NIH 1994). Revised in 1994 as a result of the women's health advocacy efforts described previously, these guidelines require that women and members of minority groups and their subpopulations be included in all NIH-supported research projects involving human subjects, unless a clear and compelling rationale and justification is provided that such inclusion is scientifically inappropriate. (Cost may not be used as a rationale for exclusion.) As stated in the guidelines, the intent of this policy is to ensure that all future NIH-supported biomedical and behavioral research involving human subjects will be carried out in a manner sufficient to elicit information about individuals of both genders and the diverse racial and ethnic groups and, in the case of clinical trials, to examine differential effects on such groups.

Although in one place the guidelines say that "Principal Investigators should assess the theoretical and/or scientific linkages between gender, race/ethnicity, and their topic of study," elsewhere the guidelines make clear that the review of applications will only assess appropriate representation of "both genders." The gender comparisons that are required only relate to statistical comparisons of outcomes by sex.

It is common, therefore, to see reference in NIH-supported studies to "gender differences" when in fact biological males and females are simply being compared on some dependent variable or outcome measure. Typically, these studies offer no analysis of how gender as a social and cultural construction is operating to produce whatever differences are observed by sex. However, it is important to note that in the past few years, specific attention to the dynamics of gender—in the way feminist scholars mean it—has emerged at the programmatic level at NIH.

For example, in the area of HIV and AIDS research, as the proportion of women contracting HIV infection from heterosexual relations has increased throughout the world, it has become clear to all involved in AIDS research that it is essential to better understand the ways in which unequal power in interpersonal relationships, based on cultural norms about gender roles and responsibilities, confers risk for HIV infection upon women in many societies. Although feminist scholars and advocates have made this point from the beginning of the global epidemic, even in the United States, where women were a minority of HIV and AIDS cases until recently, it has taken harsh epidemiological data to bring more mainstream AIDS researchers and policymakers to the same conclusion. So in the past few years, not only women but also the dynamics of gender have risen on the list of priorities for research in HIV prevention and care, and an increasing number of grants in these areas have been funded in recent years. The current emphasis on developing vaginal microbicides for preventing sexual transmission of HIV that women can use without the knowledge of or negotiation with men is particularly illustrative of this change (NIH 1999).

But other contributions from feminist social scientists largely have been unincorporated (if not ignored) in the federal science agenda. In particular, feminist critiques of the social organization of science, including the ways in which training for and conduct of scientific research may be gendered, are not commonly funded areas of research. As argued earlier, the reticence to fund such research is related to antipathy toward social science research in general as well as to discomfort about challenging existing social structural arrangements from which most policy shapers currently benefit.

STRATEGIES FOR
GREATER IMPACT

The impact of feminism on federally funded S&T can easily be seen as a "glass is half-empty or glass is half-full" phenomenon. Clearly, much progress has been made, but much work remains to be done to have the goals and analyses of feminist politics and scholarship fully realized. There are some simple, but useful, strategies that may help move things along even further, although they often require intellectual and political compromise that is too difficult for some feminists to accept.

First, many of the gains made by feminist scholars, and women generally, in the federal S&T arena have been made stealthily. Rather than explicitly promoting a straightforwardly feminist program, many feminist women and men have moved their agendas forward by using what appear to be less threatening approaches to their audiences. For example, rather than arguing the importance of redressing gender inequality in biomedical research, savvy advocates for increased funding for breast cancer research instead appealed to the paternalism of male members of Congress (and society at large) by focusing on the possibility that their mothers, wives, or daughters might be afflicted. Cast in this way, women's health research became something even very conservative congressmen could, and did,

support. Choosing frameworks and words carefully can be an effective strategy.

A second and related strategy is to translate complex questions and analyses into simpler and more familiar language. This is a particular challenge for intellectuals of any discipline, because we hold our concepts and our claims very dear and have engaged in many contests to defend them within the scientific community. To then have to distill and translate them into what to us seem more banal and incomplete terms can feel like an assault on our intellectual integrity. From the perspective of affecting policy action, however, conceptual fidelity is much less important than providing policymakers tools that they can understand, find persuasive, and then use among their colleagues to influence change.

This point leads to a third strategy for increasing the impact of feminism, and that is to make our research fit the funders' missions and priorities. All federal agencies have mandates and missions spelled out in their authorizing legislation. In addition, most agencies that fund research have operational agendas, or "strategic" plans, that outline their scientific programs and funding priorities. In many cases, academic researchers have been involved in the processes of developing such plans and priorities (federal agencies usually engage outside constituency groups in these efforts), so their agendas may already be woven within those of the agencies. In any event, potential grantees should pay careful attention to the stated priorities of the funders. This does not mean that one cannot do the research that most excites one; rather, it means that one must develop ways of framing that research within the priorities of the funders. Here, too, some concessions may have to be made with respect to the concepts, terms, and frameworks employed or at least how they are described in a grant application. But savvy grantees usually manage to conduct the research they want by finding ways to articulate their projects within the agendas of the funders.

CONCLUSION

Late-twentieth-century feminist politics and feminist scholarship have had a significant impact on the process and content of federally funded S&T, which may not be entirely evident to people outside the federal enterprise. The impact may be more observable to those of us on the inside because we can directly see—and appreciate—the incremental nature of change, given what we know about the bureaucratic and political processes operating. Those on the outside may be less patient, especially if it is their research that is not (yet) being funded. But, by better educating themselves about the dynamics of science policymaking and budgeting, and by being better political actors themselves—for example, by making their scholarship understandable and relevant to policymakers in order to get it on their radar in the first place—feminist social scientists can help hasten the process of change.

References

Auerbach, Judith D. 1999. From the SWS President: Gender as Proxy. *Gender & Society* 13(Dec.):701-3.

Auerbach, Judith D. and Anne E. Figert. 1995. Women's Health Research: Public Policy and Sociology. *Journal of Health and Social Behavior* (Extra issue):115-31.

Garnett, Shannon E. 1999. NINDS, Parkinson's Advocates Testify Before Congress. *NIH Record LI* 25:1-4.

Narrigan, Deborah, Jane Sprague Zones, Nancy Worcester, and Maxine Jo Grad. 1997. Research to Improve Women's Health: An Agenda for Equity. In *Women's Health: Complexities and Differences*, ed. S. B. Ruzek, V. L. Olesen, and Adele E. Clarke. Columbus: Ohio State University Press.

NIH (National Institutes of Health). 1994. NIH Guidelines on the Inclusion of Women and Minorities as Subjects in Clinical Research. *NIH Guide for Grants and Contracts*, vol. 23, no. 11, 18 Mar.

———. 1999. *National Institutes of Health Fiscal Year 2001 Plan for HIV-Related Research*. Bethesda, MD: National Institutes of Health, Office of AIDS Research. Available at http://www.nih.gov/od/oar.

———. Human Resource Program Support. 1999. Data from the Human Resource Data Base.

NSF (National Science Foundation). 1999a. Table 1: Federal obligations for total research by detailed field of science & engineering and selected agency: fiscal years 1970-99. Available at www.nsf.gov/sbe/srs/srs99345/htmstart.htm.

———. 1999b. Women, Minorities, and Persons with Disabilities in Science and Engineering: 1998. NSF 99-338.

Zitner, Aaron. 1999. Health Legislation Turns Personal. *Boston Globe*, 23 Nov.

Feminism and Family
Studies for a New Century

By MAXINE BACA ZINN

ABSTRACT: Feminism has revolutionized family studies. This article traces the impact of feminism on the family field in the last quarter of the twentieth century, focusing on (1) academic representations of the family before feminism; (2) second-wave feminism's unmasking of the gender-structured family; (3) how feminist pluralism enlarged the family field; (4) current feminist debates on family diversity and change; and (5) connections between feminist scholarship on the family and public policy.

Maxine Baca Zinn is professor of sociology at Michigan State University, where she is also senior researcher at the Julian Samora Research Institute. The coauthor of Diversity in Families *(fifth edition, 1999), she has written widely on gender, families, and racial inequality.*

THESE are extraordinary times for study of the family. Accelerated social changes in the United States and the world are reshaping family life across the social spectrum. As society experiences major earthquakes, feminist thinking about family life is undergoing seismic shifts as well. This article examines the intellectual contributions and challenges to the family field posed by feminism over the past three decades. Although there is no single feminist perspective on families, feminist thinkers have demonstrated that family forms are socially and historically constructed, not monolithic universals that exist across time and space, and that family arrangements are not the natural result of biological differences between women and men. Feminist thinkers have produced a vast scholarship that spans the disciplines and recasts family life through a gendered lens. Today, new branches of feminism reveal how other complexities, such as race and class, shape families. They offer wider, more inclusive frameworks to guide family scholarship in the new century.

This article traces the impact of feminism on the family field. Taking a chronological approach, I begin with a brief look at family studies before feminism engaged the field in the 1970s. I then address the ways in which second-wave feminism's unmasking of gender and power relations in families utterly transformed a prosaic subject that had fallen from favor among progressive scholars. Turning, then, to current feminism, I focus on the emergent themes of inequality and family variation. New attention to family and household patterns as they diverge in different segments of society is redirecting the feminist agenda. I conclude with a discussion of how feminist-fueled family debates are reflected in public discourse. Unfortunately, I cannot cite many of the influential feminist works and foundational texts; space constraints require that I paint with broad brush strokes a picture of how the field has changed with time.

FAMILY STUDIES BEFORE FEMINISM

To revisit the origins and development of family studies is to appreciate feminism's revolutionary impact. In the late nineteenth and early twentieth centuries, the field of family study emerged out of a deep, fundamental belief in the need to document and ameliorate social problems (Thomas and Wilcox 1987). Social observers bemoaned the deterioration of traditional family life caused by rapid change, calling for wholesome families as a way of strengthening the social fabric. The family was thought to be the "building block of society." It was conceived as a private sphere, distinct and separate from the world at large and especially from work and the marketplace. Family was women's sphere, while men toiled in the workplace. This division of labor was a critical feature of the modern world. All families immersed in society would converge into a single family arrangement. Although this was not a full-blown theory of the family, the emphasis on separate spheres, equating men with the public and women with the private, dominated early thought.

Early family scholars were pro-family, but they did not endorse any family form. They were influenced by the Chicago school of American sociology and were preoccupied with the transition from traditional to modern social forms. Ideas about modernization ordained the nuclear family as the norm even though there were many varieties of families in different regional, economic, racial, and ethnic groups. Although they were liberal or reformist on most social issues, "early family thinkers were extremely conservative in regard to family" (Osmond 1987, 113). Ignoring the economic circumstances and social discrimination that produced distinctive family patterns, they confused difference with disorganization.

By mid-century, a mythical family prototype had become entrenched in structural functionalism, the dominant social science framework of the era. Structural functionalism was a theory of society and a sociological refinement of popular ideas about the family. The theory's central image was a society composed of interdependent parts linked together for the good of the whole. Social order was maintained by a high degree of consensus and a division of labor between the various components of society. The most basic component was the family, "organized around a unique and unalterable type of role structure operating for something larger than itself" (Kingsbury and Scanzoni 1993, 170). Men's instrumental roles linked families with the outside world, while women's expressive roles ensured family solidarity. Structural functionalism made role differentiation an essential feature of families and the larger social order as well. The division of society into public and private components with a corresponding division of men's and women's roles was viewed as a complementary arrangement well suited to advanced, industrial societies. The conjugal family was a haven of consensus in an increasingly competitive public world. It socialized the next generation and trained youths to take their places in society. Like past family thought, the strategy of structural functionalism was to posit one family type (by no means the only family form, even then) and define it as "the normal family" (Boss and Thorne 1989). The authority structure consisting of father as provider and head and mother as caretaker and heart was the dominant family framework in the 1950s and 1960s. It glorified a historically specific and class-specific family form of the 1950s as the benchmark for families in modern society. In effect, structural functionalism made the modern nuclear family a falsely universal construct. It ignored difference, even though race and class differences were at the very foundation of family experience.

THE EARLY FEMINIST TRANSFORMATION

The family has long held an intrinsic appeal for feminists. Early frameworks seeking to understand the position of women in society often made kinship and domestic relations a theoretical priority. Liberal feminism, radical feminism, and socialist feminism offered different answers to questions about why women have lesser social status and fewer advantages than men. Despite their differences, each implicated the family in one way or another and sparked disputes about how to bring about liberating social changes. "Smash monogamy" and "abolish the nuclear family" were early rallying calls that generated fierce controversies.

From the late 1960s and through the 1970s, feminist scholars unmasked an idealized vision of the family that supported women's oppression. Feminist critiques developed in the context of the social and political upheavals of the times. Radicals, people of color, and feminists questioned functionalism's basic premises. They mounted strong opposition to the model created by past family experts. They challenged the unified family because it obscured women's experiences. Where the mainstream family model saw the family as a cohesive system resting on integrated sex roles, feminists argued that the family was the primary site of women's oppression. What functionalism saw as role differentiation feminists identified as the core of family politics.

As feminists posed new questions and offered new ways to see family life, they also took careful stock of their own impact on the family field (Ferree 1990; Glenn 1987; Osmond and Thorne 1993; Targ 1989; Thompson and Walker 1995; Thorne 1992; Walker and Thompson 1984). These works provide excellent reviews of the feminist knowledge explosion in family studies. Osmond and Thorne (1993) outline the distinctive features of feminist family scholarship including (1) the centrality of women's experiences; (2) the social construction of gender as a central concept; (3) attention to sociohistorical context; (4) the empirical reality of multiple family forms; and (5) the commitment to social change and value-oriented approaches to studying family life.

By deconstructing family worlds, feminists began to fashion alternative definitions of what families are. For example, they demonstrated that the concept of family is an ideological concept, which conceals varied meanings and configurations. To move beyond symbolism and idealization, family should be distinguished from household. A family is a construct of meanings and relationships; a household is a residential and economic unit (Osmond and Thorne 1993; Rapp 1978). To put it another way, "family" designates the way things should be, while "household" refers to the manner in which women, men, and children actually come together in domestic units (Fernandez-Kelly and Garcia 1990, 141). Feminists also deconstructed the daily activities that take place within domestic units. For example, housework was redefined as work, and concepts such as caring work were introduced to describe many of the unpaid and often unrecognized tasks that women perform for the benefit of others. The feminist themes that revolutionized family studies in the 1980s are summarized in the following.

Gender is pervasive in family life

Gender organizes every aspect of family life, including roles, everyday practices, images, and power. From this vantage point, the family takes on a different meaning, especially the conception of the family as a unified whole, treated as a harmony of interests between family members. This conventional view, however, neglects power relations making up families, the entanglement of love and domination that often makes the family "an arena of struggle" for women and men (Hartmann 1981). Ever since Jessie Bernard's classic work on marriage revealed that there are two marriages in every marital union—his and hers—and that his is better than hers (Bernard 1972), family scholars have shown that women and men experience the family in different ways.

Families are linked with larger institutions and structures

The image of the family as a haven or domestic retreat sets family relations apart from the world at large. "The myth of separate worlds" (Kanter 1984) was an early focal point for feminist scholars who argued that the public-private dualism romanticized the family, obscured family dilemmas, and denied social inequities that often preclude the family ideal. Feminism exposed many ways in which broader social systems enter into family dynamics, reproducing macrostructural divisions inside microstructural family worlds.

Families are socially constructed and historically changing

Feminist viewpoints have challenged the tendency to treat families as if they were natural and inevitable human arrangements. Instead, feminism has argued that families are social. They differ dramatically across time, space, and social strata. Even "stages we take for granted like childhood, adolescence, and adulthood are not timeless entities built into human nature but aspects of the human condition that have been reshaped with historical changes" (Skolnick 1993, 45).

Individual families are the product of human agency

Families are not molded from the outside in. While feminist frameworks emphasize the situations and contexts that construct families, they do not ascribe to a rigid social determinism. Family members are neither robots nor lumps of clay. Human agency is critical in understanding how people cope with, adapt to, and often change families to create meaningful lives for themselves. Facing different contingencies, women, men, and children shape their families through their own actions and behaviors. The concept of family adaptive strategies can be useful for illustrating ongoing interaction between family members and their social environments.

NEW FEMINIST PERSPECTIVES ON FAMILY LIFE AND INEQUALITY

As these themes swept feminism in the 1980s, they refocused the family field. Gender and inequality together with the feminist understanding of structural influences gradually emerged as core issues. At the same time, creative tensions within feminism shaped the feminist framework and its influence on the field as a whole.

Since the late 1960s, minority scholars and their allies have charged that mainstream scholarship was not alone in misrepresenting the family. Women of color argued that the family means different things to different groups. Treating gender as the main cause of women's inequality obscured women's multiple and contradictory family experiences. As they analyzed families from an insider's perspective, many other women began to interrogate and reformulate earlier feminist generalizations. Their scholarship revealed that, in the absence of outside support, many women found collective strength in family life. Some women joined forces with husbands, brothers, and other community men to forge political struggles against racial and class-based oppression. While mainstream feminists had indicted the "patriarchal family" as the primary site of women's oppression, new research identified a far more complex reality. Though most families and households were indeed patriarchal, they were also sites of racial and class-based solidarity—places to resist discrimination and exploitation (Caulfield 1974; Stack 1974; Glenn 1987; Baca Zinn 1975; Kibria 1994; Pessar 1995). Under certain circumstances, gender divisions are less important as families strive to be strong and united in the face of external pressures.

Early feminist claims that wage work outside of the family would emancipate women fell short in light of race and class differences. Women's work patterns have always varied by race. For example, African American women have had a long history of being out to work, a trend that increased only modestly after World War II. Much greater rates of increase occurred among white, Latina, Chinese, and Filipina women even before the advent of the feminist movement of the 1970s. But because their paid work has been bound up with race and class inequalities, the employment of women of color has not produced equality. They often have labored in race- and gender-segregated occupations—work that may create temporary shifts in day-to-day family living but does not change the traditional marital division of labor (Zavella 1987). Family relations between women and men do not occur in a vacuum. By incorporating race and class into the analysis, other feminists offered a fresh view of the opportunities people (both women and men) have to go to work, to form families, and to shape their lives in the face of restricted resources.

By the end of the 1980s, an emergent discourse on family diversity was pressing academic feminism for a redefinition of the key issues in the field. Lesbian and gay feminists underscored compulsory hetersexuality as a key component of family organization. They showed that, like race and class, sexuality is a system of inequality, which constrains same-sex relationships. With more knowledge about the family experiences of marginalized groups, a powerful lesson took hold: feminist generalizations are not applicable regardless of social context (Collins 1994, 62).

In the last two decades of the twentieth century, feminist thought has turned to particular contexts and their effects on family life. One important framework is multiracial feminism, which examines the interactive influence of gender, race, and class and posits racial inequality as a major factor influencing family formation. Central to this perspective is that different privileges and disadvantages accrue to family members as the result of their location in a racially stratified, class-based society. Different social locations are the difference that make a difference. They structure work, wages, and the social and legal supports crucial to family life. Much of the new scholarship emerging from multiracial feminism examines racial-ethnic families and shows that diversity is not an intrinsic property of different groups but the product of power relations that structure the experience of all families, albeit in different ways (Baca Zinn 1994, 305).[1]

Multiracial feminism has been fruitful in developing new avenues for family study by redirecting attention from power relations exclusively within families to power relations between families as well. This reveals how advantaged families and disadvantaged families are intertwined (Baca Zinn 1994; Dill 1994; Glenn 1992; Collins 1997). As Dill (1994) shows, the histories of racial-ethnic families in the United States were not a matter of simple coexistence with dominant race and class groups. Instead, the opportunities of some families rested on the disadvantages of other families. Social and economic conditions produce interconnected family patterns today as well. For example, many professional lifestyles in dual-career families depend on race and class privileges to hire immigrants and other women of color as child care and domestic workers. In the context of such power relations, the family lives of domestic workers often suffer. Particular circumstances require different adaptations and different understandings of the social conditions affecting families.

In the twenty-first century, the issues raised by multiracial feminism will become more urgent. Changing demographic realities and their accompanying social divisions pose great challenges to family scholars and society at large. Indeed, the future of the United States as a modern industrial democracy may well depend on improving the status of its diverse racial groups and their families. Efforts to refocus family study through difference stand out in several end-of-the-century family anthologies (Hansen and Garey 1998; Coontz with Parson and Raley 1999; Ferguson 1998) and in the important new *Handbook of Family Diversity* (Demo, Allen, and Fine 2000).

As academic feminism on the family has matured, gender has remained an anchor point. But a more complex understanding of the family's relation to society (especially how that relationship is influenced by class, race, and sexuality) stretches gender in many ways. Once understood oppositionally, as a simple difference between women and men, feminist approaches began to see gender as a range of relations between differently situated people. This permitted us to see that gender relations occur between women and between men. It has also paved the way for careful examination of men's family experiences (Arendell 1995; Coltrane 1996).

FEMINIST PERSPECTIVES AT CENTURY'S END

At the end of the twentieth century, the family field is forever changed. Although not all family scholars have worked from an explicitly feminist perspective, many feminist concerns are now at the heart of family studies. Even in the most mainstream venues and in highly quantitative studies, themes of gendered conditions in families are being addressed. Diversity, inequality, and conflict are now woven through family studies, replacing the old themes of family uniformity, convergence, and consensus. Much of this scholarship is built upon the feminist reconstruction begun in the decades of the 1960s and 1970s. Yet by grounding family studies in the experiences of different groups of people, a new model of family life is firmly in place. The scholarship of feminists, gays and lesbians, profeminist men, and racial minorities has swept the field with such perturbing ramifications that "business as usual [is] no longer possible" (Doherty et al. 1993, 15). David Cheal (1991) refers to this stage of development as "the big bang," a dramatic period of diversification in family studies (53). Other family scholars agree that a paradigm shift has occurred (Allen and Demo 1995; Mann et al. 1997; Skolnick 1993).

Many social changes of the century's last three decades have set the stage for the transformation. Families and the world in which they are anchored have changed dramatically. Broad social trends like women's increasing workplace participation, high divorce rates, growing class inequalities, greater racial and ethnic diversity in the United States, and the movement of lesbians and gays into the mainstream of society have destabilized domestic life. The family is now a tangled array of relationships. The form once idealized as natural is declining throughout the industrial world. The conditions of postindustrial capitalism are replacing an arrangement that Judith Stacey calls "the modern family"—an intact nuclear household composed of a breadwinner husband, a homemaker wife, and their dependent children. In place of this model are a variety of patterns including widespread female-headed households and growing impoverishment of women and their children. As women create innovative ways to cope with economic uncertainty and domestic upheaval, their households expand and contract as spouses, lovers, children, and friends leave and return. The "postmodern family" is fluid, unsettled, and recombinant (Stacey 1990).

Postmodern families are not created by economic transformations alone. Several forces in the postindustrial world have given way to an era of opportunities for families to expand in new directions. The recent visibility of lesbian and gay families illustrates an important cultural shift. "Families of choice" add to the unprecedented variety of contemporary family arrangements (Demo and Allen 1996; Weston 1991). Whereas "lesbian/gay" and "family" were once treated as antithetical, Stacey (1996) contends that same-sex couples bearing children are "one of the only new, truly original, and decidedly controversial genres of family formation and structure to have emerged in the West during many centuries" (110).

The postmodern rubric applies well to immigrants, whose family configurations are in constant flux. Migration entails separation from families, homes, jobs, and communities in one locale to be rebuilt in another. As migrants make their way amid economic and political changes now sweeping the world, they adjust to their new surroundings through "binational," "transnational," and "multinational," families—arrangements induced by global changes in work opportunities in the United States and the world (Chavez 1992; Hondagneu-Sotelo and Avila 1997). Historical research, too, highlights the elastic qualities of immigrant families. It turns out that family fluidity is structural and a commonplace adaptation.

CONTEMPORARY DEBATES

Although feminist thinkers share a broadly defined perspective on the family, they also differ on many issues. Three questions capture some current areas of disagreement. First, to what extent has feminism reshaped the family field? Whereas many feminist and family scholars herald a paradigm shift, others disagree. For example, Dorothy Smith argues that despite feminist alternatives, the field's conception of the family is as conventional as ever—a legally married couple sharing a household, with an adult male in paid employment whose earnings provide the economic basis of the family household. The adult female may also earn an income, but her primary responsibility is the care of husband, household, and children. Smith (1993) calls this model the Standard North American Family (SNAF), an ideological code that orders theory, governs public policy, and infects even progressive elements within family studies.

Second, does the new emphasis on family diversity preclude a unified family analysis? In other words, does the deconstruction of the family defy generalizations? This tension reflects familiar social science concerns about the current preoccupation with difference. For example, some scholars fear that too much emphasis on diversity will blind us to the commonalities that exist between families (Doherty et al. 1993; Skolnick 1998). For others, multiplicity need not lead to an empty pluralism of infinite family configurations or lifestyle choices. Instead, it invites more rigorous scholarship. Family diversity is implicated in different economic orders and the global shifts that accompany them. Scholars have suggested that the multiplicity of household types is one of the chief props of the world economy (Smith, Wallerstein, and Evers 1985). The new challenge is to set about finding unities and commonalities while being attentive to specificities—as Karen Sacks (1989) puts it, "to conceptualize unity in diversity" (535). Coontz and Parson (1997) note that converging strands in women's family and work experiences go hand in hand with ever expanding variations by race and class. As women from every group struggle to mesh paid work and motherhood, their efforts "interact differently with racist institutions, cultural resources, and socioeconomic trends, producing different dynamics and outcomes" (447). Far from being only about marginalized families, the new structural diversity approaches illuminate family conditions in dominant social locations as well. Most important, they offer a unified analysis of how families in different social locations are linked through structural conditions.

The third question highlighting disagreement between researchers is, How important is family structure? Shifting patterns of marriage and childbirth, together with the rise of new family forms, are producing lively feminist debates. Whereas some lament the declining predominance of the two-parent family, others are less pessimistic about it. Despite varying positions on the two-parent family, feminists tend to agree that end-of-the-century demographic and economic changes are the result of trends set in motion long ago and that conditions of postindustrial capitalism are exacerbating family change throughout the world. Even in different societies, families and households are undergoing similar shifts as a result of global economic changes. But feminists disagree on the meaning of such changes for women and on how children are affected by this aspect of family transformation. Some, for example, highlight growing inequalities that accompany family diversity such as the difference between dualearner couples and single-mother families in economic well-being (McLanahan and Casper 1995, 3).

Some feminists have argued that macroeconomic shifts and the family trends that accompany them—rising levels of women's labor force participation and female-headed households—are not entirely burdensome for women. Instead, these trends have positive consequences in that their new freedoms from marriage foster women's autonomy (Hartmann 1987). Another interpretation, however, is cautious of generalizing about women's independence from men, due to the disproportionate levels of poverty in female-headed households (Baca Zinn 1987; Pessar, 1995).

But while they differ on the details, feminists agree on several major points. They agree that the decline in marriage, the rise of female-headed households, and the increasing incidence of single parenthood are consequences of social, economic, and political dislocations rather than the cause, as so many would have us believe. Feminists agree that the problem is not simply a matter of family structure per se but the broad issue of social support for families—whether headed by one parent, two parents, or a collection of "fictive kin." These points of agreement generate considerable resistance in today's political climate.

A FEMINIST PARADOX: RECOGNITION AND REJECTION

Family issues are at the heart of religious, political, and philosophical ideologies. Liberals, conservatives, and progressives (including most feminists) are divided over marriage, women's equality, gay and lesbian rights, child rearing, and welfare. When these issues are debated in the media, in Congress, and in state legislatures, feminists are often morally condemned on the grounds that their views are self-indulgent. Many critics view feminism as a threat to the family. For them, broad shifts in gender arrangements represent family decline and are morally framed as a national loss of family values. For

anti-feminists, excessive personal freedom has spawned a divorce culture and unmarried parenthood, which are responsible for our worst social problems. By reinvoking ideas deeply rooted in conventional thought, the rhetoric of family values galvanizes public opinion around the idealized two-parent, heterosexual family (Nicholson 1997; Stacey 1996; Dill, Baca Zinn, and Patton 1998).

Feminism in the family field confronts a growing paradox. In spite of a rich storehouse of knowledge, and feminist advocacy organizations such as the Institute for Women's Policy Research, feminist scholarship has not influenced lawmakers in the creation of a national, official, overall family policy. Nor did feminists prevent the enactment of recent legislation ending the federal safety net for poor families. False assumptions about the working family provided the rationale for the 1996 welfare reform legislation, which ignored the conclusions of feminist and other progressive social science research that welfare reform would not end poverty as we know it. Feminists have repeatedly pointed out, albeit to political deaf ears, that for better or for worse, the traditional family cannot predominate in the postmodern world. These conclusions have been ignored because they challenge the dominant family ideology. Much as it did a century ago, a mythical family image remains a constant thread in popular and policy discourses.

If feminist scholarship is ignored by policymakers, it is often attacked by conservatives. The Institute for

American Values has waged a public campaign to restore the traditional family. In 1997, the institute released to the media a right-of-center review of college textbooks. Claiming that widely used family textbooks are anti-marriage and a national embarrassment (Glenn 1997), the report pilloried feminist texts for denigrating the beneficial consequences of marriage for individuals and society.

Given the political obstacles to progressive feminist scholarship, is there a possibility that feminism will prevail in the media and in policy arenas as it has in academic settings? A new national organization, the Council on Contemporary Families, was recently formed to serve as an agent of social change. The council seeks to promote the strengths and welfare of all families. Its major goal is to foster better public understanding of what contemporary families need and how these needs can be met. Reflecting the diversity of families that it seeks to serve, its members are researchers and clinicians drawn from a wide variety of fields within and outside of academe, all committed to bringing the best of research and experience to a wider public (Council on Contemporary Families 1999).

Feminism has redefined family studies as it existed in the first three-quarters of the twentieth century. This is an important accomplishment. But if feminism is to have its fair share of influence on families and society, the paradigm shift is not enough. At the threshold of the new century, feminism finds itself in a moment of opportunity. We have answers, not all by any means, but many answers to the pressing family issues of our times. What better way to further feminist advances than to shape public agendas and mobilize political support for the nation's families, whatever their form?

Note

1. The term "racial-ethnic" refers to groups that are socially subordinate and remain culturally distinct within U.S. society. It is meant to encompass (1) the systematic discrimination against socially constructed racial groups and (2) their distinctive cultural arrangements. Historically, the categories of African American, Latino, Asian American, and Native American were constructed as both racially and culturally distinct. In each group, members share a distinctive culture, have a common heritage, and have developed a common identity with a larger society that subordinates them (Baca Zinn and Dill 1994, 11-12).

References

Allen, Katherine and David H. Demo. 1995. The Families of Lesbians and Gay Men: A New Frontier in Family Research. *Journal of Marriage and the Family* 57 (Feb.):111-27.

Arendell, Terry. 1995. *Fathers and Divorce*. Thousand Oaks, CA: Sage.

Baca Zinn, Maxine. 1975. Political Familism: Toward Sex Role Equality in Chicano Families. *Aztlan* 6(1): 13-26.

———. 1987. Structural Transformation and Minority Families. In *Women, Households and the Economy*, ed. Lourdes Beneria and Catharine R. Stimpson. New Brunswick, NJ: Rutgers University Press.

———. 1994. Feminist Rethinking from Racial Ethnic Families. In *Women of Color in U.S. Society*, ed. Maxine Baca Zinn and Bonnie Thornton Dill. Philadelphia: Temple University Press.

Baca Zinn, Maxine and Bonnie Thornton Dill. 1994. Difference and Domination. In *Women of Color in U.S. Society*, ed. Maxine Baca Zinn and Bonnie Thornton Dill. Philadelphia: Temple University Press.

Bernard, Jessie. 1972. *The Future of Marriage*. New York: Bantam Books.

Boss, Pauline and Barrie Thorne. 1989. Family Sociology and Family Therapy: A Feminist Linkage. In *Women in Families*, ed. Monica McGoldrick, Carol M. Anderson, and Froma Walsh. New York: W. W. Norton.

Caulfield, Minna Davis. 1974. Imperialism, the Family, and Cultures of Resistance. *Socialist Revolution* 20:67-85.

Chavez, Leo R. 1992. *Shadowed Lives: Undocumented Immigrants in American Society*. Orlando, FL: Harcourt Brace.

Cheal, David. 1991. *Family and the State of Theory*. Toronto: University of Toronto Press.

Collins, Patricia Hill. 1994. Shifting the Center: Race, Class, and Feminist Theorizing About Motherhood. In *Mothering: Ideology, Experience, and Agency*, ed. Evelyn Nakano Glenn, Grace Chang, and Linda Rennie Forcey. New York: Routledge.

———. 1997. African-American Women and Economic Justice: A Preliminary Analysis of Wealth, Family, and Black Social Class. *University of Cincinnati Law Review* 65(3):825-52.

Coltrane, Scott. 1996. *Family Man: Fatherhood, Housework, and Gender Equity*. New York: Oxford University Press.

Coontz, Stephanie and Maya Parson. 1997. Complicating the Contested Terrain of Work/Family Intersections. *Signs* 22(2):440-52.

Coontz, Stephanie with Maya Parson and Gabrielle Raley. 1999. *American Families: A Multicultural Reader*. New York: Routledge.

Council on Contemporary Families. 1999. Newsletter 2(May).

Demo, David H. and Katherine R. Allen. 1996. Diversity Within Gay and Lesbian Families: Challenges and Implications for Family Theory and Research. *Journal of Social and Personal Relationships* 13:413-34.

Demo, David H., Katherine R. Allen, and Mark A. Fine, ed. 2000. *Handbook of Family Diversity*. New York: Oxford University Press.

Dill, Bonnie Thornton. 1994. Fictive Kin, Paper Sons, and Compadrazgo: Women of Color and the Struggle for Family Survival. In *Women of Color in U.S. Society*, ed. Maxine Baca Zinn and Bonnie Thornton Dill. Philadelphia: Temple University Press.

Dill, Bonnie Thornton, Maxine Baca Zinn, and Sandra Patton. 1998. Race, Family Values, and Welfare Reform. *Sage Race Relations Abstracts* 23(Fall):4-31.

Doherty, William J., Pauline G. Boss, Ralph La Rossa, Walter R. Schumm, and Suzanne K. Steinmetz. 1993. Family Theories and Methods: A Contextual Approach. In *Sourcebook of Family Theories*, ed. William J. Doherty, Pauline G. Boss, Ralph La Rossa, Walter R. Schumm, and Suzanne K. Steinmetz. New York: Plenum Press.

Ferguson, Susan J. 1998. *Shifting the Center: Understanding Contemporary Families*. Mountain View, CA: Mayfield.

Fernandez-Kelly, Maria Patricia and Anna M. Garcia. 1990. Power Surrendered, Power Restored: The Politics of Home and Work Among Hispanic Women. In *Women and Politics in America*, ed. Louise Tilly and Patricia Gurrin. New York: Russell Sage Foundation.

Ferree, Myra Marx. 1990. Beyond Separate Spheres: Feminism and Family

Research. *Journal of Marriage and the Family* 52(4):866-84.

Glenn, Evelyn Nakano. 1987. Gender and the Family. In *Analyzing Gender*, ed. Beth B. Hess and Myra Marx Ferree. Newbury Park, CA: Sage.

———. 1992. From Servitude to Service Work: Historical Continuities in the Racial Division of Paid Reproductive Labor. *Signs* 18(1):1-43.

Glenn, Norval D. 1997. A Critique of Twenty Family and Marriage Textbooks. *Family Relations* 46(July):197-208.

Hansen, Karen V. and Anita Ilta Garey. 1998. *Families in the U.S.: Kinship and Domestic Politics*. Philadelphia: Temple University Press.

Hartmann, Heidi I. 1981. The Family as the Locus of Gender, Class, and Political Struggle. *Signs* 6(3):366-94.

———. 1987. Changes in Women's Economic and Family Roles in Post World War II United States. In *Women, Households, and the Economy*, ed. Lourdes Beneria and Catharine R. Stimpson. New Brunswick, NJ: Rutgers University Press.

Hondagneu-Sotelo, Pierrette and Ernestine Avila. 1997. I'm Here, But I'm There: The Meanings of Latina Transnational Motherhood. *Gender & Society* 11(Oct.):548-71.

Kanter, Rosabeth Moss. 1984. Jobs and Families: Impact of Working Roles on Family Life. In *Work and Family*, ed. Patricia Voydanoff. Palo Alto, CA: Mayfield.

Kibria, Nazli. 1994. Migration and Vietnamese American Women: Remaking Ethnicity. In *Women of Color in U.S. Society*, ed. Maxine Baca Zinn and Bonnie Thornton Dill. Philadelphia: Temple University Press.

Kingsbury, Nancy and John Scanzoni. 1993. Structural Functionalism. In *Sourcebook of Family Theories*, ed. William J. Doherty, Pauline G. Boss, Ralph La Rossa, Walter R. Schumm, and Suzanne K. Steinmetz. New York: Plenum Press.

Mann, Susan A., Michael A. Grime, Alice Abel Kemp, and Pamela J. Jenkins. 1997. Paradigm Shifts in Family Sociology? Evidence from Three Decades of Family Textbooks. *Journal of Family Issues* 18(May):315-49.

McLanahan, Sara and Lynn Casper. 1995. Growing Diversity and Inequality in the American Family. In *State of the Union: America in the 1990s*, ed. Reynolds Farley. Vol. 2. New York: Russell Sage Foundation.

Nicholson, Linda. 1997. The Myth of the Traditional Family. In *Feminism and Families*, ed. Hilde Lindemann Nelson. New York: Routledge.

Osmond, Marie Withers. 1987. Radical-Critical Theories. In *Handbook of Marriage and the Family*, ed. Marvin B. Sussman and Suzanne K. Steinmetz. New York: Plenum Press.

Osmond, Marie Withers and Barrie Thorne. 1993. Feminist Theories: The Social Construction of Gender. In *Sourcebook of Family Theories*, ed. William J. Doherty, Pauline G. Boss, Ralph La Rossa, Walter R. Schumm, and Suzanne K. Steinmetz. New York: Plenum Press.

Pessar, Patricia. 1995. On the Homefront and in the Workplace: Integrating Immigrant Women into Feminist Discourse. *Anthropological Quarterly* 66(Jan.):37-47.

Rapp, Rayna. 1978. Family and Class in Contemporary America: Notes Toward an Understanding of Ideology. *Science and Society* 42:278-300.

Sacks, Karen. 1989. Toward a Unified Theory of Class, Race, and Gender. *American Ethnologist* 16(3):534-50.

Skolnick, Arlene. 1998. Public Dreams, Private Lives. *Contemporary Sociology* 27(May):233-35.

Skolnick, Arlene S. 1993. Changes of Heart: Family Dynamics in Historical Perspective. In *Family, Self, and Society: Toward a New Agenda for Family Research*, ed. Philip A. Cowan, Dorothy Field, Donald A. Hansen, and Arlene S. Skolnick. Hilsdale, NJ: Erlbaum Associates.

Smith, Dorothy E. 1993. The Standard American Family: SNAF as an Ideological Code. *Journal of Family Issues* 14(1):50-65.

Smith, Joan, Immanual Wallerstein, and H. D. Evers. 1985. *The Household and the World Economy*. Beverly Hills, CA: Sage.

Stacey, Judith. 1990. *Brave New Families: Stories of Domestic Upheaval in Late Twentieth Century America*. New York: Basic Books.

———. 1996. *In the Name of the Family: Rethinking Family Values in the Postmodern Age*. Boston: Beacon Press.

Stack, Carol B. 1974. *All Our Kin: Strategies for Survival in a Black Community*. New York: Harper & Row.

Targ, Dena. 1989. Feminist Family Sociology: Some Reflections. *Sociological Focus* 22(3):151-60.

Thomas, Darwin L. and Jean Edmundson Wilcox. 1987. The Rise of Family Theory. In *Handbook of Marriage and the Family*, ed. Marvin B. Sussman and Suzanne Steinmetz. New York: Plenum.

Thompson, Linda and Alexis Walker. 1995. The Place of Feminism in Family Studies. *Journal of Marriage and the Family* 57:847-66.

Thorne, Barrie. 1992. Feminism and the Family: Two Decades of Thought. In *Rethinking the Family: Some Feminist Questions*, ed. Barrie Thorne and Marilyn Yalom. Boston: Northeastern University Press.

Walker, Alexis and Linda Thompson. 1984. Feminism and Family Studies. *Journal of Family Issues* 54(Dec.): 545-70.

Weston, Kath. 1991. *Families We Choose*. New York: Columbia University Press.

Zavella, Patricia. 1987. *Women's Work and Chicano Families: Cannery Workers of the Santa Clara Valley*. Ithaca, NY: Cornell University Press.

ANNALS, *AAPSS*, **571**, September 2000

Feminism in Criminology: Engendering the Outlaw

By DANA M. BRITTON

ABSTRACT: This article assesses the progress of and prospects for feminism in criminology. The focus is on the last 25 years of feminist research and theorizing about women offenders, victims, and workers in the criminal justice system. A general overview is provided of the directions of this scholarship, and key debates between mainstream and feminist perspectives are reviewed. The article also examines the contributions of feminist activists both within and outside the discipline to concrete social change for women victims and offenders. The article closes with a discussion of emerging trends in feminist criminology. New research and theorizing about women's experiences with crime challenge and subvert the traditional divisions and domains of mainstream criminology.

Dana M. Britton is an assistant professor of sociology at Kansas State University. Her research and teaching interests are in the areas of gender, work, criminology, and social control. She has published articles based on her research on gender and prison work in a number of academic journals and is writing a book drawing on this work.

CRIMINOLOGY remains one of the most thoroughly masculinized of all social science fields; certainly, it is one of the last academic bastions in which scholars regularly restrict their studies to the activities and habits of men without feeling compelled to account for this (Rafter and Heidensohn 1995). The reason lies, at least in part, in the fact that criminology is in possession of one of the most consistently demonstrated findings in all of the social sciences: as long as statistics have been collected, they have revealed that men are considerably more likely than women to engage in activities defined as criminal. Students are thus attracted to criminology courses by the promise of studying dangerous men; so, too, have scholars been fascinated for decades by the allure of the male outlaw, "hoping perhaps that some of the romance and fascination of this role will rub off" (Chesney-Lind 1995, xii).

In this context, the phrase "feminist criminology" may well seem something of an oxymoron. However, while the vast overrepresentation of men as criminals has served some as a rationale for ignoring women, for others, it has been a point of departure for considering them. The founding of feminist criminology can be somewhat arbitrarily fixed at 1976, with the publication of Carol Smart's *Women, Crime and Criminology: A Feminist Critique*. Though a handful of earlier works had addressed some of the general themes she raised, Smart's book brought them together in a systematic critique of the treatment (or lack thereof) of women offenders in mainstream criminology and the neglect of women's experiences as victims in an attempt to set out some directions for the new field of feminist inquiry.

Almost 25 years later, a substantial body of research has accumulated in the areas specified in Smart's pioneering work, and the field has moved considerably beyond these boundaries. As has been the case for many disciplines, however, the feminist revolution in criminology is still incomplete. Some universities do now routinely offer courses like "Women and Crime," and the Division on Women and Crime has taken its place among other specialty sections in the American Society of Criminology. Even so, these labels bespeak the marginalization of feminist criminology, which is still regarded, by and large, as something outside the mainstream. Feminist criminologists have made great strides in terms of adding women in at the margins of the discipline, but they have, as yet, been less successful in deconstructing its central frames of reference and theoretical and methodological assumptions (Morris and Gelsthorpe 1991).

As is the case in most areas of academic feminism, there is ongoing debate over what the aims of feminist inquiry in criminology should be and over what counts as work that can carry the name. I will not attempt to resolve this debate here. The emerging subject divisions in the field are easier to discern. Feminist criminology may be divided into work that focuses on women as criminal offenders, women as victims of crime, and women as workers in the criminal justice system. Reviews of the field generally do not include the third category, which is something of a hybrid, attracting scholars from both criminology and the sociology of work. I will focus here, however, on all three areas, attempting to give readers a very brief sense of what we know, a review of some key work and important debates, and a sense of the directions in which the field seems to be moving. I will conclude with a discussion of some of the central challenges that remain for feminist criminology.

Before moving on, a caveat is necessary. Although I have referred to the discipline thus far as if it existed as a unified set of frameworks and assumptions, this is not really the case. There are a wide variety of theoretical and methodological perspectives in criminology, and some (for example, critical, interactionist, and Marxist approaches) have been more receptive to feminism than others. My focus here, however, will be on the mainstream in criminology, which I take to be a set of theoretical and methodological frameworks and empirical studies aimed at understanding the etiology of crime (a category taken to be a given) and proposing, implementing, and evaluating methods of crime control. This kind of criminology has historically been very closely allied with state mechanisms of social control, and it is the state that provides the lion's share of research funding in these areas. Therefore, while one might accurately say that there are a variety of criminologies currently extant, mainstream criminology is clearly hegemonic and has most thoroughly marginalized feminist research and

theory. It will be my focus in the analysis to follow.

WOMEN AS OFFENDERS

Women are vastly underrepresented as criminal offenders. Of course, any data claiming to represent the facts about crime are always the end product of an interaction between the responses of social control authorities and the behaviors of the individuals involved. Even so, there is no serious dispute among criminologists that the extant data substantially misrepresent the actual sex ratio of criminal offending. The primary source of such data, the Uniform Crime Reports (UCR) program of the Federal Bureau of Investigation (FBI), reports detailed information on eight index crimes (these are homicide, forcible rape, robbery, aggravated assault, burglary, larceny-theft, motor vehicle theft, and arson). Women composed 26 percent of those arrested for these offenses in 1997. The UCR also reports statistics for less serious offenses, which constitute the bulk of all arrests. For men and women, these offenses are consistently similar, with larceny-theft (a category largely of petty theft, including shoplifting), simple (nonaggravated) assault, drug offenses, and driving under the influence of alcohol (DUI) topping the list for women in 1997, accounting for 45 percent of women's arrests. For men, the top four offenses were drug crimes, DUI, simple assault, and larceny-theft, composing 38 percent of men's arrests (Maguire and Pastore 1999).

These data indicate that men and women are actually quite similar in terms of the offenses for which they are most often arrested and that the majority are crimes that most would view as petty, for example, larceny-theft. The most striking difference is the absolute level of men's and women's offending. Although larceny-theft accounts for 16 percent of arrests of women, men's arrest rate for this crime is almost 2.5 times higher. Data for violent offenses illustrate this pattern in much clearer detail. In 1997, women were only 16 percent of those arrested for the index offenses of homicide, forcible rape, robbery, and aggravated assault (known collectively as the index of violent crime). Men's arrest rate for homicide was 9 times higher than women's; for rape, 83 times higher; for robbery (defined as the taking or attempted taking of property by force or fear), 10 times higher; and for aggravated assault, 5 times higher. The only offenses for which women's arrests exceed men's are prostitution, for which women are 60 percent of those arrested, and running away from home (a juvenile offense), for which girls were 58 percent of those arrested in 1997.

Arrest rates vary by race as well. In 1997, whites were 63 percent of those arrested for all index offenses; African Americans were 35 percent. For violent index offenses, whites accounted for 57 percent of arrests, versus 41 percent for African Americans. The FBI does not publish arrest statistics by sex and race. We do know, however, that African American men and women are overrepresented among those arrested.

Studies of unpublished UCR data and self-reports show that African American women have higher rates of arrest and participation in homicide, aggravated assault, and other index offenses than white women (Simpson and Elis 1995). For some offenses, such as larceny-theft, arrest rates for African American women most closely match those for white men (Chilton and Datesman 1987); black men's arrest rates are the highest; white women generally rank at the bottom, regardless of the offense.

This statistical picture illustrates some of the challenges facing feminist criminology. The sex ratio of offending is remarkably constant, which seems to indicate the need for theory that would account for why it is that women are so much less likely than men to offend. Indeed, this was the place that criminology, when it considered women at all, often began. Paradoxically, however, rather than being viewed as successes, women have been seen by mainstream theorists as aberrant because they do not commit crime. Newer feminist work in this vein has viewed women's conformity in a somewhat more positive light, relying, for example, on Carol Gilligan's theories of moral development to suggest that women's "ethic of care" makes them less likely to offend (Steffensmeier and Allan 1996). Even a cursory examination of the statistics on sex and race, however, reveals the dangers that can come from viewing women as a unitary category. Differences in arrest rates between African American and white women are often dramatic, and feminist criminology has only just begun to grapple with the implications of these differences (Daly and Maher 1998). Even more problematic is the almost complete lack of data about criminal offending among other racial groups, such as Asian or Hispanic women.

The first studies of women and offending that fell, at least putatively, in the realm of feminist criminology appeared in 1975, with the publication of Freda Adler's *Sisters in Crime* and Rita James Simon's *Women and Crime*. Though these books differ slightly in focus, both make the same general theoretical argument, which has come to be known as emancipation theory. Adler and Simon both contended that women's lower rates of participation in criminal activity could be explained by their confinement to domestic roles and by discrimination that limited their aspirations and opportunities (Daly and Chesney-Lind 1988). With the advent of the women's movement, the situation could be expected to change, however. Adler saw increasing participation in violent crime as inevitable as women became more like men as a result of their social and political emancipation. Simon believed that opportunities created by women's higher levels of formal labor market activity would lead to higher arrest rates for property and occupational crimes, such as fraud, larceny, and embezzlement. Adler did consider race, arguing that black women's higher rates of participation in crime could be explained by their more liberated status: "If one looks at where Black women are as criminals today,

one can appreciate where white women are headed as liberated criminals in the coming years" (154).

This argument has obvious appeal for opponents of the feminist movement, but empirically, the theory has received very little support. While women's rates of violent crime have increased, in absolute terms, their rates relative to men's have not changed substantially since 1960 (Steffensmeier 1995). Contrary to popular mythology, there is simply no evidence of the large-scale existence of a new, more violent female offender (Maher 1997). Women's rates of property offending relative to men's have increased since the 1960s, but almost all of the increase has come from higher rates of arrest for larceny-theft, mostly shoplifting (Chilton and Datesman 1987). Rather than reflecting expanding opportunities, however, this increase is more likely due to women's increasing economic marginalization and changing views of women by social control authorities (Morris 1987). There is also no evidence that women with more feminist attitudes are more likely to be criminal; in fact, the opposite is true (Simpson 1989). Although there is now fairly broad consensus that Adler's and Simon's work would not fall within the purview of feminist criminology (Morris and Gelsthorpe 1991; cf. Brown 1986), these books did put women's crime on the empirical agenda for the discipline, and they were groundbreaking in their attempts to build a theory that would explain men's as well as women's crime.

In addition to documenting the levels of women's criminal offending, feminist criminologists have drawn attention to women's (and men's) treatment by police, the courts, and the prison system. Contradicting popular stereotype, studies of women's experiences with the criminal justice system have revealed that women do not benefit, at least not uniformly, from chivalry at the hands of police, prosecutors, and judges. In some instances, such as juvenile status offenses, girls are subject to much harsher treatment than boys (Chesney-Lind 1989). Some research reveals that African American women receive more negative treatment by police, are more likely to be sentenced to prison, and receive longer sentences than white women (Mann 1995), although there is still considerable debate around this issue. A series of studies (for example, Daly 1987) has shown that women who are married and have children do sometimes receive more leniency than other defendants. This effect is double edged, however; women who do not conform to traditional stereotypes of wives and mothers or who are perceived to shirk their responsibilities may be dealt with especially severely (Morris and Wilczynski 1994).

The kinds of quantitative studies reviewed here have provided some answers to the question of how women's rates of offending and treatment by the system compare to men's and, as such, are a crucial first step. This equity approach (Cain 1990) has been guided largely by liberal feminist precepts, conceptualizing gender as an independent variable and seeing men and women as essentially equal and therefore deserving of equal treatment (Daly and Maher 1998). The fundamental limitation of such a strategy is put best by Cain (1990):

Equity studies do not enable us to pose the question whether or not even absolutely equal sentences might be unjust . . . too high or too low in themselves, or [whether] behaviour . . . should not, from some standpoints at least, be subject to penalty. A concern with equity leaves the substance of what is being equalised un-analysed. (2-3)

This kind of liberal feminist approach poses men as the criminal yardstick and equates justice with equality. Larger questions about the processes of criminalization of some acts, rather than others, and the inherent justice or injustice of the system are left unanswered. Such studies also fail to question the meanings and active construction of the categories of sex, race, and class, taking them simply as givens.

More recently, a substantial body of ethnographic and interview research has appeared that takes as its central focus the construction and meaning of such categories. This work has substantially deepened our understanding of the lives of women involved in crime. Mirroring overall trends in feminist theory, the best of this work is moving toward a nuanced and contingent conception of women's agency, one that sees women neither exclusively as victims nor as unfettered actors. Lisa Maher's richly textured ethnographic study of women involved in street-level sex and drug markets (1997) is a particularly good example. Maher convincingly demonstrates that the women she studies are not liberated drug kingpins, but nor are they mindless slaves, willing to sink to any depth of depravity to serve their addictions. Rather, they actively work within the constraints of the male-dominated informal economy, rarely controlling significant resources; they perform a range of gender-typed tasks, such as "copping" (buying) drugs for customers fearful of being arrested. While women do sometimes initiate violence, they are more likely to be the targets of victimization by police, male partners, and "tricks."

Feminist research and theorizing on women's offending has also been closely connected with activism. This has been the case on a number of fronts but has perhaps been most visible in the area of women's imprisonment. America is in the throes of an imprisonment binge—since 1990, our prison population has grown by about 6.5 percent per year. Women constitute only about 7 percent of those incarcerated, but their rates of imprisonment have been rising much faster than men's. Between 1988 and 1997, arrests for men increased by only 11 percent, and the number of men incarcerated increased by 96 percent. For women, the situation was much starker: arrests increased by 40 percent, and women's prison population increased 146 percent. This increase fell particularly heavily on Hispanic and African American women, whose rates of incarceration, respectively, are 3.5 and 8.0 times those of white women (Maguire and Pastore 1999).

Advocates for women in prison have been instrumental in bringing these facts to light and in generating public concern over women's rising rates of imprisonment. They have also brought about practical changes that have improved the lives of women inmates, including the elimination of some laws that imposed harsher (indeterminate) sentences on women, the expansion of medical services, improvements in job training and educational opportunities, and even some in-prison nurseries, such as the pioneering program at New York's Bedford Hills (Price and Sokoloff 1995). This work has also generated serious policy alternatives that take into account men's and women's different life histories (for example, women in prison are six times more likely to report prior sexual abuse than their male counterparts), the context of their offending (women are much more likely than men to be first-time offenders or to have committed only nonviolent offenses previously), and women's much lower rates of recidivism compared to men (Chesney-Lind 1996; Davis 1997).

WOMEN AS VICTIMS

As in the case of offending, women are underrepresented as victims of crime, at least as victimization is measured by the statistics most widely used by criminologists. The primary source of data derives from the National Crime Victimization Survey (NCVS), conducted annually since 1973 by Census Bureau personnel for the Bureau of Justice Statistics. The NCVS is administered to approximately 101,000 individuals, who are asked questions about their crime victimization. NCVS data consistently show that men are more likely to be victimized by all kinds of violent crime than are women, except rape and sexual assault. Men's overall rate of violent crime victimization in 1997 was 45.8 (per 1,000 population aged 12 years or older); women's was 33.0. Data on homicide, collected by the FBI, show that men are three times as likely to be victims.

NCVS data also indicate that African Americans and Hispanics are more likely to be victims of violent crime than whites and that the young and those with lower incomes also have higher rates of victimization. Unlike the UCR, the NCVS does publish victimization statistics that are disaggregated by sex and race combined, and the dramatic differences they reveal again demonstrate the danger of treating women (or men) as a unitary category. For homicide, white women have the lowest rates of victimization; African American women's rates are about four times higher, and African American women are more likely even than white men to be victims. African American men's rates of homicide victimization—eight times higher than those of white men—starkly testify to an epidemic level of violence, as does the persistent finding that for violent crimes other than homicide, African American men are about one and a half times as likely to be victims as white men. Among women, African Americans are generally much more likely than whites to be victims of all kinds of violent crime; generally, their rates of victimization most closely match white men's rather than white women's.

Feminist criminology has perhaps made its greatest impact on mainstream criminology in the area of women's victimization. The realm in which this has happened, however, has been somewhat limited, as the literature has generally focused on the kinds of offenses of which women are most likely to be victims. As the foregoing data suggest, rape has been a central concern and so, too, has intimate violence. NCVS data indicate that, although women's levels of violent victimization are lower than men's overall, their victimization is much more likely to be personal; from 1992 to 1996, women were five to eight times more likely than men to be victimized by intimates (Maguire and Pastore 1999). Though there is little question that women face specifically gendered violence of this kind, concentrating only on these offenses has had the effect of highlighting the differences between men and women as victims and excludes an analysis of the ways in which other kinds of victimization (which account for far more incidents overall) may be gendered (Chesney-Lind 1995). Even so, feminist research in these areas has clearly been influential; mainstream criminology texts now invariably include sections on rape and intimate violence, and many discuss feminist empirical work and theory.

Unlike studies of female offenders, which did exist before feminist criminology drew attention to them in the 1970s, there simply was no comparable research in mainstream criminology on women's experiences of victimization or on the crimes that disproportionately affect women. A rare exception is Menachem Amir's *Patterns in Forcible Rape* (1971). Although this was one of the first attempts to untangle the dimensions along which rape offending varies (for example, sex, race, class, circumstances), the study paid no attention to the experiences of the victims themselves. The effect of this omission becomes particularly clear in Amir's introduction (or perhaps official legitimation) of the concept of "victim-precipitated" rape, which he claimed accounted for about 19 percent of the cases in his study:

[Victim-precipitated rape occurs in] those rape situations in which the victim actually, or so it was deemed, agreed to sexual relations but retracted before the actual act or did not react strongly enough when the suggestion was made by the offender(s). The term applies also to cases in risky situations marred with sexuality, especially when she uses what could be interpreted as indecency of language and gestures, or constitutes what could be taken as an invitation to sexual relations. (266)

Feminist critics, both within and outside criminology, quickly charged that this notion clearly placed criminology in collusion with the rapist, who can apparently claim sexual access whenever he deems that his victim has aroused him (Schwendinger and Schwendinger 1983).

The first influential feminist studies of women's victimization appeared during the 1970s and focused on wife battering and rape. Susan Brownmiller's work (1975), in particular, is a deft synthesis of mainstream criminological research on rape offenders (including Amir's study) with a radical feminist perspective that views rape as the sine qua non of men's control of women under patriarchy. Both in content and in timing, these early feminist accounts posed a powerful challenge even to radical criminology, which was rising to prominence during the 1970s. At the heart of the radical perspective was a view of crime as resistance to class and race domination (Taylor, Walton, and Young 1973) and a conceptualization of the offender as the "rogue male" using the only resources available to him in fighting an unjust system. Radical criminologists were caught off guard by the rising tide of radical feminist research on the experiences of women who disproportionately suffered at the hands of such outlaws (Gelsthorpe and Morris 1988). Roger Matthews and Jock Young, two leading British radical criminologists, have admitted that feminist research convinced them of "the limits of the romantic conception of crime and the criminal" (Matthews and Young 1986, 2). Subsequently, radical criminology has taken a more "realist" turn, attempting to come to terms with women's victimization as well as the fact that the poor and working classes are disproportionately the victims of crime (DeKeseredy 1996).

Unlike research on women's offending, which has been guided largely by liberal feminist ideas and methodologies, women's victimization has been a central issue for radical feminists. The relationship with mainstream criminology has been an awkward one, complicated both by radical feminism's antipositivist assumptions and by its advocacy of social change. Modern mainstream criminology, born at the turn of the twentieth century, is also called the positivist school. To oversimplify, this means that most traditional criminologists have used the tools of the scientific method, such as the social survey and statistical methodology, to document what has been conceptualized as a universe of pre-existing social categories. Such inquiry has been framed as value neutral, and it posits the discovery of facts about the social world as an eventual goal. In criminology, scholars have gone about measuring crime and victimization as if these behaviors were readily apparent, uncontested, and invariant in their meaning across social groups. The equity studies discussed previously are examples of this approach, and some of its limitations have already been noted.

Radical feminists take this critique one step further. Radical feminist accounts, like Brownmiller's, have argued that violence against women cannot simply be equated with the victimization of men but, rather, that it takes on a different meaning in the context of a social system in which men are dominant over women. Thus women's violence against men is not the same as men's violence against women. Radical feminists have also pointed to the role of social institutions (such as the criminal justice system and the family) and social norms around sexuality and violence in working together to erase and normalize women's victimization. As a result, victims of rape and battery are often persuaded that such things are either normal or justified, and their victimization may not be apparent, even to themselves. This stance clearly renders any mere quantification of experiences of victimization necessarily incomplete. In addition, radical feminists have argued for the use of research as a tool for social change, a position also at odds with mainstream criminology.

Fault lines have formed around a number of issues, but the ongoing debate over statistics on women's victimization is a particularly apposite case. As noted earlier, the NCVS serves as the primary source of victimization data used by criminologists. Yet before 1992, this instrument did not query sample respondents specifically about rape or sexual assault, asking instead only whether they had been "beaten up" or attacked in other ways. Nor did the survey specifically attempt to measure victimization in the home, inquiring only whether "anyone" had committed violence against the respondent. An extensive redesign process, prompted in part by criticisms from feminist advocacy groups (although general methodological criticisms had also been raised by others), led to the inclusion of questions specifically about rape as well as an item addressing victimization in the home. After the redesign, overall estimates of personal victimization increased by 44 percent, but rape and sexual assault victimization rates increased by 157 percent. The new instrument also produced a 72 percent increase in women's reporting that they had been victimized by intimates, and a 155 percent increase in reports of victimization by other relatives (Bachman and Saltzman 1995). There is little doubt that the statistical picture has become a more accurate one.

Even so, criminology has remained resistant to the implications of radical feminism's assumption that women may not see violence against them in terms of standard legal categories, such as those used in the NCVS. Much feminist empirical work on women's victimization has employed substantive definitions of these acts, asking respondents in general terms if they, for example, have had sex against their will due to force, threat of force, or incapacity to consent. Such studies typically yield higher prevalence estimates than those reflected in official statistics. For example, while 14.0 percent of the ever-married women in Russell's sample (1982) reported incidents of victimization by their husbands that fit the legal definition of rape, only 0.9 percent of these women mentioned these experiences when asked directly if they had ever been the victim of a rape or an attempted rape. Such research has been the subject of a considerable backlash from critics, however, who typically rely on official statistics, such as the UCR and NCVS, to assert that feminists have vastly inflated the extent of women's victimization.

A second area of dispute has arisen around the radical feminist assumption that any analysis of victimization is incomplete without an understanding of the patriarchal context that shapes the meaning of these acts (Hanmer and Maynard 1987). The implication of this critique is that any simple count of

events, no matter how accurate, will necessarily fail to tell the whole story. Perhaps the best example of this controversy is the debate over statistics on rates of partner or spousal violence, which has crystallized recently around the mutual combat hypothesis. Briefly, this notion arose from research employing an instrument (the Conflict Tactics Scale) that directs respondents to count instances of their own use of a wide spectrum of physically aggressive techniques against their partners during marital or relationship conflicts (Straus, Gelles, and Steinmetz 1980). Surprisingly, studies using this instrument indicate that women are just as likely to use physical violence as men. This result has been offered as a fundamental challenge to feminist constructions of marital violence as a problem experienced primarily by women in the patriarchal context of marriage. Calls for attention to the problem of battered husbands have followed, and the mutual combat hypothesis has achieved wide cultural and disciplinary currency. Criminology texts now largely refer to "partner" or "spousal" violence; I recently reviewed a criminology textbook-in-development that began the section on violence in marriage by framing the problem as one of mutual combat.

Feminist critics have responded that the context in which violence is experienced is crucial. Women are much more likely than men to use violence in self-defense, more likely to be injured by acts of intimate violence directed against them, more likely to feel seriously threatened by it, less likely to be able to effectively defend themselves, and less likely to have the resources to leave violent relationships (Nazroo 1995; for a review, see Gelles and Loeske 1993). Again, this controversy illustrates the uneasy relationship between criminology's positivist tradition and the antipositivist implications of the assumptions that undergird radical feminist research and theorizing on women's experiences of violence. A similar controversy exists in research on fear of crime, an area in which women's much higher rates of expressed fear are seemingly unaccounted for by their lower rates of victimization. Pioneering work by Elizabeth Stanko (1990) and others, however, has revealed that much of women's victimization is hidden (that is, not accounted for by official statistics), routine, and socially legitimated (Madriz 1997) and that women have ample reason to express high levels of fear.

As in the case of women offenders, activism both within and outside the discipline has been instrumental in framing women's victimization as a legitimate social problem and in making concrete changes in the criminal justice system. Presumptive arrest policies regarding domestic violence incidents, now in place in the majority of U.S. jurisdictions, were prompted in large part by empirical research conducted by criminologists (Sherman and Berk 1984). While such a strategy represents an important symbolic step, indicating that such violence is finally being taken more seriously by the system, subsequent research (Sherman 1992) indicates that such policies are not working as well as

their proponents had hoped, and in some cases, they appear to increase the chances of repeat violence. Debate and research within criminology continue to be influential in shaping policy in this area. Other significant legal and political changes include revisions in laws defining rape or sexual assault; the passage of "rape shield" laws, which do not allow the discussion of victims' sexual histories in court; and the recent passage of the Violence Against Women Act, which defines gender-based victimization as a hate crime and allocates increased funds for battered women's shelters, rape crisis centers, and policing and research efforts directed to reducing the number of crimes against women.

WOMEN AS WORKERS

During the last 25 years, increasing numbers of women have entered criminal justice occupations. Most research to date has addressed women's experiences in policing, prison work, and law, and these will be my focus here. Before the 1970s, few women were employed in any of these jobs. A variety of factors eased women's entry. As has been the case with most male-dominated occupations, legislative change and legal pressure have been most influential; Title VII and the Equal Employment Opportunity Act formally opened all of these occupations to women. Title IX was also important for women in law, as it struck down policies that had either barred them from law schools entirely or kept their numbers to a minimum. Even so, administrators, coworkers, and clients did not immediately welcome women. Lawsuits challenging recruitment and promotion practices, among other things, were necessary to fully open the doors for women's entry (Martin and Jurik 1996).

Women have also benefited from demographic changes. The sheer number of people employed in all of these jobs has increased dramatically over the last two decades, and women have filled the gap as the supply of male workers has not been adequate to meet the rising demand. This effect has been particularly dramatic in prison work. Between 1983 and 1995, the number of staff in prisons and jails increased 187 percent, but the number of female staff almost quadrupled, increasing by 372 percent (American Correctional Association 1984; Maguire and Pastore 1999). Additional factors, specific to law, policing, and prison work, have also contributed to women's increasing representation in these fields. By 1998, women constituted 12 percent of all police officers, 24 percent of all prison officers, and 34 percent of all attorneys (Bureau of Labor Statistics 1999).

Increasing access has not necessarily meant equal rewards. There is a considerable wage gap in each occupation; women's incomes in policing are only 86 percent of those of their male counterparts; in prison work, 89 percent; and in law, 70 percent. The relatively smaller gaps in policing and prison work are undoubtedly due to the fact that the employer in these cases is the government, a labor market sector in which

recruiting and promotion practices are at least somewhat formalized. Law, on the other hand, is practiced in highly diverse settings, each with its own set of employment practices and its own reward structure. Regardless, women in all three occupations are likely to be found at the lowest rungs of their respective occupational ladders. In policing, for example, women are 16 percent of municipal officers but only 7 percent of state police (National Center for Women in Policing 1999). Women in prison work continue to face blocked access to supervisory positions (Britton 1997), and women in law are concentrated in the least prestigious specialties (for example, family law and public defense) and work in the lowest-paid settings (Pierce 1995).

While there have always been women criminals and women victims, until a quarter-century ago, there was a paucity of women working in criminal justice occupations. What this means is that, although mainstream criminological research existed on police, prison workers, and attorneys prior to 1975, these studies essentially focused on "the men and their work" and lacked an analysis of gender. Subsequently, a considerable volume of literature on women in criminal justice occupations has appeared. I will not attempt to cover the literature on each occupation here (for a review, see Martin and Jurik 1996). Two clear, though sometimes overlapping, areas of research have emerged in studies of women's experiences in all three occupations, however. The first has involved a focus on difference, asking questions about how or whether women perform their jobs differently from men and about the unique gendered characteristics women bring to their work. The second line of research has contended that these jobs and the organizations in which they are performed are themselves gendered and has looked at the ways in which gendered organizational structures, ideologies, policies and practices, interactions, and worker identities assume and reinforce inequality.

Theoretical and empirical work in the first vein is in some ways a response to critics who have long argued that women, on account of their gender, do not possess the characteristics necessary for success in these heavily masculinized and male-dominated occupations. As a male attorney interviewed by Pierce (1995) put it, "I think Clarence Darrow once said women are too nice to be lawyers. I think he was right. It's not that I don't think women are bright or competent—they just don't have that *killer* instinct" (26). Similar, and usually less charitable, sentiments can be found in both popular and academic discussions of the role of women in prison work and in policing. Research from the difference perspective has attempted to turn this critique on its head, arguing that women are not the same as their male counterparts but that the gendered qualities that they bring with them are actually assets.

In some ways, this line of argument represents a return to the discourse employed by women criminal justice system reformers of the nineteenth century. Claims that women were simply inherently better able to

deal with women victims, suspects, clients, and prisoners were largely successful in persuading state and local governments to hire policewomen, whose main responsibility was to deal with delinquent women and girls and to build reformatories, staffed exclusively by women, to hold women inmates (Appier 1998; Freedman 1981). The principal change is that such rhetoric is now being used to argue for the integration of women into male-dominated occupations, rather than the establishment of separate, sex-segregated jobs and institutions. Menkel-Meadow (1987), for example, argues that women bring a "different voice" to the practice of law and that women, by virtue of their socialization and experiences, will be less adversarial, more interested in substantive justice (rather than strict procedural fairness), and will ultimately seek to empower their clients, rather than themselves. Advocates for women in policing have long contended that women's supposedly superior communication skills will make them better at resolving conflicts through dialogue, rather than force, and that they will be more empathetic and effective in working with victims and suspects (Appier 1998; Martin 1997). A similar argument has been made for increasing the number of women officers in men's prisons, where their presence is held to "normalize" and "soften" the work environment (Britton 1997).

On balance, however, empirical research and experience have not been supportive of these kinds of claims. Neither policing, nor prison work, nor law have been radically transformed or even become much kinder and gentler as women have increasingly moved into these occupations. The reason lies, in part, in a factor left out of the difference equation, the gendered structure of occupations and organizations themselves. This has been the focus of the second line of research. Pierce (1995), for example, finds that the adversarial structure of the legal profession, and litigation work in particular, leaves women few options; to succeed, they must adopt the tactics of their successful male peers, developing qualities such as aggression, intimidation, and impersonality. This creates a double bind for women, as those who take on this role are usually perceived more negatively than their male counterparts. Some women do resist, but most do so at the cost of success, at least as it has been defined by others. The gendered structure of the practice of litigation leaves little room for the meaningful assertion of difference, even if women lawyers were so inclined. Further, the masculinization of these occupations and of the organizations in which they are performed means that the rewards that accrue to difference vary dramatically by sex. Britton (1997) finds that male officers in men's and women's prisons benefit from asserting their unique abilities to use physical force. Women's purportedly unique gendered abilities, such as higher levels of empathy, emotionality, and communication skills, are often seen by administrators and coworkers, particularly in men's prisons, as either dangerous or extraneous.

These kinds of findings should not be taken to mean, however, that difference is immaterial. Women in these occupations do often differ from their male counterparts, particularly in relationship to issues like balancing work and family. Research also demonstrates that many do see themselves as different, both in terms of work styles and personality. It is also clear that we can meaningfully speak of characteristics that have been more or less associated with masculinity and femininity. Whether they display these characteristics or not, research and experience tell us that individual workers will be held accountable for them. An emerging trend in research on women in criminal justice occupations (and research on women and work more generally) recognizes this but at the same time argues that organizational and occupational structures are also important. This approach is in some ways a synthesis of the two perspectives outlined earlier and contends that the crucial issue is context; some work settings are more amenable to, or at least less penalizing of, gendered characteristics associated with women workers (Britton 2000). Miller (1999), for example, finds that community policing draws on traits like empathy, a service orientation, and communication skills and that women are often drawn to the work for this reason. Ely (1995) finds that women in law firms with a higher proportion of women in positions of power are less likely to see feminine-stereotyped characteristics as impediments to success and are more flexible in their ideas about gender overall. Anleu's research (1992) indicates that women have greater career opportunities in corporate legal departments than in private law firms, at least partly because occupational demands and domestic responsibilities are not as incompatible. Taken together, these findings suggest that while increasing the number of women in these occupations is an important step, structural changes in policing, prison, and legal organizations are also necessary to produce significant change in the direction of equality for women.

EMERGING ISSUES

Kathleen Daly and Lisa Maher (1998) divide feminist criminology into two periods. The first phase, into which much of the work previously described falls, has focused on the tasks of filling in gaps, comparison, and critique. With little knowledge about women offenders, victims, and workers in the criminal justice system available, the first chore of feminist criminology was to provide this information. Though a substantial beginning has been made, it is likely that research in these areas will continue.

The second phase is characterized by work that disrupts the existing frameworks of criminology in more fundamental ways, resulting in the growth of a body of research and theory that Maureen Cain (1990) has called "transgressive criminology." For example, some feminist criminologists have crossed the traditional division between offending and victimization. As research on women

offenders accumulated, it became clear that they were usually also victims, having experienced substantial physical and verbal abuse at the hands of intimates. The "blurred boundaries" thesis argues that women's offending is intimately linked to their previous victimization; a central task for feminist criminology in the years to come will be filling in the black box (Daly 1992) that connects the two. Undoubtedly, this will require a new, more nuanced conception of women offenders that disrupts the dichotomy in which they have been seen only either as innocent victims or as hardened criminals. Some work in this vein has already appeared; Lisa Maher's research (1997), described earlier, is but one example.

This dichotomy is deeply racialized, and this presents yet another challenge for feminist criminology. There is little doubt that the face of the much-mythologized new, more dangerous, female offender is that of a woman of color and that the most innocent victims have always been white. Feminist criminology is just beginning to come to terms with this. Whatever the difficulties posed by official statistics, research and theorizing must continue to reject the essentialism inherent in treating women as a unitary category (Simpson 1989). We already know much about the ways in which race, class, and sexual inequality interweave with women's experiences as victims, offenders, and workers. The challenge for feminist criminology in the years to come will lie in formulating theory and carrying out empirical studies that prioritize all of these dimensions, rather than relegating one or more of them to the background for the sake of methodological convenience.

Given men's overrepresentation as offenders and victims, the screaming silence in criminology around the connection between masculinity and crime has always been something of a paradox. Feminist criminology has recently begun to draw attention to this issue. Messerschmidt's (1993) was one of the first significant theoretical contributions in this area; it argues that, for men who lack access to other resources, crime can serve as an alternate means of doing masculinity. More recent accounts (see Newburn and Stanko 1994 for a review) have begun to untangle the contexts in which this use of crime is more or less likely and to explore the kinds of masculinities that result. A similar line of research has very recently begun to inquire into the social construction and reproduction of gendered identities among women involved in crime. On a parallel track, studies of work in criminal justice occupations are drawing attention to the individual and organizational construction of gender among both men and women workers (Britton 1997; Miller 1999; Pierce 1995). This research represents a promising direction for the field, both because it finally acknowledges men as men and because it moves us beyond dichotomized, static, individualistic notions about gender.

Finally, one of the most important issues facing activists in the discipline during the coming years will undoubtedly lie in rethinking feminist criminology's relationship with the state. Those working on issues connected to women offenders have already recognized the perils of the liberal strategy of strict legal equality. Such policies, when imposed in an already unequal and gendered context, have almost invariably disadvantaged women. Victimization activists have been more enthusiastic about the criminal justice system as a force for change but find that even well-intentioned policies, such as presumptive arrest for domestic violence offenders, have had unanticipated negative consequences. Women in policing, prison work, and law have also found that obtaining the legal right of access to these jobs is not enough to ensure equality.

Simply creating new laws to enforce, providing more offenders to incarcerate, and allowing women to work in the system have done little to disrupt its underlying structure, which is deeply gendered and racialized. As Carol Smart (1998) notes, the turning point for feminist criminology will come in realizing that "law is not simply . . . a set of tools or rules that we can bend into a more favourable shape" (31). Smart herself, arguably one of the founding mothers of feminist criminology, has recently disavowed the project entirely, arguing instead for a deconstructionist approach that disrupts and subverts criminology's traditional categories and frames of reference (Smart 1995). Rethinking feminist criminology's relationship to the state and to the criminal justice system does not necessarily mean that feminists in the discipline (or elsewhere) should reject efforts directed toward legal change. What this critique does suggest is that in feminism's continuing encounter with criminology, conceptions of justice, rather than law, should occupy a much more central place in our thinking (Klein 1995).

References

Adler, Freda. 1975. *Sisters in Crime: The Rise of the New Female Criminal*. New York: McGraw-Hill.

American Correctional Association. 1984. *Juvenile and Adult Correctional Departments, Institutions, Agencies and Paroling Authorities, United States and Canada*. College Park, MD: American Correctional Association.

Amir, Menachem. 1971. *Patterns in Forcible Rape*. Chicago: University of Chicago Press.

Anleu, Sharon Roach. 1992. Women in Law: Theory, Research and Practice. *Australian and New Zealand Journal of Sociology* 28(3):391-410.

Appier, Janis. 1998. *Policing Women: The Sexual Politics of Law Enforcement and the LAPD*. Philadelphia: Temple University Press.

Bachman, Ronet and Linda E. Saltzman. 1995. *Violence Against Women*. Washington, DC: Bureau of Justice Statistics.

Britton, Dana M. 1997. Gendered Organizational Logic: Policy and Practice in Men's and Women's Prisons. *Gender & Society* 11:796-818.

———. 2000. The Epistemology of the Gendered Organization. *Gender & Society* 14(3):418-435.

Brown, Beverley. 1986. Women and Crime: The Dark Figures of Criminology. *Economy and Society* 15(3): 355-402.

Brownmiller, Susan. 1975. *Against Our Will: Men, Women, and Rape*. New York: Simon & Schuster.

Bureau of Labor Statistics. 1999. *Highlights of Women's Earnings in 1998*. Washington, DC: Government Printing Office.

Cain, Maureen. 1990. Towards Transgression: New Directions in Feminist Criminology. *International Journal of the Sociology of Law* 18:1-18.

Chesney-Lind, Meda. 1989. Girls' Crime and Women's Place: Toward a Feminist Model of Female Delinquency. *Crime and Delinquency* 35(1):5-29.

———. 1995. Preface. In *International Feminist Perspectives in Criminology: Engendering a Discipline*, ed. Nicole Hahn Rafter and Frances Heidensohn. Philadelphia: Open University Press.

———. 1996. Sentencing Women to Prison: Equality Without Justice. In *Race, Gender, and Class in Criminology: The Intersection*, ed. M. D. Schwartz and D. Milovanovic. New York: Garland.

Chilton, Roland and Susan K. Datesman. 1987. Gender, Race, and Crime: An Analysis of Urban Arrest Trends, 1960-1980. *Gender & Society* 1(2):152-71.

Daly, Kathleen. 1987. Discrimination in the Criminal Courts: Family, Gender, and the Problem of Equal Treatment. *Social Forces* 66(1):152-75.

———. 1992. Women's Pathways to Felony Court: Feminist Theories of Lawbreaking and Problems of Representation. *Southern California Review of Law and Women's Studies* 2:11-52.

Daly, Kathleen and Meda Chesney-Lind. 1988. Feminism and Criminology. *Justice Quarterly* 5:497-538.

Daly, Kathleen and Lisa Maher. 1998. Crossroads and Intersections: Building from Feminist Critique. In *Crimi-*

nology at the Crossroads, ed. Kathleen Daly and Lisa Maher. New York: Oxford University Press.

Davis, Angela Y. 1997. Race and Criminalization: Black Americans and the Punishment Industry. In *The House That Race Built*, ed. Wahneema Lubiano. New York: Pantheon.

DeKeseredy, Walter S. 1996. The Left-Realist Perspective on Race, Class, and Gender. In *Race, Gender, and Class in Criminology*, ed. M. D. Schwartz and D. Milovanovic. New York: Garland.

Ely, Robin J. 1995. The Power in Demography: Women's Social Constructions of Gender Identity at Work. *Academy of Management Journal* 38(3): 589-634.

Freedman, Estelle. 1981. *Their Sister's Keepers: Women's Prison Reform in America, 1830-1930*. Ann Arbor: University of Michigan Press.

Gelles, Richard and Donileen Loeske, eds. 1993. *Current Controversies on Family Violence*. London: Sage.

Gelsthorpe, Loraine and Allison Morris. 1988. Feminism and Criminology in Britain. *British Journal of Criminology* 28(2):93-110.

Hanmer, J. and M. Maynard. 1987. *Women, Violence, and Social Control*. London: Macmillan.

Klein, Dorie. 1995. Crime Through Gender's Prism: Feminist Criminology in the United States. In *International Feminist Perspectives in Criminology: Engendering a Discipline*, ed. Nicole Hahn Rafter and Frances Heidensohn. Philadelphia: Open University Press.

Madriz, Esther. 1997. *Nothing Bad Happens to Good Girls: Fear of Crime in Women's Lives*. Berkeley: University of California Press.

Maguire, Kathleen and Ann L. Pastore. 1999. *Sourcebook of Criminal Justice Statistics*. Washington, DC: Government Printing Office. Available at http://www.albany.edu/sourcebook.

Maher, Lisa. 1997. *Sexed Work: Gender, Race, and Resistance in a Brooklyn Drug Market*. New York: Oxford University Press.

Mann, Coramae Richey. 1995. Women of Color and the Criminal Justice System. In *The Criminal Justice System and Women: Offenders, Victims, and Workers*, ed. Barbara Raffel Price and Natalie J. Sokoloff. New York: McGraw-Hill.

Martin, Patricia Y. 1997. Gender, Accounts, and Rape Processing Work. *Social Problems* 44(4):464-82.

Martin, Susan E. and Nancy C. Jurik. 1996. *Doing Justice, Doing Gender: Women in Law and Criminal Justice Occupations*. Thousand Oaks, CA: Sage.

Matthews, Roger and Jock Young. 1986. *Confronting Crime*. London: Sage.

Menkel-Meadow, Carrie. 1987. Portia in a Different Voice: Speculating on a Women's Lawyering Process. *Berkeley Women's Law Journal* 1(1):39-63.

Messerschmidt, James W. 1993. *Masculinities and Crime*. Boston: Rowman & Littlefield.

Miller, Susan L. 1999. *Gender and Community Policing*. Boston: Northeastern University Press.

Morris, Allison. 1987. *Women, Crime, and Criminal Justice*. New York: Basil Blackwell.

Morris, Allison and Loraine Gelsthorpe. 1991. Feminist Perspectives in Criminology: Transforming and Transgressing. *Women & Criminal Justice* 2(2):3-26.

Morris, Allison and Ania Wilczynski. 1994. Rocking the Cradle: Mothers Who Kill Their Children. In *Moving Targets: Women, Murder, and Representation*, ed. Helen Birch. Berkeley: University of California Press.

National Center for Women in Policing. 1999. *Equality Denied: The Status of*

Women in Policing, 1998. Arlington, VA: Feminist Majority Foundation.

Nazroo, James. 1995. Uncovering Gender Differences in the Use of Marital Violence: The Effect of Methodology. *Sociology* 29(3):475-94.

Newburn, Tim and Elizabeth A. Stanko, eds. 1994. *Just Boys Doing Business? Men, Masculinities and Crime.* New York: Routledge.

Pierce, Jennifer. 1995. *Gender Trials: Emotional Lives in Contemporary Law Firms.* Berkeley: University of California Press.

Price, Barbara Raffel and Natalie J. Sokoloff, eds. 1995. *The Criminal Justice System and Women: Offenders, Victims, and Workers.* New York: McGraw-Hill.

Rafter, Nicole Hahn and Frances Heidensohn. 1995. Introduction: The Development of Feminist Perspectives on Crime. In *International Feminist Perspectives in Criminology: Engendering a Discipline,* ed. Nicole Hahn Rafter and Frances Heidensohn. Philadelphia: Open University Press.

Russell, Diana E. H. 1982. *Rape in Marriage.* New York: Macmillan.

Schwendinger, Julia R. and Herman Schwendinger. 1983. *Rape and Inequality.* Newbury Park, CA: Sage.

Sherman, Lawrence A. 1992. *Policing Domestic Violence.* New York: Free Press.

Sherman, Lawrence A. and Richard A. Berk. 1984. The Specific Deterrent Effects of Arrest for Domestic Violence. *American Sociological Review* 49(2): 261-92.

Simon, Rita James. 1975. *Women and Crime.* Lexington, MA: Lexington Books.

Simpson, Sally S. 1989. Feminist Theory, Crime, and Justice. *Criminology* 27: 605-31.

Simpson, Sally S. and Lori Elis. 1995. Doing Gender: Sorting out the Caste and Crime Conundrum. *Criminology* 33(1):47-81.

Smart, Carol. 1976. *Women, Crime and Criminology: A Feminist Critique.* Boston: Routledge & Kegan Paul.

———. 1995. *Law, Crime and Sexuality: Essays in Feminism.* London: Sage.

———. 1998. The Woman of Legal Discourse. In *Criminology at the Crossroads,* ed. Kathleen Daly and Lisa Maher. New York: Oxford University Press.

Stanko, Elizabeth. 1990. *Everyday Violence.* London: Pandora.

Steffensmeier, Darrell. 1995. Trends in Female Crime: It's Still a Man's World. In *The Criminal Justice System and Women,* ed. Barbara R. Price and Natalie J. Sokoloff. New York: McGraw-Hill.

Steffensmeier, Darrell and Emilie Allan. 1996. Gender and Crime: Toward a Gendered Theory of Female Offending. *Annual Review of Sociology* 22:459-88.

Straus, Murray A., Richard J. Gelles, and Suzanne Steinmetz. 1980. *Behind Closed Doors.* New York: Doubleday.

Taylor, Ian, Paul Walton, and Jock Young. 1973. *The New Criminology.* London: Routledge & Kegan Paul.

ANNALS, *AAPSS*, **571**, September 2000

From Pornography
to Sadomasochism:
Reconciling Feminist Differences

By LYNN S. CHANCER

ABSTRACT: Stemming from a belief in the deeply interconnected character of private and public events, sexuality was a key part of second-wave feminist thought in the 1960s and 1970s. In turn, feminism influenced academic interest in sexuality throughout the 1980s and 1990s. Yet, the sex debates, or sex wars, of the later decades have resulted in a recurrent division between feminists. Some have emphasized the structural character of sexist subordination; others have paid relatively greater attention to individual experiences of sexual repression. This split between sexism and sex manifested itself in polarized feminist positions over a variety of issues. This article focuses specific attention on feminist divisions over pornography and sadomasochism, and it suggests synthetic positions beyond either-or divides. Suggestions are made for a third wave of feminism that avoids divisive pitfalls and includes considerations of both differences and commonalities between women.

Lynn S. Chancer is associate professor of sociology at Fordham University. She is the author of Sadomasochism in Everyday Life *(1992);* Reconcilable Differences: Confronting Beauty, Pornography and the Future of Feminism *(1998); and* Provoking Assaults: When High Profile Crimes Become Divisive Social Causes *(forthcoming). She has written numerous articles and book chapters about gender and crime, feminist theory, and American culture.*

THE second-wave feminist movement of the 1960s and 1970s played an important part in the growth of sexuality as an influential topic of women's studies and social science research by the year 2000. After the publication of radical feminist works like Kate Millett's *Sexual Politics* (1970) and Shulamith Firestone's *Dialectic of Sex* (1970), investigating sexuality and studying power became intimately connected. No longer was sex seen as a merely private matter, somehow immune from public critiques of dominance and subordination to which issues such as the economy, or racism, had often been subjected. Rather, breaking down conventional barriers between power exerted publicly and privately, politically and personally, became key to defining gender studies. In the wake of early feminism, it was now legitimate to explore problems of sexual oppression and sexual repression that had historically plagued women and that had negative consequences for men as well.

But by the 1980s and 1990s, other developments also tied the feminist movement to the study of sexuality. Broadly speaking, no longer was there any illusion that feminists spoke in a single voice; substantive differences were even more blatantly visible than common concerns. One well-known manifestation of conflict was over second-wave presumptions that all women were equal. By the 1980s and 1990s, feminism had spawned a range of feminisms that quite properly called attention to racial, class, and sexual divergences in women's experiences and perspectives. Regarding sexuality in particular, though, feminists started to disagree across these social differences about where emphasis should be placed: relatively speaking, should sexual oppression or sexual repression be given more attention?

This dispute took the form of a series of so-called sex debates, or sex wars, which have become familiar in the last two decades not only to feminist activists but also to feminist researchers interested in the subject of sex. In and of themselves, these sex debates might be viewed as harmless, indeed as testimony to feminism(s)'s strength as a growing and increasingly diverse U.S. social movement. Yet arguments between feminists over sexuality have unfolded in a striking pattern. This article contends that the divisions have unfolded repetitively insofar as some feminists have consistently focused on the problem of sexist oppression, while others have emphasized sexual repression. Moreover, it is my intention to show that this recurrent divide has unintentionally weakened the movement from within during the same period when conservative reactions were feeding a "backlash" from without (see Faludi 1991).

But what exactly was this split between sex and sexism, as I call it (Chancer 1998), that evolved from common concerns about "sexual politics" into a recurrent manifestation of difference? On the side of the debate highlighting sexism, some feminists focused on the oppressive character of patriarchal societies writ large. Here, women protested institutional inequities of power—in the law or at workplaces—where gendered discrimination takes place. Other feminists accorded relatively greater priority to achieving sexual freedom for women, recognizing that male-dominated societies often restrict women's desires as a fundamental form of control (elevating heterosexuality, for instance, to a privileged status). Highlighting sex on this side, individual defiance was valued just as much as critiques of institutions; sexual practices that challenge traditional constraint became a mode of rebellion and a personal politic.

This split can be traced back through at least five issues where it recurred in a similar form, even as its contents shifted, through the 1980s and 1990s. First, and perhaps most well known, the issue of pornography became bitterly divisive. Going back even further, to the 1970s, some feminists favored censoring sexually explicit materials that they believed oppressed women vis-à-vis particularly sadistic representations of violence. In particular, Catharine MacKinnon and Andrea Dworkin proposed an ordinance that, if enacted, would have outlawed the subset of these pornographic images that was perceived to be most objectionable. Other feminists, among them Ellen Willis and Carol Vance, were opposed to legally mandating restrictions; on the contrary, they argued, some women experienced pornography as sexually liberating. Though neither side entirely disagreed with the other—more precisely, their disagreements were about emphasis—the former position highlighted systemic patriarchal ills bequeathed from the past. In contrast, feminists holding the latter position stressed a need for sexual freedom in the present.

A second example of a feminist split between sexism and sex manifested itself at the now-notorious 1982 Barnard Conference on Sexuality. This conference made clear that some feminists regarded sadomasochistic sexual practices as inseparable from patriarchal hierarchies based on relations of dominance and subordination (for example, Linden 1982). This view diverged from other feminists' view that sadomasochistic practices constituted a legitimate form of consensual sexual activity that women were entitled to enjoy without fear of discriminatory judgment by society or other feminists. Yet a third instance of the division between sexism and sex involved polarized feminist interpretations of sex work. For some feminists, including Laurie Schrage (1989), prostitution was inseparable from the systematic exploitation of women (see also Barry 1979; Hoigard and Finstad 1992); for others, including many sex workers themselves, women's involvement was felt to be legitimate and to offer greater excitement and enjoyment than many other occupations (for example, Bell 1987; Delacoste and Alexander 1987). Linked to the former position was a commitment to maintaining prostitution's criminalized status; on the other hand, those who believed in sex work's legitimacy sought to decriminalize the conditions under which they believed women had a right to labor freely and safely.

A fourth division has centered on the issue of violence against women.

Representative of the sexual-subordination side in this case was the stance of well-known feminist author Susan Brownmiller. In *Against Our Will* (1975), Brownmiller argued that sexual assault was inseparable from the oppressive character of male domination in general; even if a particular woman had not experienced rape, fear of violence exerted intimidating controls over her own and the lives of all women. Later however, in *The Morning After* (1993), Katie Roiphe contended that radical feminists had exaggerated the existence and dangers of violence against women. For Roiphe, placing herself provocatively in opposition, this perspective overlooked various situations in which apparently objectionable heterosexual interactions were experienced as involving erotic ambiguity and play. Relatedly, and published that same year, Naomi Wolf's *Fire with Fire* (1993) pitted the idea of "power feminism" against a "victim feminism," which she, too, claimed had become an outdated by-product of older feminist approaches to problems of dominance and subordination.

Last and most recent is a similarly shaped feminist division between sexism and sex over the subject of beauty. Ironically, Wolf's better-known earlier book *Beauty Myth* (1991) offered a classic contemporary statement of the sexist subordination position. The author objected to the debilitating character of patriarchal expectations that women look eternally young, thin, and attractive. But this view, too, came to be the subject of feminist controversy through the 1990s as some women,

approximating the sex side of the debate, expressed the belief that beauty could be a source of pleasure as well as pain. Exemplifying this most recent schism, Kathy Davis has described being attacked by Kathryn Morgan over the issue of cosmetic surgery: in *Reshaping the Female Body* (1995), Davis documented many women's feelings that such surgery was desired and was experienced to be "empowering." For Morgan, however, women's belief that they needed cosmetic surgery could not be separated from subordination to patriarchal expectations of beauty, which were badly in need of change (Morgan 1991).

If this split between sexism and sex has recurred in feminist debates over one issue after another—pornography, sadomasochism, prostitution, violence against women, and, most currently, beauty—why has this been the case? Before addressing this question, an ensuing section elaborates on the sexism-sex divide as it unfolded around two of the aforementioned issues: pornography and sadomasochism. This section suggests that more synthetic third positions are both possible and needed if feminists are not to become distracted from making agreed-upon external changes by spending energy attacking each other's divergent views. The rigid character of these ongoing divisions makes it difficult to discern commonalities as well as differences between feminists, and it has led to the paying of greater attention to the political weaknesses of this incipient social movement than to its strengths. After this brief discussion of divided feminist views concerning pornography and sado-masochism, a final section reviews three factors that may have produced the recurrent divide between sex and sexism. Here, in conclusion, I suggest how further incarnations of the split might be avoided in a feminist third wave of the future.

THE PORNOGRAPHY ISSUE: THESIS, ANTITHESIS, POSSIBLE SYNTHESIS?

In 1988, I was reminded of the extent of acrimony between feminists over this issue after attending a New York City conference entitled "Sexual Liberals and the Attack on Radical Feminism." Not only were radical feminists discussing attacks against their own position, but speakers were attacking sexual liberals as well. Indeed, pro-censorship feminist speakers on what I am calling the sexual-subordination side denounced feminists on the sexual-pleasure side for failing to join a campaign against pornography. Women who defended pornography's legality were portrayed as traitorous; specifically, Catharine MacKinnon referred to Willis and others as the "Uncle Toms of the movement" (Chancer 1988).

Yet the position represented by MacKinnon and Dworkin itself failed to address three substantive points being made by feminists with whom they disagreed. First, a problem raised on the sex side by the Feminist Anti-Censorship Task Force was that MacKinnon and Dworkin's position potentially abridged civil liberties: anti-pornography ordinances introduced in the cities of Minneapolis and Indianapolis posed dangers to First Amendment freedoms by using vague criteria to outlaw particular images; for this reason, the two ordinances were struck down by the U.S. Supreme Court. However, after the Canadian Supreme Court kept the issue alive by ruling that the ordinances were constitutional at least north of the United States, a book written by Dworkin herself was seized on the U.S.-Canada border (Chancer 1998).

Second, as Willis and Vance, among other members of the Feminist Anti-Censorship Task Force, pointed out, an anti-pornography position was likely to be experienced by many women as in favor of sexual repression. According to this argument, some pornographic images are experienced as liberating in their effects, especially when expression of any sexual feelings has often been historically tabooed based on gender. Of concern, then, was whether the sexual-subordination side paradoxically threatened to remove what was for some women a valued medium of experienced pleasures. Finally, a third objection raised by Willis and others revolved around a danger not only to individual women but to feminism as a social movement: was it a problem to focus so much attention on a single issue? In and of itself, little reason existed to expect that censoring pornography would transform male-dominated relations of power that are multifaceted and complex in their origins and effects.

Although those wishing to legally restrict pornography had little response to these objections (rather, they seemed to malign the feminists who raised them), it also makes little sense to overlook valid points made on the anti-pornography side of this debate. Two things can be possible simultaneously. As students of representation have underscored, cultural imagery can both circulate consensually and lawfully—in the process allowing quite genuine feelings of pleasure to be experienced—all the while such images nevertheless contribute to the reproduction of dominant-subordinate relationships in an inequitably organized society. In this regard, one might refer to the persistence of what could be deemed a "hegemonic pornography." By this, I mean that as long as a given society remains largely politically, economically, and culturally male-dominated, certain sexual representations are likely to become ideologically predominant—or "hegemonic"—over others. Accordingly, many of the cultural images and narratives present in contemporary pornography are likely to represent male desires and fantasies disproportionately. Thus even though Willis, Vance, and others suggest that some women experience pleasure by viewing or participating in the making of pornography, other women are likely to feel alienated by the hegemonic pornography they encounter in movies, magazines, or books. Within much contemporary pornography, they may have good reason to feel that their own sexual needs, feelings, and desires do not find authentic self-reflection.

Consequently, a problem with the pornography debate as it has divided feminists since the 1970s is that it has not left adequate room for combining valid points from each of these two sides. Ironically, even though feminist theory has been distinctive in advocating the advantages of both-and positions, the pornography debate has tended to be waged in either-or form. Yet perhaps less divisive positions are possible and could emerge from synthesizing excessively polarized sets of considerations. On the one hand, it makes little sense to censor pornography, thereby removing a source of pleasure from some women and contributing to the diminution of important First Amendment freedoms for both sexes. Moreover, granting pornography too much attention can indeed be deradicalizing in effect, distracting attention from wide-ranging and multi-issued perspectives that fueled feminism's vibrancy in prior periods.

On the other hand, nothing about an anti-censorship position prevents protesting the following problem: even if pornography were not restricted by law, women do not equally occupy positions of ownership and authorship when it comes to representations of their sexuality. Consequently, just as it makes little sense to censor some pornography, it is likewise unnecessary to abandon efforts aimed at transforming the institutional contexts within which the pornography industry has thrived. For instance, critiques of sexual socialization within traditional nuclear families relate secondarily, but significantly, to altering pornography—namely, how and where sexual desires are channeled—in a broader sense. Similarly germane is how women make decisions to work in the sex industry at all or why men are still largely in control of pornography's profits and production. In other words, questions of gender and class interaction need not be left far away but can be melded into a reconsidered third feminist position on pornography. But a similar analysis may also assist in clarifying feminist divides over the issue of sadomasochism.

SADOMASOCHISM, FEMINISM, AND EVERYDAY LIFE

Reflecting the academic tinge of these debates even as they seeped into popular cultural cognizance, a feminist split over the issue of sadomasochism first became controversial in a conference setting. In 1982, the Barnard Conference on Sexuality was the site of a controversy over sex versus sexism as to whether women from a pro-sadomasochism West Coast group (SAMOIS) ought legitimately be included on a conference panel. According to the organizers, feminists in SAMOIS had a right to participate in sadomasochistic sex; it was a form of consensual sexual pleasure, they argued. An even more central issue was entailed for many women who thereby found themselves on the sex side of this next schism: had feminists concerned with sexual subordination, like MacKinnon and Dworkin, become too rigid, allowing a brand of political correctness to become predominant and limiting? To the extent that this had occurred, a feminist superego may have started to intimidate women whose experiences of sexuality did not conform to a sanitized and idealized vision. Women might begin to fear acknowledging pleasure they

found in heterosexuality, pornography, or sadomasochistically oriented sexual practices—whether politically correct or not. Thus, these feminists contended that by repressing the verity of many women's psychic and sexual realities, feminism risked reproducing another version of sexual repression—paradoxically, since this was a central component of the oppression against which feminists initially rebelled.

But, as with the pornography issue, the validity of these objections did not necessitate eschewing any and all sensible points on the other side of this debate. Rather, two inter-related arguments, neither of which was adequately addressed this time through the sexual-pleasure position, need to be blended into any satisfactory third-wave synthesis. First, it should be noted that the sex side of this feminist debate made only narrow usage of the term "sadomasochism": in and outside the Barnard conference, the concept was associated almost exclusively with sexuality. While this was the connotation originally intended by Freud, other intellectual traditions have linked sadomasochism to a much wider array of social interactions involving dominance and subordination; these encompass, but are not limited to, the sexual. For example, in attempting to link psychoanalytic and Marxist thought, Frankfurt School theorist Erich Fromm (1941) and feminist theorist Jessica Benjamin (1988) both employed "sadomasochism" to refer to broad-based desires for controlling or being controlled. For Fromm, systems of power that have authoritarian psychosocial bases—

including, in quite different ways, capitalism and fascism—rely on sadomasochistic defense mechanisms for their sustenance. For Benjamin, sadomasochistic interactions often characterize familiar relationships between spouses, or between parents and child, which need not be overtly sexual in character.

Applying this point to the feminist debate over sadomasochism, then, raises a second problem, which those on the sex side of this debate tended to overlook. In contrast to the sexual-pleasure side's usage of the term to describe consensual relationships, sadomasochistic dynamics are often coercive. For instance, the situation of a battered woman—often unable to escape due to financial and psychic constraints and fearing the sadistic other with whom she has been involved—diverges dramatically from that of a woman in a sadomasochistic sexual situation. Only the latter can presumably halt sadomasochistic activity when and if she chooses. Moreover, it is not only within violent gendered relationships that lack of choice distinguishes what I have elsewhere called coercively "sadomasochistic dynamics" (Chancer 1992): far more broadly, women living in patriarchal societies often find themselves situated masochistically in a host of day-to-day situations not of their own making. So-called normal processes of gender socialization have traditionally placed women in a predicament Simone de Beauvoir ([1952] 1974) dubbed that of "the second sex"; in this sense, the conventionally (mis)used idea of masochism in

women has little to do with seeking pleasure in pain and much to do with the socially constructed ramifications of sexist subordination.

Therefore, it seems again that a third position is required that would be capable of incorporating two perspectives at once. In this second example, a more synthetic approach would neither repressively judge women who enjoy sadomasochistic sex consensually explored in the present nor ignore the seriousness of coercive social situations bequeathed to women (and men) from the past. On the one hand, it is problematic to ignore that in many sexual situations, playfulness indeed may be involved; on the other hand, to fail to indict institutional arrangements that make sadomasochistic dynamics common, in and beyond their sexual manifestations, is to let society off the hook. Hardly does the feminist movement gain from overlooking how "sadomasochistic dynamics" (Chancer 1992) characterize a variety of compulsively generated social situations. In addition to gendered interactions that may or may not involve violence, workplace interactions too often feature a sadomasochistic texture: especially in capitalistic contexts, fears about the punitive consequences of questioning or challenging a job may maintain hierarchical relations that have little to do with choice. Moreover, as is analogous with the previously cited example of domestic violence, sexual harassment poses a problem for feminists precisely because it often entails coercive dynamics of both gender and class. Like a particular batterer, many harassers may know only too well that power in a given situation stems from an employee's economic need, not only from her sex.

But, with this, one comes back to the question of why feminists across a range of issues, including pornography and sadomasochism, have not insisted on more synthetic and less divisive approaches. It is inadequate simply to state the importance of doing two things at once: namely, both promoting sexual freedom and transforming ideas and institutions that limit choices outside and inside the bedroom. Thus, remaining to be investigated is why the split between sexism and sex developed in the first place and what this analysis suggests could help to avert its patterned recurrence.

TOWARD A THIRD WAVE OF FEMINISM: IN CONCLUSION

Three reasons can be cited that, in combination, have contributed to a repetitive splitting of sexism and sex in feminist debates of the 1980s and 1990s. A first factor has already been mentioned: as Susan Faludi (1991) suggested, a conservative backlash against feminism through these decades may have generated defense reactions; overwhelmed by external obstacles, political activists may have unwittingly turned against one another. To the extent that such internalization has occurred, second-wave American feminism is by no means alone. Other social movements, too, including a 1960s anti-racist movement that became divided into civil rights and nationalistic segments and a character-istically factionalized U.S. Left, have experienced acrimonious divisions. These may likewise stem from difficulties in effecting deep-seated changes in American society without encountering severe backlashes orchestrated in reaction.

A second explanation relates to cultural characteristics of the press. As Todd Gitlin (1980) and Stuart Hall et al. (1978), among other students of media, have noted, editors and reporters are attracted to sharply antagonistic oppositions between issues and spokespersons. Not only are such either-or polarities believed to sell news but presenting only two sides of a story serves an ideological function by appearing democratic; nevertheless, these authors argue, such disputes tend to neutralize the critical effects of points made by each opposing party. Applied to feminist debates of the 1980s and 1990s, this suggests that perhaps the media have publicized only antagonistic two-sided positions—for instance, MacKinnon and Dworkin versus Willis and Vance on the pornography issue—even though a wider range of ideas actually characterizes feminist thought in concrete instances.

But while these first two external factors help to elucidate the question of feminist splitting in the 1980s and 1990s, a third explanation may have the most potential for altering feminist reactions from within. Even though editors and reporters favor two-sided antagonisms, attending feminist conferences and reading feminist writings about each of the five issues mentioned here—

pornography, sadomasochism, prostitution, violence against women, and beauty—make clear that the sex wars have not simply been a product of journalists' imaginations. Thus in the thick of political practice, it may be quite difficult for even feminists to enact theoretical commitments to both-and rather than either-or visions of the social world. Widespread dualisms—mind versus body; culture versus nature; masculinity versus femininity—are far more deeply embedded and familiar ways of thinking and feeling.

Even granting this trio of difficulties, though, both-and perspectives that respect rather than demean the various sides of debated issues are a crucial part of third-wave feminist approaches. To avoid the fractious divisions that have weakened the movement from within during several decades of conservative reaction, any revitalized movement has to incorporate several sets of considerations simultaneously into its activities as well as its theories. Happily, exactly such synthetic approaches have appeared in literatures concerning a number of the debates this article reviewed. For example, both-and approaches to the sex debates have characterized the work of Susan Bordo (1993) on the subject of sexist expectations of women's appearance and the work of Wendy Chapkis (1997) with regard to false splits between feminists over attitudes toward sex work (and sex workers).

Overall, then, the next wave of feminism stands to gain from incorporating both a capacity for respecting diversities of agency and an ability to make collective demands; both considerations of differences and commonalities are worth remembering and encompassing. More specifically, by "diversities of agency," I mean that it is counterproductive for feminists to divide over whether an individual woman likes and is aroused by pornography or not; enjoys sadomasochistic sexual practices or not; decides to undertake cosmetic surgery or not; wishes to engage in sex work or not.

These decisions may reflect valid differences of opinion between women who otherwise share similar overall goals. For example, what individuals like or do not like sexually about pornography, for instance, need not deflect attention from targeting sexism in the pornography industry overall. Collective demands can be made, challenging institutionally based power and raising questions of political economy; at the same time, valid differences between women are left to stand. Analogously, individuals' attitudes and actions regarding cosmetic surgery need not obscure another collective concern: transforming a media industry that still overvalues young, thin, and often white women's bodies. Nor do disagreements about an individual woman's engagement with sex work need to deflect feminist attentions away from the larger social context in which that woman often does not experience genuine economic choice. Finally, a two-pronged feminist strategy toward a third wave might be able to protest the sadomasochistic character of a given culture, at the same time recognizing that sadomasochistic desires are likely to characterize many individuals' experiences of desire.

Across differences of class and race and sexual preference, feminists share interests in both criticizing systemic subordination and respecting individual diversities. Perhaps greater awareness of false dichotomies that have divided feminists in the recent past—such as the one analyzed here between sexism and sex—will ensure the realization of increasingly multifaceted goals in a not-too-distant feminist future.

References

Barry, Kathleen. 1979. *Female Sexual Slavery*. New York: New York University Press.

Beauvoir, Simone de. [1952] 1974. *The Second Sex*, ed. H. M. Parshley. New York: Vintage.

Bell, Laurie, ed. 1987. *Good Girls / Bad Girls: Feminists and Sex Trade Workers Face to Face*. Seattle: Seal.

Benjamin, Jessica. 1988. *The Bonds of Love: Psychoanalysis, Feminism, and the Problem of Domination*. New York: Pantheon.

Bordo, Susan. 1993. *Unbearable Weight: Feminism, Western Culture, and the Body*. Berkeley: University of California Press.

Brownmiller, Susan. 1975. *Against Our Will: Men, Women, and Rape*. New York: Simon & Schuster.

Chancer, Lynn S. 1988. Pornography Debates Reconsidered. *New Politics* 2(1):72-84.

———. 1992. *Sadomasochism in Everyday Life: Dynamics of Power and Powerlessness*. New Brunswick, NJ: Rutgers University Press.

———. 1998. *Reconcilable Differences: Confronting Beauty, Pornography and the Future of Feminism*. Berkeley: University of California Press.

Chapkis, Wendy. 1997. *Live Sex Acts: Women Performing Erotic Labor*. New York: Routledge.

Davis, Kathy. 1995. *Reshaping the Female Body: The Dilemma of Cosmetic Surgery*. New York: Routledge.

Delacoste, Frederique and Priscilla Alexander, eds. 1987. *Sex Work: Writings by Women in the Sex Industry*. Pittsburgh, PA: Cleis.

Faludi, Susan. 1991. *Backlash: The Undeclared War Against American Women*. New York: Crown.

Firestone, Shulamith. 1970. *The Dialectic of Sex: The Case for Feminist Revolution*. New York: Morrow.

Fromm, Erich. 1941. *Escape from Freedom*. New York: Holt, Rinehart, & Winston.

Gitlin, Todd. 1980. *The Whole World Is Watching: Mass Media in the Making and Unmaking of the New Left*. Berkeley: University of California Press.

Hall, Stuart, Chas Critcher, Tony Jefferson, John Clarke, and Brian Roberts. 1978. *Policing the Crisis: Mugging, the State, and Law and Order*. London: Macmillan.

Hoigard, Cecilie and Liv Finstad. 1992. *Backstreets: Prostitution, Money, and Love*. University Park: Pennsylvania State University Press.

Linden, Robin R., ed. 1982. *Against Sadomasochism: A Radical Feminist Analysis*. San Francisco: Frog in the Well.

Millett, Kate. 1970. *Sexual Politics*. New York: Doubleday.

Morgan, Kathryn Pauly. 1991. Women and the Knife: Cosmetic Surgery and the Colonization of Women's Bodies. *Hypatia* 6(3):25-53.

Roiphe, Katie. 1993. *The Morning After: Sex, Fear, and Feminism on Campus.* New York: Little, Brown.

Schrage, Laurie. 1989. Should Feminists Oppose Prostitution? *Ethics* 99:347-61.

Wolf, Naomi. 1991. *The Beauty Myth: How Images of Beauty Are Used Against Women.* New York: Morrow.

———. 1993. *Fire with Fire: The New Female Power and How It Could Change the Twenty-First Century.* New York: Ballantine.

ANNALS, *AAPSS*, **571**, September 2000

Feminist Scholarship in Archaeology

By KELLEY HAYS-GILPIN

ABSTRACT: Archaeologists have been slow to embrace feminist scholarship. Although most still avoid the term "feminism," an archaeology of gender has emerged and thrived. This article explores the history of women and feminism in archaeology, examines a few of the central issues addressed by feminist and gender-oriented archaeologists, briefly addresses equity issues for women archaeologists, and identifies some future directions.

Kelley Hays-Gilpin is assistant professor of anthropology at Northern Arizona University. She served as a tribal archaeologist for the Navajo Nation and now collaborates with the Hopi Cultural Preservation Office. She coedited Reader in Gender Archaeology *with David S. Whitley and is currently working on the manuscript for a book on gendered imagery in rock art.*

WHAT is archaeology? The popular view of scientists digging in the ground for artifacts is not entirely accurate. Some, but by no means all, archaeologists dig. Many study surface evidence, from large-scale settlement patterns to symbolic landscapes. Many perform chemical studies of stone and clay objects and their geological source materials. Some decipher ancient writing systems, while others study paintings, pottery decoration, and sculpture. Many archaeologists spend their time in laboratories making and breaking pottery or studying pollen, bones, and seeds. A number of archaeologists negotiate preservation policy in federal, state, local, and tribal governments. Most archaeologists study material evidence for events and processes that took place in the past, but a few focus on relationships between humans and material culture in the present. An example of the latter is the University of Arizona's Garbage Project, which studies relationships between contemporary Americans and garbage.

The present article will explore the history of women and feminists in archaeology and will outline what they have accomplished, often in the face of indifference and resistance. A complete or even representative review of this burgeoning field is impossible; I will focus on archaeology in the United States, with a few examples from other parts of the world. For reasons that will be discussed, not all contributors to what I have defined here as feminist and feminist-influenced archaeology have used the term "feminism" to describe their work. Many favor the expressions "gender archaeology" or "archaeology of gender." My goal is to show that, however we label them, women, feminist, and gender archaeologists are transforming the discipline in many ways.

HISTORY OF WOMEN IN ARCHAEOLOGY

Women have always taken part in archaeology. Early-twentieth-century women archaeologists, like their male counterparts, were often financially independent and came from upper- and middle-class backgrounds. Many had kinship or marriage connections to male archaeologists or other scientists who helped them gain access to the appropriate education, training, and field opportunities. Women working on their own often held laboratory or museum positions, rather than taking part in field research. Joan Gero (1985, 344) characterizes such jobs as "archaeological housework," extensions of gender-appropriate roles typical of Western society.

Class and race have also influenced who did which archaeological tasks. In the 1930s and 1940s, working-class women recruited to Works Progress Administration (WPA) jobs excavated Moundbuilder sites in the southeastern United States; these women included as many as 160 African American women in Alabama and Georgia. Distribution of WPA supervisory positions followed traditional gender lines, however; University of Chicago doctoral candidate Madeline Kneberg Lewis became a laboratory director at the University of Tennessee, while male students were hired to supervise field crews (Sullivan, in Claassen 1994). In the Southeast,

a class and race based definition of femininity encouraged educated white supervisors to seek poor women as unskilled laborers in the field as early as 1935 but repelled educated white women from the field in the United States until the late 1960s and continues to keep them out of the field in the Mediterranean area today. (Claassen 1994, 5)

Since at least the 1920s, one of the first steps to becoming a professional archaeologist has been participation in the field school—practical, hands-on excavation and site survey done for college credit. Until about the 1960s, women had fewer choices of field schools than did men. Unfortunately, proving that women could do fieldwork as well as men did not open many doors, especially in the eastern United States and England. Many male field directors felt that women distracted male crew members and got in the way of highly valued masculine activities such as cursing and working without shirts. Susan Bender writes that "women [were] seen as incompatible with the tightly defined all-male social setting of the excavation, where easy companionship and consequent productivity reign[ed] until a woman threaten[ed] to disrupt it." Nonetheless, "despite the existence of such discrimination, women . . . found ways to do field archaeology, and . . . [were] consistently . . . aided in doing so by a variety of supportive male colleagues" (Bender 1991, 213).

Women archaeology students in the U.S. Southwest, to draw from the area I know best, encountered a wider range of reactions, perhaps because individualism and resistance to Eastern propriety have long been hallmarks of the so-called wild west. Edgar Lee Hewett allowed women to attend his University of New Mexico (UNM) field school in Chaco Canyon in the 1930s. His program became a magnet for ambitious young women. Some, like Bertha Dutton, came from working-class families. While a student, Dutton served as Hewett's secretary, but she graduated to a long professional museum career and took Girl Scouts on summer archaeological tours and digs. Hewett hired University of Arizona graduate Florence Hawley as UNM's first female archaeology professor in 1934, just after she completed her Ph.D. at the University of Chicago. Yet ethnologist Charles Lange noted that Hewett "provided opportunities to women in part because he was fair and in part because he could pay them less than he would have to have paid their male counterparts" (Cordell 1993, 220).

Former UNM student Florence Lister recalls two pieces of advice from Florence Hawley, her mentor, in the early 1940s: to break into the discipline, a woman must "find some aspect of the work that the men did not enjoy and then to become a specialist in it," and "Your best bet is to marry an archaeologist" (Lister 1997, 5-7). Lister became a pottery specialist and married a National Park Service archaeologist she met at the Chaco Canyon field school. For many decades, she and Robert Lister worked as partners in the southwestern United States and Mexico. Lister seems not to have fretted over having both children and career. The couple took their children along even to remote field locations.

A. V. Kidder, the father of Southwestern archaeology, not only permitted women to do fieldwork but, following a training session in which men and women students worked together at Pecos Pueblo, he assigned Isabel Kelly, Frances Watkins, and Eva Horner to direct excavations at Tecolote ruin as part of his 1929 field school (Preucel and Chesson 1994). Watkins later publicly advocated archaeology as a profession for women, writing, "We proved that women with a good background of laboratory and theoretical education, plus a few weeks of practical intensive field training under expert direction, could lead and manage an expedition and do reconnaissance quite as well as any young man with similar experience" (Watkins 1931, 176). Watkins, like many early women archaeologists, became a museum curator. Isabel Kelly became a prominent ethnographer of the Great Basin Paiute peoples.

In a 1930 field diary, young University of Arizona instructor Clara Lee Tanner complained that field school director Dean Byron Cummings occasionally left her and a female student at base camp to babysit the children of their hosts and outfitters. On 31 July 1930, for example, Tanner wrote, "The Dean leaves in search of a cave site, while Mrs. W. leaves for Flagstaff. We are left in charge of the brats." The next day, she noted, "What a night! Great being a mother to a sick baby, walking the floor turning a flashlight on cats and what not, and so on." Tanner eventually abandoned her archaeological ambitions, instead becoming a foremost authority on Native American art and material culture. She taught archaeology and other subjects at the University of Arizona for 48 years, with less pay and a heavier course load than her male counterparts, but she told me that she did as she pleased in spite of discrimination and never considered herself a feminist. Early women in archaeology displayed more rugged individualism than collective resistance to bias. A friend who began her archaeological career in Arizona in the 1950s says flatly, "We never thought of those things."

My friend's response echoes those of more than 20 women archaeologists who declined Jonathan Reyman's invitation to take part in a 1989 Society for American Archaeology symposium entitled "Women in Archaeology" for one of three reasons: not having anything significant to say about the topic, not having experienced discrimination in their archaeological careers, and seeing the role of women in archaeology as no different from that of men. Many men, however, responded that a symposium on women in archaeology would be a waste of time, and one suggested it would be "just another hen party" (Reyman 1992, 71-72).

As recently as 1987, the University of Arizona employed about a dozen men and no women archaeology professors. Whether or not overt discrimination played a role is actively debated. Opinions differ among those who should know, and much depends on defining discrimination. Professor Carol Kramer's hiring in the late 1980s came as a direct result of activism by women graduate students, myself included, and a National Science Foundation grant program (Visiting Professors for Women in Science and Engineering) that placed women visiting professors in departments with no female faculty. We felt that all students need mentors of both sexes but that women, who made up more than half of the graduate students in the department, also needed access to the network of women archaeologists that continues to grow in direct response to a perceived old-boy network. But we did not all call ourselves feminists. Today, professors Carol Kramer, Barbara Mills, and Mary Stiner teach and mentor Arizona archaeology graduate students of both sexes.

Many women in archaeology eschew the feminist label. Many see feminism as political, and they believe that politics do not belong in science. But as feminist archaeologist Roberta Gilchrist (1991) has argued, politics of many kinds are there already. Alison Wylie (1992), who has analyzed the impact of feminism on archaeological theory, shows that feminism leads to better science, not anti-science. Many fear that men will not take work labeled "feminist" seriously, or do not wish to exclude excellent work being done along similar lines by men. Just what might be termed "feminism" in archaeology, when it is labeled as such, bears its own historical telling.

HISTORY OF FEMINIST ARCHAEOLOGY

In this section, I discuss the history of explicitly feminist research within archaeology, starting with obstacles that delayed its acceptance. Some have attributed archaeology's resistance to feminism in part to the ecosystems paradigm that dominated the discipline from the late 1950s through the early 1980s (Conkey and Spector 1984). The ecosystems view tends to treat all humans as largely interchangeable producers and consumers of resources. Culturally specific details, including gender, were thought to be inaccessible to scientific measurement. Moreover, many archaeologists believe that biology determines gender roles and that sexing skeletons is relatively straightforward, despite evidence to the contrary from sociocultural and biological anthropology. They conclude, then, that gender is unproblematic and unworthy of special attention.

Joan Gero (1985, 344) attributes the resistance to feminist approaches to white, middle-class males' domination of the profession of archaeology. A self-image that characterizes archaeologists as masculine, strong, and active—as the "cowboys of science"—promotes a system of negative rewards for publicly engaging in feminist discourse of any kind. Alison Wylie (1997) suggests that feminism could not have arisen in archaeology until a critical mass of women had entered the discipline and women's achievements in general had disrupted core assumptions about gender roles in archaeology.

Emma Lou Davis was one of the earliest women archaeologists to call herself a feminist, and she did so at a time when women in archaeology were few. She took her archaeology degree in 1964, late in her life, after an eclectic career as an artist and Communist activist. Reporting her field research on Paleoindians of southern California, she promoted three feminist goals: challenging the prevailing view of male hunting as the most important aspect of early cultures; demonstrating that including feminine voices in archaeological narrative resulted in a more complete and accurate portrayal of the past; and writing personal narrative about doing research. Describing a book of hers, she wrote,

This is a very female book. Hopefully, it contributes a different voice, different attitudes and values from male traditions of archaeological writing in which, somehow, the actors become lost in the gimmicks and stage props. . . . This is not a book about full-time Elephant Hunters (a male myth, not substantiated by our information). It is about peoples of the marsh: setting snares for musk-rats and nets for ducks; gathering eggs on a spring morning when brant were feeding; when there was enough dried horse meat in camp to tide the family over until the next camel. (Davis 1978; reprinted in Hays-Gilpin and Whitley 1998, 353)

Many feminist archaeologists initially set out to make women and their work visible, to counter interpretations that portrayed only men as actively making and doing things. In 1983, Janet Spector asked questions about how to find evidence for women's activities, and she developed a set of methods she called the "task differentiation approach" to make gender an explicit axis of analysis. The method relies on potentially biased records of what Plains Indian women and men did in historical times. Perhaps because of its reliance on historical records, "dirt archaeologists" and prehistorians ignored it. Because it relied on normative, binary male-female gender categories as well, Spector herself has repudiated the method and moved on to more complicated approaches. Spector, together with Margaret Conkey, argued in 1984 (Conkey and Spector 1984) that for archaeologists to study gender, much more was needed than simply "finding women" in the past and that studying gender would lead to significantly better understandings of the past. They presented a list of topics that seemed to be missing from the archaeological literature at that time, for example, "Gender Arrangements and the Emergence of Food Production." Patty Jo Watson subsequently took up this challenge. Previous theories of plant domestication in the Eastern Woodlands of North America had suggested that, as plants and humans evolved together, plants effectively domesticated themselves or that male shamans' domestication of gourds for ritual use led to farming food plants. Watson and her student Mary C. Kennedy concluded instead that women probably domesticated plants and produced new strains of maize, because throughout the world, "food plants in foraging societies are women's business" and they likely had the most intimate knowledge of wild plants and where and how they grew. In addition, women are responsible for horticulture in historical tribes in the area, and women are just as likely as men to have been active, inventive, and curious (Watson and Kennedy 1991, 269).

Feminist archaeology has always been more popular in Europe than in the United States. Feminist critique emerged earliest in Scandinavian archaeology, where a 1979 conference asked, "Were they all men?" (Bertelsen, Lillehammer, and Naess 1987), and a 1985 conference resulted in the founding of a journal now entitled *Women in Archaeology in Norway*. In England in the 1980s, several young archaeologists, including Ian Hodder, Michael Shanks, and Christopher Tilley, championed a reflexive "post-processual archaeology" in opposition to the mainstream "culture process" school, which emphasized a scientific, generalizing, and largely impersonal approach to interpreting the past. They included feminism in a list of new approaches that archaeologists should pursue to produce multivocal, contextually situated, and interpretative archaeological narratives. As Ericka Engelstad (1991) notes, however, the post-processualists nonetheless focused on issues thought to interest men, such as power and prestige; uncritically accepted binary thinking as a human universal; and sometimes produced overtly misogynist interpretations. Nonetheless, discussions of gender and feminism have taken place at annual meetings of the Theoretical Archaeology Group since 1982, and students at Cambridge published a special

issue of the *Archaeological Journal from Cambridge* devoted to feminist approaches in 1988.

Although little explicit consideration of gender difference, feminist theory, or equity issues attracted widespread attention in the Americas until the 1990s, several earlier efforts set the stage. Historical archaeologist Suzanne Spencer-Wood produced a feminist critique of Western gender stereotypes in some classic ethnological texts as early as 1971, and she applied feminist methods to archaeological analysis in 1981 but was unable to publish anything with an explicitly feminist focus until 1987 (Spencer-Wood 1996, 123). Alice Kehoe and Sarah Nelson organized a gender-oriented archaeology session at the 1987 American Anthropological Association annual meeting. Convinced that using the words "feminist" or "gender" in the title would doom the session to rejection by those who screened the archaeology panels, they called it "Powers of Observation: Alternative Views in Archaeology" and invited some men with other perspectives to take part. The session was accepted, and its proceedings were published in 1990 (Nelson and Kehoe 1990; Nelson 1997, 40).

Margaret Conkey and Joan Gero invited a select group of scholars (men as well as women) to contribute papers using gender as an explicit line of inquiry in 1988. The first compendium of feminist papers in historical archaeology in the Americas appeared in 1991 (Seifert 1991), following regular colloquia since 1988 at the Society for Historical Archaeology annual meetings. Inspired by a visit from philosopher and feminist Alison Wylie, archaeology students at the University of Calgary chose gender as the focus for their 1989 Chacmool Conference. To their surprise, they attracted about 100 speakers, the largest turnout for the annual conference to that date. At least 80 percent avoided the term "feminism" in the abstracts for their papers, however (Hanen and Kelley 1992). Nearly half dissociated themselves from feminism, and many others expressed ambivalence about the label in a survey by Alison Wylie (1997). Cheryl Claassen convened the Anthropology and Archaeology of Women Conference at Appalachian State University in 1991 (Claassen 1992). Its successor, the Gender and Archaeology Conference, still held every other year, attracts archaeologists, art historians, and classicists (Claassen and Joyce 1997; Rautman 2000). Also in 1991, Hilary du Cros and Laurajane Smith convened the first of several Australian Women in Archaeology Conferences and gave it the subtitle "A Feminist Critique" (du Cros and Smith 1993). A wide, international network of archaeologists interested in gender, most of them women, has resulted. Women still seem more interested than men in understanding social identities and roles, especially in investigating who women were, what they did, and how they experienced life. Each successive year, however, the mix of speakers as well as audience seems to include more men and more of those who self-identify as other-gendered.

In addition to studying gender in the past, feminists study equity issues within the practice of archaeology (Nelson, Nelson, and Wylie 1994). Gender stereotypes projected into the past and present-day inequalities are related. Joan Gero shows that most archaeologists assume that men made most stone tools in the past and that present-day stone tool specialists—especially those who replicate and use ancient tool types thought to have been used for hunting and butchering—are almost all men (Gero 1985, 1996). Linda Hurcombe (1995) summarizes, "The study of gender in ancient societies seems inseparable from the place of gender in our own society" (87). Many of Hurcombe's British female students wanted to find evidence that women in the past hunted game animals, not because such evidence is abundant and suppressed by sexist archaeologists (it is not) but because hunting "was the task *they* valued" more than plant gathering (96). After all, hunting in Britain is culturally coded as an upper-class, leisure activity as well as a manly one.

Gender archaeology is now moving from a somewhat segregated milieu to the mainstream. Timothy Taylor's *Prehistory of Sex: Four Million Years of Human Sexual Culture* (1996) provides a creative and humorous summary of recent anthropological and archaeological thought on sex and gender for a general audience. Articles addressing gender issues increasingly appear in major professional journals such as *Antiquity* and *American Antiquity*. Long-term, collaborative team projects now include gendered perspectives. For example, in a monograph on prehistoric twined yucca fiber sandals from shallow caves in Arizona, my colleagues and I not only included standard information about textile technology, tree-ring dating, and where the artifacts were found but also discussed how these and other elaborately decorated artifacts might have been used in social contexts to signal and even negotiate gender identities, roles, and statuses (Hays-Gilpin, Deegan, and Morris 1998).

FEMINIST CONTRIBUTIONS
TO ARCHAEOLOGY

Feminists and gender archaeologists have already made significant contributions to our understanding of long-term changes and variations in gender roles, hierarchies, and ideologies in many parts of the world. I will touch on a few examples: the role of hunting in human evolution, the origins of women's oppression, ancient goddess worship, and nonbinary gender systems.

One of the first feminist critiques of traditional archaeology and biological anthropology was an attack on the "man the hunter" model of human evolution. In a widely cited example of feminist revisionism, Sally Linton ([1971] 1975) argued that "woman the gatherer" provided a more accurate model for early human lifeways on the African savannahs. Frances Dahlberg's 1981 edited volume *Woman the Gatherer* brought together ethnographic studies of recent hunter-gatherer societies, our chimpanzee relatives, and the fossil record of early humans to challenge the androcentric notion that hunting large game by males played the most important role in shaping human evolution. This research demonstrated that for living hunter-gatherers of southern Africa, plant resources provided more food and a more reliable food supply than meat. Many researchers now refer to such societies as "gatherer-hunters." The authors also showed that the gatherer-hunter division of labor is very flexible. Men, women, and children routinely collect plant, insect, and rodent foods and hunt small game, while men and sometimes women, even pregnant and lactating women, hunt larger game. In spite of often verbalizing ideal gender roles, in practice, everyone does any task necessary.

While ethnographers can observe living people, archaeologists face many obstacles to documenting gendered divisions of labor in the distant past. In the absence of unambiguous evidence of task differences, most archaeologists have simply assumed that men hunted, made stone tools, and functioned in public and ritual roles, while women cared for children, prepared food, made crafts of "soft" materials, such as textiles, baskets, and pottery, and confined their activities to domestic or household spheres. In some cultures, these distinctions tend to apply; in some, they do not. In all, the reality is more complicated than Western stereotypes imagine. Feminist critique has spurred archaeologists to look for evidence and to challenge unsupported assumptions about sex and gender.

One enduring hope for a feminist archaeology is that detailed study of material remains from past societies will provide evidence of the origins of women's oppression today and perhaps will demonstrate that oppression is not inevitable. However, it is nonarchaeologists who tend to raise this issue, while those in the profession rarely approach it (Nelson 1997), perhaps because many archaeologists see research on the origins of anything as problematic at best and as a sign of pandering to popular interests at worst (Conkey with Williams 1991; Tringham and Conkey 1998). But the question has not gone away; is women's oppression due to the institutionalization of private property, the rise of states, or some other cultural development rather than innate and unchanging sex or gender inequalities? As with most origins research, the more thorough and detailed the investigation, the more the question seems to dissolve in contradictions and complexities.

Consideration of power and hierarchy in the past has broadened to include sources of power other than wealth or control of material resources. Western taken-for-granted dichotomies such as public-domestic and sacred-profane, their gender associations, and their relative importance now receive critical attention. Scholars now raise the possibility that many past societies were organized "heterarchically,"

with multiple sources of power that did not necessarily coincide in one set of vertical power relationships, or "hierarchy." For example, men and women in Bronze Age Denmark did not divide their activities according to public-sacred and domestic-profane contexts; rather, distribution and contexts of ritual and exotic artifacts show that both men and women performed ritual roles. Men took part in processions and ritual combat, depicted in rock carvings, and women made votive offerings of decorated metal items in watery places. Both men and women seem to have had access to exotic objects and materials, such as bronze and gold, and to the ritual roles and knowledge implied by their use. The diversity and relative importance of men's and women's activities fluctuated, with increased investment in women's votive offerings in times when militarism and expansion lessened (Levy 1999, 64-68). The debate over the origin of women's inferior position is thus beginning to focus on specific kinds of power held by women and men and on intersections of gender with age and class.

Many feminists want archaeologists to explore whether any prehistoric societies serve as gender-egalitarian models for society. In 1978, Ann Barstow argued that archaeology could provide feminists with alternative histories for women. She chose an unfortunate example, James Mellaart's work on the Neolithic Goddess at the Anatolian site of Çatal Hüyük. Most professional archaeologists regard Mellaart's interpretations (1967) of figurines, sculpture, and wall-paintings as little more than romantic speculation. But interest in "the Goddess" became a lively topic of debate among archaeologists, scholars in other disciplines, and the adherents of women's spirituality movements. Popular books by Marija Gimbutas (1987, 1991) assert that female figurines spanning a period of at least 20,000 years over the whole of Europe demonstrate ancient belief in a Mother Goddess, deposed by marauding patriarchal Indo-European speakers in later prehistoric times. Gimbutas failed to address a number of questions other archaeologists find important: did the figurines represent deities or other spiritual beings or individuals—the artists, or family members? How would we know? Why are so many figurines sex-ambiguous? Investigation of archaeological materials has yet to yield evidence for past matriarchies worshiping a universal Great Mother Goddess or even a pan-European Goddess. Recent research suggests that past gender ideologies were far more diverse and complex, offering many models of feminine power, not only nurturing and mothering but also destructive or simply ambiguous. The fact that the majority of figurines in many times and places, including the European Ice Age, show no evidence of sexual features at all (and a few are surely male) suggests that projecting a present-day essential or ideal of the feminine onto the past on the basis of these data is misguided (Goodison and Morris 1998; Meskell 1995). In efforts to preserve jobs and funding, archaeologists in Communist countries such as the USSR and China routinely identified prehistoric matriarchies, as predicted by Marx and Engels, in their interpretations of data so skimpy they could not support any hypothesis about social organization. Do Western expectations of ancient matriarchies also derive from outdated models of social evolution, or do the infiltration of popular culture by Freudian thought and simple wishful thinking play roles? Most archaeologists, including many feminist ones, have difficulty understanding why some women want scientific support for using feminine images from the past to validate present-day, and often highly personal, beliefs that seem to restrict rather than broaden the range of possible identities and roles for women. The topic deserves further dialogue and is sure to receive it.

Aside from revising old myths (and some relatively new ones), does the archaeological study of sex and gender systems in past cultures make new and significant differences in the way archaeologists interpret evidence for past lifeways? Early on, positivist archaeologists, like most Euroamericans, assumed that biology determined social identities. For example, in studying graves, some archaeologists carefully measured bones and forced the results into one of four categories: male, female, juvenile, or indeterminate. Others assigned skeletons to these same categories on the basis of goods found in graves: weapons must accompany males, and adornment signified females. Any contradiction between grave goods and skeletal metrics could be dismissed as "problematic." Next, with the 1980s theoretical shift toward postpositivism, including a healthy skepticism about everything from objectivity to the nature-nurture debate, archaeologists interested in gender argued for distinguishing sex (a binary biologically based but socially constructed categorization) from gender (the social values inscribed on sex, which may have more than two categories, may change through time or cross-culturally, and may not coincide with sex). Thus, frequent occurrence of weapons in female-sexed graves might mean that fighting was part of a feminine gender identity in the culture, while rare occurrences of weapons in female graves might reflect a society in which some females fulfilled a masculine role in society or a society with more than two gender categories.

Age, class, and ethnicity also receive more attention under this framework. Gender intersects with many other kinds of social identities and cannot be studied in isolation. Careful study of Classic period (circa A.D. 1150-1350) Hohokam burials in the Phoenix, Arizona, area shows that some postmenopausal women have a wider variety of grave goods than do women of child-bearing age. These include ritual items more often found with men of all ages. Before we argue that older women served as ritual specialists in this society, we must note that this pattern appears only in some Hohokam villages and only in the platform mound structures occupied by elite members of the society, so class, community, age, and gender intersect to define privilege here (Crown and Fish 1996).

Most recently, some archaeologists have scrutinized even the sex-gender dichotomy and found it wanting (Yates 1993; Meskell 1996). Uncritical generalizing and classifying mask variation that could provide far more interesting interpretations of the past. Sex and gender, these archaeologists argue, should be decoupled entirely. Gender should be viewed as multidimensional and continuous, and archaeologists should focus on individuals and their life experiences. For example, many human figurines display elaborate sexual features in some times and places and not in others, and instead have elaborate facial or costume features in some times and places and not in others, showing that different artists emphasized different kinds of features depending on the contexts of making and using figurines, not on universal sex and gender categories. Furthermore, making, displaying, or playing with figurines may have functioned in defining, negotiating, and performing gender identities, kin relationships, and rites of passage (Knapp and Meskell 1997).

CURRENT AND
FUTURE TRENDS

Feminism is making inroads into archaeology, although the terms "gender archaeology" and "archaeology of gender" are firmly established and rarely described as "feminist," at least by Americans. The situation has changed because recent developments, such as post-processual archaeology, have introduced some degree of self-reflexivity and because archaeologists have recognized that good scientists must take care not to project present-day stereotypes onto the past. Feminists and others have demonstrated that information about gender and other social identities is often accessible through careful study and that gender is a complicated and multifaceted process. Moreover, considering gender makes a difference in our interpretations of past lifeways and human evolution and experience in the long term. Feminism makes what we do more accessible and interesting to wider audiences.

Gender research is not solely by and about women. Men have been involved from the outset and increasingly raise questions about the fact that masculine identities were also multiple, varied, and changing in the past. Investigation of the roles of children and their activities in the past increases our understanding of past societies. The archaeology of sexuality, including homosexuality, and the application of queer theory promise to be important topics (Taylor 1996; Yates 1993). Historical archaeologists are pioneering an archaeology of and for the working class. For example, Phil Duke and Dean Saitta are excavating the site of a turn-of-the-century mine strike and massacre in Colorado. Perhaps most important, a great deal of archaeology is now carried out in collaboration with descendant people, from working-class African Americans of Annapolis, Maryland, to Australian Aboriginals' tribally controlled cultural preservation programs. Even when approaches and conclusions conflict, including multiple voices from project

planning to final report or exhibit production is now accepted and encouraged by many.

In the 1998 School of American Research Senior Seminar, "Doing Archaeology as a Feminist: Moving from Theory to Practice," Alison Wylie, Margaret Conkey, and other senior scholars of feminist archaeology concluded that one of the most highly valued contributions feminism has made to archaeology is the use of nonstandard media, presentation formats, and writing styles to present results and interpretations. These include biographical narratives and personalized accounts of the research experience (Davis 1978; Spector 1993), dialogue (Joyce 1994; Tringham 1991), and hypertext; for example, Ruth Tringham and Ian Hodder post their archaeological field data on the World Wide Web and foster on-line discussion of results and interpretations. The School of American Research conference publication will include transcripts of the discussion during the conference itself and subsequent e-mail texts as well as the papers prepared for the conference. This format will emphasize and extend the collaborative structure of the seminar and provide a concrete example of feminist archaeology in action.

Although feminist ideas are entering the archaeological mainstream, concerns remain that they are being grafted onto discourse that remains androcentric. This discourse variously denies the importance of gender differences; emphasizes difference but uncritically applies binary classifications such as men-women, public-private, active-passive, and dominant-subordinate; or focuses on fixed social categories at the expense of understanding individual experience. For example, a colleague at a recent conference identified parts of his Southwest Archaic site as women's work areas because there were plant-processing tools and small mammal remains there, and those are things that women use. True, a few decades ago, only a few archaeologists thought about women's work at all, but it is not enough to simply assume that women always did the same tasks or that all cultures have binary divisions of labor.

On the other hand, we risk focusing on individual experience at the expense of recognizing that social categories, including gender, were also constituted, negotiated, and reconstituted in the past, although such categories were different from those we see today and take for granted. Some of my most radical colleagues have advised me that classifying human representations in rock engravings by sex or gender, even when genitals are apparently depicted, is a hopelessly biased act. They argue that archaeologists can never know how individuals constructed their own gender identities at any given moment; therefore, when I identify recurring images of a corn maiden and a phallic flute player in Southwest rock art as having something to do with ancestral Hopi and Zuni concepts of fertility and gender complementarity (Hays-Gilpin 2000), I am projecting my own stereotypes onto the data, regardless of whether oral traditions of the artists' descendants concur,

and they do. But archaeological methods are at their best when focused on looking for patterns and assessing their potential significance. For example, Elizabeth Brumfiel (1996) has examined Aztec figurines that seem to include representations of individuals of different ages, genders, and statuses. Comparing figurines made in the capital and in the hinterlands revealed that rural artisans produced more individualistic and personal representations, resisting dominant ideologies expressed by the standardized figures of deities favored in the capital. Looking for such patterns does minimize some kinds of diversity in the data and introduces biases of various kinds. But the results tell us something about social processes, such as domination and resistance, that we would be unable to discuss if Brumfiel had written off all variation as the confusing result of fleeting individual experiences.

Another important concern is the exclusion of working-class women and women of color from the practice of archaeology, which steadfastly remains a middle-class, white enterprise. Active recruitment of Native Americans and African Americans into academic programs and government cultural preservation programs has begun to realize some diversification. More needs to be done. Based on my own experience in the Southwest, Navajo, Hopi, and other Native American students want to learn more about their own histories but do not want to wade through numerous method and theory courses first. I suggest undergraduate courses that immediately focus on what we know (and what we do not know) about the archaeology of the regions immediately surrounding our colleges and universities or the regions of origin of the minority groups in our student bodies. Flexible, long-term training and job programs that take into account family and religious obligations would be welcomed by many women and minority students, as would mentors who have successfully negotiated archaeological careers. Obstacles include low initial wages, lack of benefits, long periods in the field away from home, difficulty in finding child care, the undervaluing of sedentary specializations such as laboratory work, and conflicts between practices such as exhuming human remains and the traditional values of family members.

CONCLUSION

In 1979, a group of Scandinavian women archaeologists asked, "Were they all men?" and demonstrated that women as well as men were active members of past societies. Subsequent efforts sought to find archaeological evidence for women and to discover what they were doing. We have increasingly focused not on finding women but on finding out about the relationships between men and women. One of the most recent contributions of feminist thought is critical thinking about our very categories men and women, male and female, and other false dichotomies. When we are able to investigate gender as multivalent and gender difference as a continuum rather than fixed categories, we will produce more complicated, but more accurate and useful, understandings of human experience and not just in the past.

Feminist archaeologists also contribute to democratization and diversification of archaeological theory and practice, not only providing feminine perspectives but encouraging inclusion of many perspectives. Feminists are also transforming the way archaeologists present their results and interpretations to the public and are helping draw out more active public participation, especially among descendant peoples whose ancestors created the remains that archaeologists study. Feminist archaeologists have already ensured that women don't remain "people without history" (see Wolf 1982) or "those of little note" (see Scott 1994), but they still struggle to do archaeology as feminists in a field that still rewards androcentrism in so many ways.

References

Barstow, Ann. 1978. The Uses of Archaeology for Women's History: James Mellaart's Work on the Neolithic Goddess at Çatal Hüyük. *Feminist Studies* 4(3):7-17.

Bender, Susan J. 1991. Towards a History of Women in Northeastern U.S. Archaeology. In *The Archaeology of Gender: Proceedings of the Twenty-Second Annual Conference of the Archaeological Association of the University of Calgary*, ed. D. Walde and N. D. Willows. Calgary, Alberta, Canada: Archaeological Association of the University of Calgary.

Bertelsen, Reidar, Arnvid Lillehammer, and Jenny-Rita Naess, eds. 1987. *Were They All Men? An Examination of Sex*

Roles in Prehistoric Society. Stavanger, Norway: Arkeologist Museum I Stavanger.

Brumfiel, Elizabeth. 1996. Figurines and the Aztec State: Testing the Effectiveness of Ideological Domination. In *Gender and Archaeology,* ed. Rita P. Wright. Philadelphia: University of Pennsylvania Press.

Claassen, Cheryl, ed. 1992. *Exploring Gender Through Archaeology: Selected Papers from the 1991 Boone Conference.* Madison, WI: Prehistory Press.

———. 1994. *Women in Archaeology.* Philadelphia: University of Pennsylvania Press.

Claassen, Cheryl and Rosemary A. Joyce. 1997. Women in the Ancient Americas: Archaeologists, Gender, and the Making of Prehistory. In *Women in Prehistory: North America and Mesoamerica,* ed. C. Claassen and R. A. Joyce. Philadelphia: University of Pennsylvania Press.

Conkey, Margaret W. and Janet Spector. 1984. Archaeology and the Study of Gender. *Advances in Archaeological Method and Theory* 7:1-38.

Conkey, Margaret W. with Sarah H. Williams. 1991. Original Narratives: The Political Economy of Gender in Archaeology. In *Gender at the Crossroads of Knowledge: Feminist Anthropology in the Postmodern Era,* ed. M. DiLeonardo. Berkeley: University of California Press.

Cordell, Linda. 1993. Women Archaeologists in the Southwest. In *Hidden Scholars: Women Anthropologists and the Native American Southwest,* ed. N. J. Parezo. Albuquerque: University of New Mexico Press.

Crown, Patricia L. and Suzanne K. Fish. 1996. Gender and Status in the Hohokam Pre-Classic to Classic Tradition. *American Anthropologist* 98(4):803-17.

Dahlberg, Frances, ed. 1981. *Woman the Gatherer.* New Haven, CT: Yale University Press.

Davis, Emma Lou. 1978. *The Ancient Californians: Rancholabrean Hunters of the Mojave Lakes Country.* Los Angeles: Natural History Museum of Los Angeles County.

du Cros, Hilary and Laurajane Smith, eds. 1993. *Women in Archaeology: A Feminist Critique.* Canberra: Australian National University.

Engelstad, Ericka. 1991. Images of Power and Contradiction: Feminist Theory and Post-Processual Archaeology. *Antiquity* 65:502-14.

Gero, Joan M. 1985. Sociopolitics and the Woman-at-Home Ideology. *American Antiquity* 50:342-50.

———. 1996. Archaeological Practice and Gendered Encounters with Field Data. In *Gender and Archaeology,* ed. Rita P. Wright. Philadelphia: University of Pennsylvania Press.

Gilchrist, Roberta. 1991. Women's Archaeology? Political Feminism, Gender Theory, and Historical Revision. *Antiquity* 65:495-501.

Gimbutas, Marija. 1987. *The Language of the Goddess: Images and Symbols of Old Europe.* New York: Van der Marck.

———. 1991. *The Civilization of the Goddess: The World of Old Europe.* San Francisco: HarperCollins.

Goodison, Lucy and Christine Morris, eds. 1998. *Ancient Goddesses.* London: British Museum Press.

Hanen, Marsha and Jane Kelley. 1992. Gender and Archaeological Knowledge. In *MetaArchaeology: Reflections by Archaeologists and Philosophers,* ed. L. Embree. Boston: Kluwer.

Hays-Gilpin, Kelley. 2000. Beyond Mother Earth and Father Sky: Sex and Gender in Ancient Southwestern Visual Arts. In *Interpreting the Body: Insights from Anthropological and*

Classical Archaeology: Selected Papers from the Fourth Gender and Archaeology Conference, ed. Alison Rautman. Philadelphia: University of Pennsylvania Press.

Hays-Gilpin, Kelley, Ann Cordy Deegan, and Elizabeth Ann Morris. 1998. *Prehistoric Sandals from Northeastern Arizona: The Earl H. and Ann Axtell Morris Research*. University of Arizona Papers in Anthropology 62. Tucson: University of Arizona Press.

Hays-Gilpin, Kelley and David S. Whitley, eds. 1998. *Reader in Gender Archaeology*. London: Routledge.

Hurcombe, Linda. 1995. Our Own Engendered Species. *Antiquity* 69(262): 87-100.

Joyce, Rosemary A. 1994. Dorothy Hughes Popenoe: Eve in an Archaeological Garden. In *Women in Archaeology*, ed. Cheryl Claassen. Philadelphia: University of Pennsylvania Press.

Knapp, A. Bernard and Lynn Meskell. 1997. Bodies of Evidence on Prehistoric Cyprus. *Cambridge Archaeological Journal* 7(2):183-204.

Levy, Janet. 1999. Gender, Power, and Heterarchy in Middle-Level Societies. In *Manifesting Power: Gender and the Interpretation of Power in Archaeology*, ed. T. Sweely. London: Routledge.

Linton, Sally. [1971] 1975. Woman the Gatherer: Male Bias in Anthropology. In *Toward an Anthropology of Women*, ed. R. R. Reiter. New York: Monthly Review Press.

Lister, Florence Cline. 1997. *Pot Luck: Adventures in Archaeology*. Albuquerque: University of New Mexico Press.

Mellaart, James. 1967. *Çatal Hüyük: A Neolithic Town in Anatolia*. New York: McGraw Hill.

Meskell, Lynn. 1995. Goddesses, Gimbutas and "New Age" Archaeology. *Antiquity* 69(262):74-87.

———. 1996. The Somatization of Archaeology: Institutions, Discourses, Corporeality. *Norwegian Archaeological Review* 29:1-16.

Nelson, Margaret C., Sarah M. Nelson, and Alison Wylie, eds. 1994. *Equity Issues for Women in Archaeology*. Washington, DC: American Anthropological Association.

Nelson, Sarah M. and Alice B. Kehoe, eds. 1990. *Powers of Observation: Alternative Views in Archaeology*. Washington, DC: American Anthropological Association.

Nelson, Sarah Milledge. 1997. *Gender in Archaeology: Analyzing Power and Prestige*. Walnut Creek, CA: AltaMira Press.

Preucel, Robert W. and Meredith S. Chesson. 1994. Blue Corn Girls: A Herstory of Three Early Women Archaeologists at Tecolote, New Mexico. In *Women in Archaeology*, ed. Cheryl Claassen. Philadelphia: University of Pennsylvania Press.

Rautman, Alison, ed. 2000. *Interpreting the Body: Insights from Anthropological and Classical Archaeology: Selected Papers from the Fourth Gender and Archaeology Conference*. Philadelphia: University of Pennsylvania Press.

Reyman, Jonathan E. 1992. Women in American Archaeology: Some Historical Notes and Comments. In *Rediscovering Our Past: Essays on the History of American Archaeology*, ed. J. E. Reyman. Aldershot: Avebury.

Scott, Elizabeth M., ed. 1994. *Those of Little Note: Gender, Race, and Class in Historical Archaeology*. Tucson: University of Arizona Press.

Seifert, Donna J., ed. 1991. *Gender in Historical Archaeology. Historical Archaeology* 25(4).

Spector, Janet D. 1983. Male/Female Task Differentiation Among the Hidatsa: Toward the Development of an Archaeological Approach to the Study of Gender. In *The Hidden Half*, ed. P. Albers and B. Medicine. Washington, DC: University Press of America.

———. 1993. *What This Awl Means: Feminist Archaeology at a Wahpeton Dakota Village*. St. Paul: Minnesota Historical Society Press.

Spencer-Wood, Suzanne. 1996. Toward the Further Development of Feminist Historical Archaeology. *World Archaeological Congress Bulletin* 7:118-36.

Taylor, Timothy. 1996. *The Prehistory of Sex: Four Million Years of Human Sexual Culture*. New York: Bantam.

Tringham, Ruth E. 1991. Households with Faces: The Challenge of Gender in Prehistoric Architectural Remains. In *Engendering Archaeology: Women and Prehistory*, ed. J. Gero and M. Conkey. Oxford: Basil Blackwell.

Tringham, Ruth and Margaret Conkey. 1998. Rethinking Figurines: A Critical View from Archaeology of Gimbutas, the "Goddess" and Popular Culture. In *Ancient Goddesses*, ed. L. Goodison and C. Morris. London: British Museum Press.

Watkins, Frances. 1931. Archaeology as a Profession for Women. *Masterkey* 4:173-78.

Watson, Patty Jo and Mary C. Kennedy. 1991. The Development of Horticulture in the Eastern Woodlands of North America: Women's Role. In *Engendering Archaeology: Women and Prehistory*, ed. J. Gero and M. Conkey. London: Basil Blackwell.

Wolf, Eric. 1982. *Europe and the People Without History*. Berkeley: University of California Press.

Wylie, Alison. 1992. The Interplay of Evidential Constraints and Political Interests: Recent Archaeological Research on Gender. *American Antiquity* 57:15-35.

———. 1997. The Engendering of Archaeology: Refiguring Feminist Science Studies. *Osiris* 12:80-99.

Yates, Tim. 1993. Frameworks for an Archaeology of the Body. In *Interpretative Archaeology*, ed. Christopher Tilley. Oxford: Berg.

ANNALS, *AAPSS*, **571**, September 2000

Feminism
and Migration

By PIERRETTE HONDAGNEU-SOTELO

ABSTRACT: The second wave of U.S. feminism and the reconstitution of the United States as a country of immigration gained momentum in the 1970s. Recent manifestations of both feminism and immigration have left indelible changes on the social landscape, yet immigration and feminism are rarely coupled in popular discussion, social movements, or academic research. This article explores the articulations and disarticulations between immigration and feminism; it focuses particularly on the intersections of migration studies and feminist studies.

Pierrette Hondagneu-Sotelo is associate professor in the Department of Sociology and in the Program in American Studies and Ethnicity at the University of Southern California. She is author of Gendered Transitions: Mexican Experiences of Immigration *(1994), coeditor of* Challenging Fronteras: Structuring Latina and Latino Lives in the U.S. *(1997), and coeditor of* Gender Through the Prism of Difference *(1997, 2000). She is the author of the forthcoming book* Maid to Work in L.A. *and editor of a forthcoming book on gender and contemporary U.S. immigration.*

AS the twentieth century turns into the twenty-first, the United States is a very different country from what it was at mid-century. We hear a lot about some of these changes. Pundits and commentators, for example, constantly remind us that the Internet revolution and new, intensified forms of globalization have changed the way we live our lives. Other developments, however, do not seem to receive the recognition that the indelible changes they have left on the social landscape would seem to merit. Two of the most radically transformative forces in remaking the United States are feminism and immigration. In this article, I explore some of the articulations and disarticulations of U.S. immigration and feminism, focusing particularly on the intersections of migration studies and feminist studies.

While the United States has always embraced the notion of itself as "a nation of immigrants," a momentary hiatus in mass immigration—roughly from 1930 to 1970—led to a very different reality. Think back to the 1950s. The United States was still largely cast and imagined as a nation in "black and white," with Asian American and Mexican American numerical minorities concentrated in the western and southwestern regions, largely the legacy of premodern, neocolonialist, government-sponsored programs of contract labor that had recruited Mexican, Chinese, and Filipino manpower to develop primary industries (namely, railroads, mining, and agribusiness) in the West. During this assimilationist era, the English language and Anglo-American culture enjoyed virtually unquestioned hegemony, and ketchup, not salsa, was still the condiment of choice. If American cuisine is any barometer of change, we should take note that today salsa outsells ketchup, and the occasional foray to urban China-towns for chop suey has been rendered nearly obsolete by the proliferation of Thai restaurants and Vietnamese noodle parlors adorning suburban mini-malls from coast to coast.

Why does the landscape of race, language, and cuisine look so different today from only a few decades ago? After the mid-century hiatus in immigration, the last three decades of the twentieth century have witnessed a vigorous resurgence in U.S. immigration. As many commentators have observed, the new immigrants now hail not from Europe, as they did in the early part of the twentieth century, but from Asian, Latin American, and Caribbean nations. Unlike their earlier, European predecessors, they include not only poor, manual workers but also substantial numbers of entrepreneurs and highly educated urban professionals. Can we imagine how today's U.S. health care delivery system would function without Hindu doctors and Filipina nurses? Not all contemporary newcomers have come to the United States driven by the search for employment, however. Today's immigrants also include displaced peasants and refugees fleeing war and religious and political persecution. Unlike the classic image of Ellis Island immigrants, who were drawn to factory employment in urban, East

Coast cities, today's immigrants go to a wide variety of urban and suburban locales in the United States. Those who do go to central city areas may do so only as they pass through to settle in metropolitan suburban areas. The suburbanization of immigrant communities is a social fact, and it is only one indicator of how much the contours of immigrant experiences have changed over the last century.

The numbers of immigrants are staggering. According to analysis of census data by Michigan State University sociologist Ruben Rumbaut, by 1997, U.S. immigrants and their U.S.-born children numbered 55 million. Together, immigrants and their children, what Rumbaut calls the "immigrant stock," now constitute about one-fifth of the national population (Rumbaut 1998). The impact on particular regions is even more dramatic, as immigrants and their families concentrate in certain areas, including Miami and Los Angeles—where they make up, respectively, a whopping 72 percent and 62 percent of the population (Rumbaut 1998). Although the social locations of the largest groups of immigrants in those cities are antithetical to one another, with many Cubans in Miami controlling business and mass media while most Mexican immigrants in Los Angeles remain in subordinate, low-wage jobs, both Miami and Los Angeles are truly immigrant metropolises. Heavy concentrations of immigrants are found in other regions of Southern California and also in New York City, in Washington, D.C., and throughout Texas.

Feminism has also provoked far-reaching transformations on the social landscape. While those involved in promoting feminist social movements of the recent decades may rightly surmise that the feminist project of transforming society into a more egalitarian one for women and for all people is far from complete, the expansion of life opportunities for many women living in the United States has occurred at a staggering pace. Using the mid-twentieth century as a benchmark, it is startling to acknowledge the prevalence, by the late twentieth century, of women, including married women with young children, throughout the paid labor force and even in the highly coveted professions of law and medicine. While the gendered division of labor at home seems more impervious to change, even on that front there have been important shifts toward greater egalitarianism. The direct consequences of the organized feminist movements include many features of late-twentieth-century life that many Americans today take for granted. These include the proliferation of shelters for abused women; legislation against domestic violence and against legal discrimination against women and girls in sports, education, work, and politics; laws against sexual harassment in the workplace; and the expansion of reproductive rights.

Neither the improvements in the status and life opportunities available to women and girls nor the demographic transformations brought about by immigration have fallen from the sky. They have different constellations of causes, but both came about, at least in part, because of the civil rights movement.

Expanded opportunities for women and girls were fought for by the second wave of the organized feminist movement, which came directly on the heels of, and which looked for inspiration to, the civil rights movement of the 1950s and 1960s. More circuitous perhaps, but still worth acknowledging, is the role of the civil rights movement in pushing the nation to end all forms of legal discrimination, including racial exclusion provisions in immigration law. After the enactment of the Civil Rights Act in 1964, dramatic changes came about in immigration law, particularly the 1965 Immigrant Amendment. This legislation conclusively ended racial exclusionary policies that had previously denied entry to Asian immigrants. In recent years, many immigration scholars have cautioned that the 1965 law was neither the sole nor decisive factor in promoting this immigration. This is true, as the mass immigration of the late twentieth century has its root causes in structural changes in the global economy and in the changing political policies of nation-states. The extent to which many foreign-born immigrants could be legally admitted into the country, however, is part of the legacy of the civil rights movement (Bach 1978).

The civil rights movement ushered in a period of rights-based liberalism that is widely recognized as extending to racial and ethnic minorities, but it was also extended to new immigrants. In addition to the 1965 amendment, the Refugee Act of 1980 sought to eliminate the Cold War practice of granting political asylum only to those fleeing Communist regimes and to extend asylum more generally to those with well-founded fears of persecution, regardless of political bent. While the intent of immigration laws is not always realized in practice, it is important to recognize these expansionist legislative efforts that sought to expand the numbers and the rights of foreign-born people legally admitted to the United States. The gradual extension of rights to racial and ethnic minorities and immigrants from the 1960s to the 1980s is one of the most salient developments of the twentieth century in the United States, and this trend also occurred in other advanced, industrial democracies (Cornelius, Martin, and Hollifield 1994). This expansionist phase, however, also ultimately prompted new organized backlashes and immigration restrictionist efforts.

While some optimistic political organizers and media pundits proclaimed that "immigrant rights" would become the civil rights issue of the United States in the 1990s, the political tenor of the decade, especially in the early years before the robust boom in the stock market, proved to be among the most inhospitable to new immigrants. Still, in the shadows of larger xenophobic organizations and campaigns such as Proposition 187—the ballot initiative to deny health services and public education to the children of undocumented immigrants that California voters approved in 1994 but that proved to be unconstitutional in the courts—are a host of community, labor, ethnic, and church organizations that work to advocate and strengthen equal rights for all immigrants. These groups engage in efforts to end discrimination against immigrants and to end the unfair treatment of undocumented immigrants and refugees. Among these groups are the National Immigration Forum, located in Washington, D.C., which supports policies and programs designed to strengthen the incorporation of legal immigrants and refugees into the United States; the National Network for Immigrant and Refugee Rights, a federation of coalition groups from major cities around the country, which works more broadly to expand and defend the civil rights of undocumented and documented immigrants; the American Friends Service Committee, a Quaker organization, which operates the Immigrant and Refugee Rights Project, a project that encompasses over 20 sites and that concentrates on the monitoring of human rights abuses along the U.S.-Mexico border; and, finally, Latino civil rights organizations, such as the League of United Latin American Citizens, the Mexican American Legal Defense and Educational Fund, and the National Council of La Raza. Although immigrant advocates have experienced a period of retrenchment—especially since 1996, when immigration law was overhauled with some of the most draconian provisions of the twentieth century—the facility with which legal immigrants, refugees, and naturalized citizens still enjoy basic civil rights in the United States is testament to the immigrant rights movement.

The United States is a very different society at the end of the twentieth century in part because of feminism and immigration. While the feminist movement and the immigrant rights movement have changed the landscape of civil rights for women and immigrants in the United States, there have nonetheless been relatively few points of intersection between the two. Why? The feminist movement may have delayed responding to immigrant women's issues partly because immigrants, as a group, have not been a popular or powerful group around which to rally. Immigrants, although diverse, are commonly portrayed as poor, illegal, ignorant trespassers of national soil and transgressors of national sovereignty. Immigrants have no voice and until very recently, in the wake of the huge waves of naturalization applications—which were, ironically, prompted by the xenophobic campaigns of the 1990s such as Proposition 187 and which are now producing new crops of voters—immigrants have not formed any ready-made, visible constituency for politicians or lobbyists. In fact, their mere presence within the nation-state has often been questioned and seen as lacking legitimacy.

If the U.S. feminist movement was slow in responding to the needs and demands of women of color, it has yet, on a mass scale, to recognize the diverse needs of immigrant women of color. Fledgling programs and grassroots efforts exist, but, on a massive scale, the rights of immigrant women have not been embraced as a priority of feminist organizations.

Conversely, why has the immigrant rights movement not responded to feminist issues? The immigrant rights movement is a beleaguered group, really an amalgam of advocates and service providers. It lacks large-scale monetary resources. In recent decades, it has found itself preoccupied with the attacks on undocumented immigration and legal permanent residence prompted by various immigration laws.

Immigration and feminism are rarely, if ever, coupled in popular discussion, social movements, or academic research. Still, a large segment of immigration scholarship incorporates feminist views, concerns, and concepts. The remainder of this article will discuss the intersections of immigration and feminist scholarship, tracing a genealogy of the feminist impact on immigration research.

Before sketching a genealogy of feminist inflections in immigration studies, however, I wish to note that unlike many of the other articles in this volume, which focus on an academic discipline (such as anthropology, archaeology, and criminology), the study of migration is not a discipline but a topic that has received attention from numerous disciplines, especially sociology, anthropology, economics, history, and political science. In addition to multidisciplinarity, the study of migration is also characterized by cross-disciplinary research, by research that

meshes, say, perspectives and methods of anthropology and sociology or economics. Finally, and perhaps not surprisingly, there is no one paradigm that reigns.

Complicating the picture further, migration is a multifaceted, multidimensional social process. There are different patterns of human migration. Labor migration, which has predominated throughout the twentieth century, is characterized by very different features from migrations of political refugees or movements of colonizers, a type of migration that predominated in the fifteenth century. The contemporary study of labor migration, the type of migration that this article will discuss, includes the examination of the origins of migration flows, the study of how these migration patterns ebb and flow once they begin, the economic and labor market consequences of migration, and the social and cultural aspects of immigration and identity formation. Among these categories of theoretical foci, it is the latter, particularly with regard to the realm of domesticity, culture, and change, that has received the strongest feminist efforts in research. In recent years, the study of citizenship and the study of transnational connections maintained by migrant newcomers have also received increased attention. In fact, to the terms "migrants" and "immigrants" we have now added "transnational migrants," "transnational workers," and postmodernists' "(im)migrants" to our lexicon, in part to refer to the indeterminacy of place of settlement and to denote the deterritorialization of nation-states prompted by immigrant communities that now span national borders.

A GENEALOGY: FEMINISM AND IMMIGRATION SCHOLARSHIP

Tracing a genealogy of feminist-inspired immigration research brings good news and bad news. The good news is that there are no stagnant waters in this subfield. Feminist-inflected theories, concerns, and empirical research continue to develop, reaching into new arenas and showing many promising developments. The bad news is that feminist migration research remains a relatively ghettoized subfield. Feminist concerns and scholarship, and nearly all research that makes central the analytic category of gender, remain marginalized from the core of international migration research. Indicators such as publication in the major migration journals and awards for migration research attest to this continued marginalization.

Although the developments of feminist immigration research have not been as starkly linear as the manner in which I will represent them, the following sketch is suggestive of the trajectory of feminist social science scholarship that has followed from second-wave feminism. The sketch follows loosely the three stages of feminist research identified by Beth Hess and Myra Marx Ferree (1987). The review of literature presented in the following is not intended to be exhaustive. Due to space constraints, many significant and important works are not cited. My intent is to provide an aerial view of some of the major trends in feminist research of international migration.

First stage: Remedying the exclusion of women from research

The first stage of feminist scholarship in the 1970s and early 1980s, which might be labeled "women and migration," sought to remedy the exclusion of women from immigration research. Much of this early phase of research sought to address the virtual absence of women from research designs and androcentric biases. These included assumptions that women are too traditional and culture-bound or that women migrate only as family followers or associational migrants for family reunification. Developments in women's studies programs and feminist scholarship prompted both scholars and policymakers to begin paying attention to women migrants. As modest as this first stage seems to us today, it was met in many corners with casual indifference and sometimes with blatant, vitriolic hostility. British anthropologist Anthony Leeds (1976), for example, opined that "the category of 'women' seems to me a rhetorical one, not one which has (or can be proved to have) generic scientific utility," and he decried this focus as "individualistic, reductionist, and motivational." Leeds argued that focusing on migrant women would deflect scholarly attention from structural processes of capitalist labor exploitation. That in itself is telling, as it assumes that women do not act in economic or structural contexts and that women are somehow cloistered and sheltered from capitalist institutions.

While met with resistance in many academic quarters, the focus on women in migration gained momentum in the 1970s and early 1980s. Among the classic and still-relevant contributions of this era are a special issue of the *International Migration Review*, published in 1984, and a compilation of chapters in Simon and Brettel's edited book, *International Migration: The Female Experience*, published in 1986.

Given the long-standing omission of women from migration, an important first step involved adding women to the research picture. Those of us working today in feminist migration research salute the earlier pioneers who, in their efforts to include women in research, risked ridicule and ostracism by their colleagues (see Leeds 1976). The inclusion of women in migration research was an important first stride, but in retrospect today, we can see that many of these early efforts remained mired in an "add and stir" approach. Migrant women were added as a variable, inserted and measured with regard to, say, education and fertility, and then simply compared with migrant men's employment patterns. This sort of research characterizes much of demography's approach to the study of women in migration.

In other instances, the research spotlight focused exclusively on migrant women. This resulted in several problems, among them the tendency to produce skewed women-only portraits of immigration experiences. Commenting on this trend in historical studies of immigration, historian Donna Gabaccia (1992) observed that "the number of volumes exploring immigrant women separately from men now exceeds the volumes that successfully integrate women into general accounts" (xv). Paradoxically, this approach encouraged scholarship that marginalized immigrant women.

In retrospect, we can see that the women-only approach retards our understanding of how gender as a social system contextualizes migration processes for all immigrants, men and women. As Cynthia Cranford and I have argued elsewhere (Hondagneu-Sotelo and Cranford 1999), this preoccupation with writing women into migration research and theory stifled theorizing about the ways in which constructions of femininities and masculinities organize migration and migration outcomes. This promoted an unfortunate attachment to sex role theory, a paradigm based on atavistic assumptions. Sex role theory, which maintained that women and men learn and play out different sex role scripts, views gender as a relatively static attribute, not as a fluid practice. Migrant studies conducted in this vein typically emphasized how domestic roles anchor women and how public-sphere ties facilitate men's migration (for example, Thadani and Todaro 1984). Men's and women's activities are seen as complementary and functional, as serving the greater purpose of social cohesion. In this regard, sex role theory underemphasizes, and often ignores altogether, issues of power relations and social change. Separate spheres of public and private are emphasized, and the manner in which these are relational is glossed over.

Second stage: From "women and migration" to "gender and migration"

The earlier studies on women and migration were followed by a phase of research on gender and migration, which emerged in the 1980s and early 1990s. Prompted in part by the disruption of the universal category "women" by heightened awareness of the intersectionality of race, class, and gender relations and by the recognition of the fluidity of gender relations, this research focused on the gendering of migration patterns and on the way migration reconfigures systems of gender inequality.

In this crop of gender and migration studies are Sherri Grasmuck and Patricia Pessar's study of Dominican migration to New York City, much of which is reported in the book *Between Two Islands: Dominican International Migration* (1991), and my own research on Mexican undocumented migration to California, reported in *Gendered Transitions: Mexican Experiences of Immigration* (1994). Both of these studies take as their launching point a critique of household strategies, a model explicitly and implicitly used by many migration studies of that period. The critiques put forth in these two books, informed and driven by feminist insights, counter the image of a unitary household undivided by gender and generational hierarchies of power, authority, and resources. Families and immigrant social networks are highly gendered institutions. Both of these studies examine intrahousehold relations of power that shape migration decision-making processes, and they also look at the gendered nature of social networks and the ties between friends and family that facilitate migration.

In *Gendered Transitions*, I sought to convey the extent to which Mexican migration is gendered. Although the origins of undocumented Mexican migration lie in the political and economic transformations within the United States and Mexico and, importantly, in the linkages established between the two countries, the ways in which people respond to these migration pressures and opportunities are often determined by what happens in families and communities, and these are highly gendered spheres. In some families, for example, sons and fathers migrate easily because they are accorded the authority and the social network resources with which to do so. Meanwhile, daughters and wives may not be accorded permission or family resources with which to migrate, but in many cases, they find ways to circumvent these constraints. Through the process of migration, women may develop their own social networks that allow them to contest domestic patriarchal authority.

Not only families and communities are gendered; so are programmatic labor recruitment efforts and job demand, as Terry Repak (1995) has emphasized. We live in a society where occupational sex segregation still prevails in the labor force. The origins of Mexican migration lie in a highly organized program of gendered labor recruitment, through which nearly 5 million temporary labor contracts were handed out to Mexican workers, the vast majority of them men, between 1942 and 1964. In subsequent periods, as my research illustrates, the social networks became less exclusively male, and job demand became more diversified. Gender, together with age, intervenes in migrant social networks in ways that both facilitate and constrain migration opportunities for women and men, but these gendered patterns do not remain static over time.

This second stage of research also focused on the ways in which gender relations change through the processes of migration. After immigration, marriage patterns that once seemed set in stone may shift as spousal separations, conflicts and negotiations, and new living and working arrangements change the rules that govern daily life. Many of the Mexican undocumented families that I studied exhibited more egalitarian gender relations in household divisions of labor, family decision-making processes, and even women's everyday spatial mobility than they showed prior to migration. In her study of Vietnamese refugees resettled in Philadelphia, Nazli Kibria (1993) found similar shifts, attributable in part to the new intersecting relations of family and community. These shifts, however, were neither homogeneous nor monolithic. Still, this reconfiguration, it has been noted, often leads to men's continued attempts to return to their country of origin and to women's efforts to stay in the United States and consolidate settlement (Pessar 1986; Hondagneu-Sotelo 1994; Goldring 1996).

Does women's status always improve with migration? Many studies have continued to assess the impact of immigration on gender relations, and many studies have focused on the impact of immigrant women's employment on gender equality in the family. Research by Yen Le Espiritu (1999b) on Asian American immigrants, by Cecilia Menjívar (1999) on Salvadoran and Guatemalan immigrants in California, and by Prema Kurien (1999) on Hindu immigrant professionals in Southern California finds that there are shifts toward greater gender egalitarianism, but these are unevenly expressed in diverse contexts, and, counterintuitively to what one might expect, domestic inequalities seem to be especially marked in instances where wives earn more than their husbands. Patricia Pessar (1999), a pioneer in the field of gender and migration, has soberly reassessed some of the earlier, hasty feminist proclamations of immigrant women's liberation, rooted as they were in simplistic either-or terms that ignored intersectionalities of race and class, and in early flushes of feminist optimism. We now have a clear understanding that migration is gendered and that gender relations change with migration processes; clearly, the picture is much more complicated than it once seemed.

A primary weakness of much of this research—and my own book, *Gendered Transitions* (1994), exemplifies this debility—is that it remained focused on the level of family and household, suggesting that gender is somehow enclosed within the domestic arena. Consequently, many other important arenas and institutions—jobs, workplaces, and labor demand; notions of citizenship and changing immigration policy; public opinion and the Border Patrol, for example—were ignored by feminist research and appeared, then, as though they were devoid of gender.

*Third stage: Gender
    as a constitutive
    element of migration*

The third stage of feminist scholarship in immigration research is now emerging, and here the emphasis is on looking at gender as a constitutive element of immigration. In this current phase, research is beginning to look at the extent to which gender permeates a variety of practices, identities, and institutions. Here, patterns of labor incorporation, ethnic enclave businesses, citizenship, sexuality, and ethnic identity are interrogated in ways that reveal how gender is incorporated into a myriad of daily operations and institutional political and economic structures.

While most of the gender-inflected research continues to be produced by female scholars, men are making important contributions as well. Among the studies looking at community political mobilization by immigrants is research conducted by Michael Jones-Correa. Focusing on Latino immigrant political identity and practice in New York City and building on the research of earlier feminist inquiries that suggests that, as immigrant men lose status in the United States, they shift their orientations to their home countries and to the project of return migration, Jones-Correa (1998) reveals that immigrant women are more likely than immigrant men to participate in community organizations that interface with U.S. institutions. Looking at the other side of this coin, researcher Luin Goldring has studied the recently emergent and now quite powerful transnational Mexican hometown associations, organizations formed by Mexican immigrants in the United States that typically raise funds in the United States to assist with community development projects "back home." These can be read, Goldring (1998) persuasively suggests, as efforts that allow immigrant men to claim social status denied to them in the new society. In these transmigrant organizations, which span nation-state borders, men find a privileged arena of action, enhancing their gender status. Women participate in these associations as beauty pageant contestants or as men's helpers, and, although they remain absent from active leadership or decision making in these associations, they practice what Goldring calls "substantive social citizenship" in community organizations in the United States. The project of seeing and analyzing migrants' transnational ties, associations, and identities through a gendered lens is also being furthered by research on Salvadoran communities conducted by anthropologist Sarah Mahler (1999).

While researchers of the gendered nature of immigrant political activism and mobilization are making great strides, the topic of anti-immigrant sentiment and state immigration policies remains, in general, a less interrogated area, relatively untouched by immigration researchers, feminist or otherwise. My own feminist analysis with regard to immigration restrictionist efforts has been in regard to California's Proposition 187, which would have denied public education and health services to the children of undocumented immigrants. In an article that appeared in *Socialist Review* (1995), I argued that Proposition 187 was analogous to the repatriation efforts of the 1930s, which encouraged massive removal of Mexican immigrants as well as U.S.-born Mexican Americans to Mexico. Both programs focused not on labor and production but, rather, on the social reproduction of women, children, and families, and they targeted public assistance and social welfare. In both instances, the restrictionists targeted women and children first because they were perceived as the primary indicators of settlement and demographic transition.

In feminist scholarship, sexuality studies, inaugurated by gay, queer, and lesbian studies, has recently emerged as one of the most creative areas of inquiry. Today, the borders of sexuality studies and migration scholarship have been crossed in research conducted by psychologist Olivia Espin (1999), who has examined how immigrant women's sexual practices and identities change over time, and by sociologist Yen Le Espiritu (1999a), who has looked at the way Filipino immigrant parents and their second-generation daughters deploy sexual narratives. Espiritu finds that these narratives discipline and control the second-generation daughters and, importantly, allow Filipinos to construct the dominant group of white Americans as morally flawed and inferior. While Filipino parents and children elevate notions of Filipina chastity as a way to assert a morally superior public face, they simultaneously reinforce patriarchal control over young Filipina women's autonomy. New research by Lionel Cantu (2000) has examined how gay Mexican men's social networks and gay identities shape and promote migration to California. Meanwhile, sociologist and psychotherapist Gloria Gonzalez-Lopez (2000), inspired by gay and lesbian studies, has focused on constructions of normative heterosexuality among Mexican immigrant women, interrogating the transformations in sexual practice, ideals, and norms brought about by their migration to Los Angeles. With this body of research, we are beginning to have an understanding of how sexuality intervenes to shape migration and how migration alters sexual practices and identities.

Over a decade ago now, sociologists Judith Stacey and Barrie Thorne (1985) published what would become a defining and, sadly, almost prophetic article entitled "The Missing Feminist Revolution in

Sociology." In it they examined the mixed reception on the part of various academic disciplines to feminist scholarship, and they concluded that feminism had not succeeded in transforming basic conceptual frameworks in sociology. This is true of immigration scholarship today. Women's experiences are not seen as central in the vast majority of immigration studies, and there are still large-scale surveys conducted of immigrant men that then purport to be about all immigrants. More fundamental is this problem: gender is scarcely recognized or understood as having anything to do with relations of power. To the extent that gender is understood at all, it is seen within the framework of traditional sex roles.

Women as research subjects, and gender as an analytical category, continue to be marginalized within mainstream migration research. While migration research has grown exponentially, commensurate with demographic trends, and while there are more women actually carrying out migration research, feminist perspectives or approaches are not readily embraced or understood. On the other hand, there are new cohorts of younger male researchers, some of whom are more open to feminist perspectives in research. As I have charted in this article with the genealogy of gender and migration studies, there are many exciting developments unfolding. Still, I think it is accurate to note that feminist-inflected migration research has been more enthusiastically received by those working in gender studies, in race, class, or gender intersection-

alities, and even in postcolonial studies than it has by those working in mainstream migration studies. Will this trend continue as we move into the twenty-first century? Probably, and the real loser will be migration scholarship.

References

Bach, Robert. 1978. Mexican Immigration and U.S. Immigration Reforms in the 1960's. *Kapitalistate* 7:63-80.

Cantu, Lionel. 2000. Entre Hombres/Between Men: Latino Masculinities and Homosexualities. In *Gay Masculinities*, ed. Peter Nardi. Thousand Oaks, CA: Sage.

Cornelius, Wayne A., Philip L. Martin, and James F. Hollifield. 1994. Introduction: The Ambivalent Quest for Immigration Control. In *Controlling Immigration: A Global Perspective*, ed. Wayne A. Cornelius, Philip L. Martin, and James F. Hollifield. Stanford, CA: Stanford University Press.

Espin, Olivia M. 1999. *Women Crossing Boundaries: A Psychology of Immigration and Transformations of Sexuality.* New York: Routledge.

Espiritu, Yen Le. 1999a. "Americans Have a Different Attitude": Family, Sexuality, and Gender in Filipina American Lives. In *Gender Through the Prism of Difference*, ed. Maxine Baca Zinn, Pierrette Hondagneu-Sotelo, and Michael Messner. 2d ed. Boston: Allyn & Bacon.

———. 1999b. Gender and Labor in Asian Immigrant Families. *American Behavioral Scientist* 42(4):628-47.

Gabaccia, Donna. 1992. Introduction. In *Seeking Common Ground*, ed. Donna Gabaccia. Westport, CT: Greenwood Press.

Goldring, Luin. 1996. Gendered Memory: Reconstructions of the Village by Mexican Transnational Migrants. In *Cre-*

ating the Countryside: The Politics of Rural and Environmental Discourse, ed. Melanie DuPuis and Peter Vandergeest. Philadelphia: Temple University Press.

———. 1998. The Power of Status in Transnational Social Fields. *Comparative Urban and Community Research* 6:165-95.

Gonzalez-Lopez, Gloria. 2000. Beyond the Bed Sheets, Beyond the Borders: Mexican Immigrant Women and Their Sex Lives. Ph.D. thesis, University of Southern California.

Grasmuck, Sherri and Patricia Pessar. 1991. *Between Two Islands: Dominican International Migration*. Berkeley: University of California Press.

Hess, Beth B. and Myra Marx Ferree, eds. 1987. *Analyzing Gender: A Handbook of Social Science Research*. Newbury Park, CA: Sage.

Hondagneu-Sotelo, Pierrette. 1994. *Gendered Transitions: Mexican Experiences of Immigration*. Berkeley: University of California Press.

———. 1995. Women and Children First: New Directions in Anti-Immigrant Politics. *Socialist Review* 25:169-90.

Hondagneu-Sotelo, Pierrette and Cynthia Cranford. 1999. Gender and Migration. In *Handbook of the Sociology of Gender*, ed. Janet Saltzman Chaffetz. New York: Kluwer Academic/Plenum.

Jones-Correa, Michael. 1998. Different Paths: Gender, Immigration and Political Participation. *International Migration Review* 32(2):326-49.

Kibria, Nazli. 1993. *Family Tightrope: The Changing Lives of Vietnamese Americans*. Princeton, NJ: Princeton University Press.

Kurien, Prema. 1999. Gendered Ethnicity: Creating a Hindu Ethnic Identity in the United States. *American Behavioral Scientist* 42(4):648-70.

Leeds, Anthony. 1976. Women in the Migratory Process: A Reductionist Outlook. *Anthropological Quarterly* 49(1):69-76.

Mahler, Sarah. 1999. Engendering Transnational Migration: A Case Study of Salvadorans. *American Behavioral Scientist* 42(4):690-719.

Menjívar, Cecilia. 1999. The Intersection of Work and Gender: Central American Immigrant Women and Employment in California. *American Behavioral Scientist* 42(4):601-27.

Pessar, Patricia. 1986. The Role of Gender in Dominican Settlement in the United States. In *Women and Change in Latin America*, ed. June Nash and Helen Safa. South Hadley, MA: Bergin & Garvey.

———. 1999. Engendering Migration Studies: The Case of New Immigrants in the United States. *American Behavioral Scientist* 42(4):577-600.

Repak, Terry A. 1995. *Waiting on Washington: Central American Workers in the Nation's Capital*. Philadelphia: Temple University Press.

Rumbaut, Ruben. 1998. Transformations: The Post-Immigrant Generation in an Age of Diversity. Paper presented at the annual meeting of the Eastern Sociological Society, 21 Mar., Philadelphia.

Simon, Rita J. and Caroline B. Brettel, eds. 1986. *International Migration: The Female Experience*. Totowa, NJ: Rowman & Allanheld.

Stacey, Judith and Barrie Thorne. 1985. The Missing Feminist Revolution in Sociology. *Social Problems* 32:301-16.

Thadani, Veena N. and Michael P. Todaro. 1984. Female Migration: A Conceptual Framework. In *Women in the Cities of Asia: Migration and Urban Adaptation*, ed. James T. Fawcett, Siew-Ean Khoo, and Peter C. Smith. Boulder, CO: Westview Press.

ANNALS, *AAPSS*, **571**, September 2000

The State of Gender Studies in Political Science

By GRETCHEN RITTER and NICOLE MELLOW

ABSTRACT: What effect has the study of gender had on political science? Compared to other branches of the social sciences, political science has been among the most resistant to feminist analysis. Political science scholarship generally is divided into four main subfields: political theory, American politics, comparative politics, and international relations. There are great disparities between these areas in the types and amount of gender scholarship that has been done. While feminist theory has become an accepted part of political theory, it has had a more limited impact in the other areas. Furthermore, where gender scholarship has appeared, it is often guided by intellectually conservative epistemological and methodological assumptions. Focusing on current major themes and significant works in the discipline, this article explores the differences in gender scholarship between subfields.

Gretchen Ritter is an associate professor of American politics at the University of Texas at Austin. She is the author of Goldbugs and Greenbacks: The Antimonopoly Tradition and the Politics of Finance in America, 1865-1896 *(1997) and is working on a new book, tentatively entitled* Gender and Citizenship in American Political Development.

Nicole Mellow is a graduate student in the Department of Government at the University of Texas.

F EMINISM is not just a political phenomenon. Feminism, or gender studies, is also among the most significant intellectual movements of the late twentieth century. In recent years, useful new work on women in politics nationally and internationally has emerged. Yet, compared to anthropology, psychology, and sociology, political science has been a laggard in the area of gender studies. The purpose of this article is to consider the current state of gender studies within political science. Our focus is on what contribution the study of gender has made to the field of political science and on how scholarly conventions in the field of political science have affected the study of women and politics.

Political science is divided into four subfields: American politics (AP), comparative politics (CP), international relations (IR), and political theory (PT). Scholars in AP study political institutions and public policies of both the state and federal governments of the United States, as well as the political behavior of American citizens. Scholars of CP consider these same issues for the citizens and governments of other countries. They also engage in cross-national comparisons between countries. The field of IR is devoted to the study of transnational political issues related to war and peace, international political economy, and regional and international systems of governance such as the United Nations, the World Court, and the European Union. Finally, the field of PT is devoted to the philosophical study of issues such as justice and democracy. These commonly recognized subfields dictate course offerings, graduate training, and faculty hires in political science departments at most colleges and universities in the United States. They also influence the publication of books and of articles in leading journals.

Trends in the publication of gender-related work reflect trends in professional membership. As of 1998, about 21 percent of full-time political science faculty were women. The distribution of women in the profession, however, differs by subfield (Sarkees and McGlen 1999). At the 1999 American Political Science Association meetings, the sections that had the highest rates of participation by women included the PT sections and the race- and gender-based sections. The sections with the lowest representation of women on the program included several of the IR sections (Gruberg 1999). The growing presence of women in the profession increases the amount of work being done on gender.

In addition to this difference between subfields, there is a more informal distinction between quantitative and nonquantitative approaches to the study of politics. At the quantitative end lie scholars who specialize in formal theory, quantitative methodology, political psychology, and political behavior. At the nonquantitative end, one finds most scholars who specialize in public law, PT, political culture, and some variants of historical institutionalism. A large number of the scholars (perhaps the majority) in political science lie somewhere between these two poles and make use of both quantitative and qualitative methods. Yet, this methodological division between quantitative and nonquantitative work reflects differences in epistemological and ontological assumptions about the nature of politics and the production of knowledge.

These are divisions that matter for the study of gender in politics as well. Studies of gender and politics appear within all four of the main subfields of political science. Some of these studies are quantitative and some are qualitative, except within PT, where they are virtually all qualitative. Divisions by subfield and methodology influence the status of work on gender, the way in which gender is conceptualized, and the degree to which gender is integrated into the broader study of politics. Work that is quantitative often relies on broad assumptions about the fixed or predictable nature of political and social life. Consequently, quantitative work on gender is less likely to produce work that challenges deep-seated beliefs about the nature of politics.

Gender studies appear to have had the biggest impact on PT as a field. Feminist theorists have helped to generate new theory that challenges well-established ways of understanding topics such as justice and morality. Some have demanded that standards of justice be applied to the private realm and the family, as well as the public realm of state and civil society. Others have offered new theories of morality based upon a feminist ethics of care. PT scholars who would not identify as feminist theorists have taken note of these contributions. With the broad effect of feminist theory on the subfield as a whole, PT provides a model for other subfields to consider in integrating gender into the study of politics.

In the area of AP, much of the work on gender involves quantitative studies of political behavior. After PT scholars, it appears that AP scholars have produced the most work on gender and politics. They address the influence of gender on voting behavior, candidate selection, and the policy choices of legislators. Yet these studies are often narrowly construed and theoretically unsophisticated. Too often gender is treated as simply a descriptive characteristic. However, there are important exceptions to this trend within the field of political behavior, exceptions that may point in the direction of a new generation of scholarship that takes into account advances made in feminist theory and elsewhere. In the future, we believe that the best work on gender will incorporate both the empirical and theoretical insights from all of the subfields of political science.

While there are prominent political scientists who study gender, their work is not well represented in the leading subfield journals, including *Comparative Politics* and *International Organization*. The *American Political Science Review*, the national journal of the American Political Science Association, is regarded as the leading general journal in the subfield of AP, although it also publishes work on CP, IR, and PT. Very little work on gender has ever been published in the *American Political Science Review*. The only leading subfield journal that does have good representation in the area of gender studies is *Political Theory*.

We believe that the underrepresentation of research on gender in leading political science journals is indicative both of the resistance by many to gender as a legitimate subject of analysis and of other more general trends in political science. Scholars in some subfields favor writing books over publishing articles, and, as a result, work from certain theoretical or methodological traditions is less represented in the leading journals. Further, the division by methodology and by field has tended to work to the disadvantage of scholars whose work is intra- or interdisciplinary, as the work of scholars of gender politics often is. Consequently, while many of the leading women (and some men) in the profession work on gender politics, they often publish elsewhere— in collected volumes, interdisciplinary journals, or journals from the other social sciences or humanities. This gap between what research is being done and what research is being published in leading journals suggests that students of political science who read the leading journals lose an opportunity to learn about gender and politics. This may be why there is not a very high level of understanding about the role of gender in shaping politics within the discipline as a whole.

In the remainder of this article, we will discuss current studies in each of the major subfields of political science. Our goal is to review the major themes of this scholarship and to highlight especially significant work.

POLITICAL THEORY

Current work in gender and PT addresses foundational questions, such as the nature of political identity, epistemological concerns, the nature of morality and justice, what constitutes politics, and the divide between modernist and postmodernist approaches to the production of knowledge. There are also many more modest efforts to reread major authors and their works from a gendered perspective. In what follows, we discuss feminist readings of the work of Hannah Arendt; the debate over Nancy Hartsock's feminist standpoint theory; the debate over the ethics of care; and the somewhat amorphous literature on gender and political identity.

In recent years, the work of Hannah Arendt has generated great interest within feminist theory. Arendt is one of the few women within the canon of twentieth-century political philosophy, so she has attracted the attention of contemporary women working in this area. Arendt wrote about oppression, subordination, and violence, yet she was no progressive on gender matters. On the few occasions in which she directly addressed the issue in her writings, she appears to affirm the traditional division between the public and private realms and to call upon women to carry out their private-realm duties.

As a result, Arendt's status among feminist theorists is contested. For some, such as Seyla Benhabib, Arendt offers us the possibility of critical engagement with modernity and a revitalization of political life from a post-totalitarian perspective (Benhabib 1995). Similarly, in her book *Hannah Arendt and the Limits of Philosophy*, Lisa Disch (1994) exposes misinterpretations of Arendt to show how her work contributes to our understanding of democratic decision making, identity politics, and political judgment. Disch tries to use Arendt in order to negotiate the dispute between neo-humanist critical theorists and poststructuralists on issues of judgment. For others, including some of the authors in Bonnie Honig's edited volume *Feminist Interpretations of Hannah Arendt* (1995), Arendt's work is rife with racist and imperialist prejudices. In myriad ways, Arendt and her work provide scholars an opportunity to ponder the relationship between modern PT and feminism.

Nancy Hartsock introduced feminist standpoint theory in her 1983 book, after which it was quickly taken up for its promise of a uniquely feminist epistemology and method. The theory fell out of favor in the early 1990s as materialist approaches were coming under attack by the proponents of postmodernism and poststructuralism and as the unifying assumptions of the theory were called into question by the advocates of multiculturalism. In the last few years, there has been something of a revival of interest in feminist standpoint theory both by the advocates of feminist empiricism and by some poststructuralist feminists.

Standpoint theory argues that knowledge is experiential and dependent upon the social position of the subject. Hence, in societies in which social power and position are structured by gender, knowledge will be different for men and women (although the nature of that difference is not presumed). The main issues for standpoint theory today, according to Hartsock (1997), concern the status of experience, the construction of groups, and the connections between politics, epistemology, and epistemic privilege.

A recent special issue of *Women and Politics* on standpoint theory demonstrates the theory's widely divergent appeal among feminist empiricists, on the one hand, and feminist postmodernists, on the other. Elsewhere, Sandra Harding (1997) has written, "Feminist empiricists argue that sexist and androcentric biases are eliminated by stricter adherence to the existing methodological norms of scientific inquiry" (166). In the special issue of *Women and Politics*, Catharine Hundleby (1997) seeks to amend this approach through an enlightened union between feminist empiricism and standpoint theory: "Feminist empiricism directs us to seek out different perspectives, and standpoint theory enhances empirical resources by increasing the variety of perspectives available" (25). In contrast, Nancy Hirschmann (1997) counters postmodern critics of standpoint theory who believe that it posits a univocal perspective for women by recalling Hartsock's "notion of multiple feminist standpoints" (73). In an appealing formulation, Hirschmann ultimately argues for an approach to social experience that combines Hartsock's emphasis on materiality with the postmodernist's concern for discursive construction. Whether through the lens of postmodernism or that of feminist empiricism, standpoint theory's emphasis on lived experience makes it attractive to a variety of feminist scholars.

Another important contribution that feminism has made to the larger field of PT is in the debate over what constitutes justice and morality. In her 1982 book *In a Different Voice*, Carol Gilligan critiqued social psychology studies that found that women had a less developed sense of morality than men did. From her own studies of the moral sensibilities of men and women, Gilligan found that women had a different moral sense from men's—one she associated with an ethic of care as opposed to the more masculine ethic of justice. Gilligan's work has been enormously influential; it has been highly controversial among feminist scholars for a variety of reasons, including a tendency to essentialize women as more caring than men, as well as the presumed universality of the female experience and outlook.

Recent scholarship on the ethics of care often begins by clearly stating its anti-essentialist intent and moving instead to focus on the work of caretaking as part of a critique of liberal individualism. Two books (Hekman 1995; Bubeck 1995) examine care as an activity rather than an outlook and use the work of caregiving as a way to critique political structures that assume individualistic, autonomous, rights-bearing adults. This evocation of care as activity resonates with feminist standpoint theory's emphasis on lived experience as the basis for politics.

Finally, a great deal of work in feminist PT concerns political identity. Interest in political identity is often associated with postmodernism, poststructuralism, and multiculturalism. The first two theoretical traditions are thought to challenge modernist assumptions about ontology that posit a presocial, transhistorical "Man" who has control over his own life and collectively over human history. In contrast, multiculturalists see humans as socially and historically constituted. As a political movement, multiculturalism is associated with identity politics, or the demand for group representation as opposed to equal universal rights. To the degree that feminist theory has been concerned with exposing the way in which sex and gender are socially constituted categories that justify gender inequality, postmodernism and poststructuralism have often been positively received there.

There are some discernible themes in the PT literature of the 1990s on matters of political identity. One is the interest in expanding identity studies to include masculinity, sexual identity, and racial identity. Further, for feminist theorists there appears to be a high level of dissatisfaction with sex and gender as analytic categories (as too fixed and ahistorical) and as political categories of representation (as too universalizing across diverse groups of men and women). The response to this dissatisfaction is to search for a less foundational and more collaborative basis for politics. Positive bases for politics are often sought within the parameters of lived experience and discursive or communicative relations. Feminist contributions to theories of identity have been widely influential within PT.

In sum, the work on gender and PT ranges from critical readings of canonical texts to reconceptualizations of the nature of politics and of political knowledge. This work has clearly benefited from the normative nature of the feminist project. Feminist scholars interested in understanding gender inequality and gender hierarchy often question foundational categories and theories. This results in contentious debates but sometimes produces original and innovative insights. As a result, feminist theory has enriched both PT and the study of gender. However, political science as a whole has often failed to make much use of these insights. Greater utilization of feminist theoretical work would not only benefit empirical studies of gender; it would enliven the study of politics more generally.

AMERICAN POLITICS

Scholarship on AP covers an array of topics and approaches, and studies of gender politics are better represented in some areas than in others. How gender is treated also varies in accordance with scholars' methodological and intellectual proclivities. Most often, gender has been integrated into localized areas of study within AP by expanding traditional research questions to take women into account, though some of the most innovative scholarship challenges the bases of the research questions themselves. The result is that while there is a great deal of gender scholarship in AP, the subfield has yet to be systematically transformed by feminist insight. In a recent evaluation of the influence of feminism on political science, Staudt and Weaver (1997) suggest that AP has been tardier than other subfields in using feminist theory to change how politics is understood. They argue that the subfield has merely added the study of women into existing modes of analysis.

Since the 1960s, studies of the political behavior of citizens and elites have been standard in the AP subfield, and this area contains the greatest amount of work on gender. These studies typically examine citizens' political attitudes and behaviors or, alternatively, the different styles, behaviors, and capacities of male and female political representatives. Behavioral studies rely heavily on survey research and statistical analysis and generate an understanding of politics premised upon the individual.

Gender scholars in this area are interested in examining how, when, and why men and women differ in their political actions and attitudes. They use survey data to make statistical inferences about gender differences in the beliefs and actions of elected officials, political candidates, or the electorate. These types of studies look at the possibility of structural inequalities as well as the social, cognitive, and psychological gender differences that may affect women's success in contemporary politics. Conventional understandings of how democratic representation, pluralism, and liberalism work in America are often challenged by these studies, but it is less frequent that the very concepts themselves are subjected to a feminist critique.

Despite these limits, there are several leading scholars in political behavior whose work is exemplary. In an article on differences in social authority, communication styles, and power among male and female legislators, Lyn Kathlene (1994) criticizes a standard liberal pluralist assumption that increasing representation of marginalized groups enables them to better pursue their rights. Based on findings that male legislators became more controlling of hearings as the number of female legislators increased, she argues that "this idealized viewpoint ignores the social dynamics that subordinate women's words and actions even in 'well-balanced' male and female group interactions" (560).

Scholarship such as this draws on the insights of feminist theory to question fundamental normative assumptions about AP. Unfortunately, however, it does not appear that all behavioral gender studies are as interested in integrating feminist theory. The greater trend appears to frame traditional behavioral research questions with a specific interest in understanding how women do or do not fit into what is currently known about political behavior. This often results in refined knowledge about how people behave and how behavior affects outcomes, yet only rarely does this result in an interrogation of the foundational premises of AP.

Following behavioral studies, the areas of public policy and law in AP also contain a significant amount of scholarship on gender. These studies examine a wide range of policies and laws that pertain to women specifically in addition to examining the effect of general policies and laws on women. Specific areas of policy concern include health and sexuality, social welfare, and economic issues. Often policy studies contain a behavioral component that seeks to ascertain gender differences in opinion on such topics as abortion.

Other studies of gender, law, and policy are historical and are based on qualitative research methods. These works examine the historical development of the country's political institutions (for example, the presidency, Congress, courts) and processes and the evolution of women's involvement in the areas of political rights, political mobilization, and social movements. These works often engage questions of political identity as well. Driven by large questions of political and social theory, these works generate an understanding of politics that is macrostructural in nature, and they are often informed by feminist theory.

For example, in a 1994 article on World War II child care policies, Susan Riley argues that

wartime child care policy, like other federal programs associated with women, was shaped by a pervasive gendered ideology that . . . consisted of the customary expectations of male and female behavior, prevailing notions of the appropriately public and private, and an intense desire to limit the potential impact of wartime disruptions in traditional sex roles. (654)

In explaining the limited lifetime of this policy and the unusual circumstances surrounding its creation, Riley demonstrates how the state policymaking process has historically been informed by and reinforced an ideology of gender difference.

Research on policy in a historical context tends to be preoccupied with broad theoretical questions that are of concern to feminist and other political theorists. There is a tradition of research in the area of social welfare exemplified by scholars such as Theda Skocpol and Gwendolyn Mink that has influenced not only scholarship on American political development but interdisciplinary feminist scholarship as well. In *Protecting Soldiers and Mothers* (1992), Skocpol asserts that the early development of American social policy was shaped by a social feminist movement that advocated for the establishment of a maternalist welfare state. In *The Wages of Motherhood* (1995), Mink follows the development of this welfare state through the New Deal and argues that it was not only gendered but also racialized in ways that lowered the civic status of poor women and nonwhites. This type of policy and law research offers one of the most promising venues for integrating gender in such a way as to both critique and reformulate standard theories and interpretations of AP. Gender is being used not just to add

women to a fixed political picture. Rather, it provides an analytic concept for understanding the nature of political relations and state institutions.

Unlike the PT subfield, the study of AP has yet to be transformed in any significant or systematic way by gender analysis. This may be partly because scholars tend to study gender according to the methodological and theoretical conventions of their particular area of concentration, and thus the conventions are left largely intact. Nor does it appear that most AP scholars are interested in engaging and contributing to feminist debates in other disciplines to any significant degree. This may also contribute to the insular effect of American gender politics. Moreover, significant bodies of literature on American gender politics, such as the social policy work of Skocpol and Mink or the gender and citizenship work of scholars like Nancy Fraser and Linda Gordon (1994), are vastly underrepresented in the discipline's leading journals.

COMPARATIVE POLITICS AND
INTERNATIONAL RELATIONS

There is less new scholarship on gender in CP and IR, so we discuss these two fields together. Gender scholars in CP consider issues similar to those studied by Americanists but with a focus on other countries. Further, some comparativists study gender across multiple countries or within a region to draw conclusions about existing CP theories (for example, theories of democratization, modernization, or development). Studies of gender in IR look at gender with respect to global processes (for example, war and peace or globalization) and international organizations (such as the United Nations), as well as standard IR theories (for example, realism, liberal institutionalism, or world systems theory). Despite their underrepresentation in top journals, gender scholars in these subfields have produced relatively sophisticated studies that rely on feminist theory to challenge fundamental concepts and theories in their respective fields.

Within the CP subfield, area specialists produce a significant amount of conventional behavioral and policy pieces that are similar to that of Americanists. There are a greater number of these studies on some countries, such as advanced industrialized nations, due in part to the availability of survey and government data. A number of these area studies focus on gender and feminism vis-à-vis state activity and institutional change. An example is an analysis of gender equity in France (Mazur 1995). The author attributes the repeated failure of the French government to produce meaningful legislation on pay equity for women to the fractured nature of interest group organizing and to institutional resistance. In addition to differentiating between symbolic and real policy reform, the author illustrates the institutional sources of gender bias in the policymaking process.

Gender scholarship on the Middle East is particularly noteworthy for its theoretical sophistication. Works on Egypt by Margot Badran (1995) and on Iran by Parvin Paidar (1995), for example, examine the gender dimensions of political change in their respective countries and challenge essentialist notions of Islam. Also drawing on Iran, Parvin Ghorayshi (1996) challenges feminist essentialism by noting the diversity of women's experiences. This type of interdisciplinary work is interesting for its potential to inform debates in both CP and PT. As feminist theorists contemplate the usefulness of different identity categories, they would do well to consider the lived experience of women in diverse social and political settings.

Other comparative gender studies use a gender-informed analysis of a single country or of multiple countries to evaluate traditional comparative concerns, such as democratic transition or revolution. In an article on El Salvador, Michelle Saint-Germain (1997) argues that "the form women's participation takes in transitions is crucial to both the shape of the resulting new democracy and the subsequent impact of the new democratic institutions on building or sustaining a women's movement" (75). A volume on women and revolution, edited by Mary Ann Tetreault (1994), examines gender relations before, during, and after revolution to demonstrate how inequities are transformed and reconstituted.

By analyzing how democratization, development, or revolution affect women and are influenced by women, comparative scholars reevaluate the assumptions of classic theories in these fields. This is done both by connecting gender-informed analysis of empirical evidence to existing theories (such as that described previously) and through a rereading of classic theory from a feminist perspective. This latter task is undertaken by Catherine Scott (1995) in her book on modernization and dependency theory. As one review of her book describes, "Scott's method is to unearth key dichotomies of traditional versus modern that underpin the value systems of modernity and dependency theories, and to explore the extent to which these depend upon conceptions of gender differences and the devaluation of femininity" (Goetz 1996).

While less in quantity than CP, gender scholarship in the subfield of IR also draws on feminist theory to critique classic IR debates, such as the origins of conflict or the effectiveness of international organizations in mediating state behavior, and to offer alternative interpretations of global issues and international systems. Christine Sylvester (1994) uses various strands of feminist theory (for example, feminist empiricism, feminist standpoint) to reinterpret traditional IR debates and to argue for a postmodern feminist approach to studying IR subjects, one that includes and reflects on traditionally excluded discourses and concerns.

Similarly, contributors to a volume edited by V. Spike Peterson (1992) critique the popular IR notion of the state as a singular actor, one that has a coherent and unquestionable national interest, by looking at gender vis-à-vis such traditional state concerns as security and sovereignty. The chapters examine the ways in which the maintenance and expansion of the state rely in large part on the suppression of women, and they make clear the central role that women play in global politics. In addition, this book promotes new theoretical concepts such as that of relational autonomy, which recognize the interconnections (as opposed to the autonomy) of actors in world politics.

That these works are being published is encouraging given that IR's traditional preoccupation with war and power and its tendency, albeit increasingly contested, to view states as singularly focused on maximizing national security would seem to make it particularly inhospitable to feminist perspectives. Moreover, because gender studies in IR address current global politics as well as age-old political wisdoms about what constitutes the state and how states interact, this scholarship has far-reaching potential to transform the study of politics as well as to affect feminist scholarship more generally.

The trend in CP and IR gender studies appears to be toward reconstituting the foundational premises, concepts, and theories of their respective subfields. However, because of the limited exposure of these studies in the leading journals, the subfields are likely to remain marginalized within the discipline as a whole.

CONCLUSION

Although high-quality work is being done on gender in political science, it has had only a modest impact on the field as a whole. Part of the reason may lie in resistance to gender as a valid subject for analysis. But it is also apparent that the structure of the discipline—particularly the division by subfield and by methodological approach—has contributed to limiting the impact of gender studies on political science. Members of particular subfields tend to ignore the work produced in other subfields, just as quantitative and qualitative scholars are often skeptical of each other's work. Such boundary drawing is a significant barrier to intellectual innovation.

The most promising work on gender and politics crosses disciplinary and subfield boundaries. We found that this work is being published in interdisciplinary journals such as *Social Research*, gender journals such as *Social Politics* and *Feminist Studies*, and opinion or quasi-academic journals such as *American Prospect* and *New Left Review*. Often this work is carried out within an interdisciplinary community of scholars who meet together in smaller, specialized conferences or in larger venues such as the annual Social Science History Association meetings. The Russell Sage Foundation and the Center for Advanced Study have funded extended residential fellowships for interdisciplinary groups of scholars. While we believe that most areas of political science would benefit from such collaborative, interdisciplinary efforts, we think this is particularly the case for gender studies because it is such an interdisciplinary field.

There are important interdisciplinary journals in which political scientists play a leading role, such as *Theory and Society*; *Social Science History*; *Studies in American Political Development*; *Law & Society*; *Social Research*; and *Journal of Policy History*, to name just a few. But there is a sense of insularity within the major journals of political science. While leading scholars in political science publish in the leading journals of other disciplines (in history and sociology, for instance), leading scholars from other disciplines rarely publish in the leading political science journals. Not only is there seeming resistance to interventions from outside of the field of political science, but there seems to be a great deal of insularity among the subfields in political science as well. In reading journals such as the *American Political Science Review* or *Women and Politics*, we were struck by the lack of intersection of subfields. The subfield in which gender studies has had the greatest impact, namely PT, is the subfield that remains most removed from the others within political science.

Feminism began as a political movement for women's rights. Yet among the social sciences and humanities, it has had the least intellectual impact on political science as a discipline. The study of politics, it seems, is resistant to political influences. To make political science more receptive to such intellectual and social influences, the structure of the discipline will have to change to encourage inter- and intradisciplinary collaboration. The scholars who have participated in such efforts, who can be found in all of the subfields of political science, demonstrate in their work that the results are well worth the effort.

References

Badran, Margot. 1995. *Feminists, Islam, and Nation: Gender and the Making of Modern Egypt*. Princeton, NJ: Princeton University Press.

Benhabib, Seyla. 1995. The Pariah and Her Shadow: Hannah Arendt's Biography of Rahel Varnhagen. *Political Theory* 23(1):5-24.

Bubeck, Diemut. 1995. *Care, Gender, and Justice*. New York: Oxford University Press.

Disch, Lisa. 1994. *Hannah Arendt and the Limits of Philosophy*. Ithaca, NY: Cornell University Press.

Fraser, Nancy and Linda Gordon. 1994. Civil Citizenship Against Social Citizenship. In *The Condition of Citizenship*, ed. Bart van Steenbergen. Thousand Oaks, CA: Sage.

Ghorayshi, Parvin. 1996. Women in Developing Countries: Methodological and Theoretical Considerations. *Women and Politics* 16(3):89-109.

Gilligan, Carol. 1982. *In a Different Voice: Psychological Theory and Women's Development*. Cambridge, MA: Harvard University Press.

Goetz, Anne Marie. 1996. Review of *Gender and Development: Rethinking Modernization and Dependency Theory*, by Catherine V. Scott. *American Political Science Review* 90(1):225-26.

Gruberg, Martin. 1999. Participation by Women in 1999 APSA Annual Meeting. *PS* 32(4):761.

Harding, Sandra. 1997. Is There a Feminist Method? In *Feminisms*, ed. Sandra Kemp and Judith Squires. New York: Oxford University Press.

Hartsock, Nancy. 1983. *Money, Sex, and Power: Toward a Feminist Historical Materialism*. Boston: Northeastern University Press.

———. 1997. Standpoint Theories for the Next Century. *Women and Politics* 18(3):93-101.

Hekman, Susan. 1995. *Moral Voices, Moral Selves: Carol Gilligan and Feminist Moral Theory*. University Park: Pennsylvania State University Press.

Hirschmann, Nancy. 1997. Feminist Standpoint as Postmodern Strategy. *Women and Politics* 18(3):73-92.

Honig, Bonnie, ed. 1995. *Feminist Interpretations of Hannah Arendt*. University Park: Pennsylvania State University Press.

Hundleby, Catherine. 1997. Where Standpoint Stands Now. *Women and Politics* 18(3):25-43.

Kathlene, Lyn. 1994. Power and Influence in State Legislative Policymaking: The Interaction of Gender and Position in Committee Hearing Debates. *American Political Science Review* 88(3):560-76.

Mazur, Amy G. 1995. *Gender Bias and the State: Symbolic Reform at Work in Fifth Republic France*. Pittsburgh, PA: University of Pittsburgh Press.

Mink, Gwendolyn. 1995. *The Wages of Motherhood: Inequality in the Welfare State, 1917-1942*. Ithaca, NY: Cornell University Press.

Paidar, Parvin. 1995. *Women and the Political Process in Twentieth-Century Iran*. New York: Cambridge University Press.

Peterson, V. Spike, ed. 1992. *Gendered States: Feminist (Re)Visions of International Relations Theory*. Boulder, CO: Lynne Rienner.

Riley, Susan E. 1994. Caring for Rosie's Children: Federal Child Care Policies in the World War II Era. *Polity* 26(4): 655-75.

Saint-Germain, Michelle A. 1997. Mujeres '94: Democratic Transition and the Women's Movement in El Salvador. *Women and Politics* 18(2): 75-99.

Sarkees, Meredith Reid and Nancy E. McGlen. 1999. Misdirected Backlash: The Evolving Nature of Academia and the Status of Women in Political Science. *PS* 32(1):100-108.

Scott, Catherine V. 1995. *Gender and Development: Rethinking Modernization and Dependency Theory*. Boulder, CO: Lynne Rienner.

Skocpol, Theda. 1992. *Protecting Soldiers and Mothers: The Political Origins of Social Policy in the United States*. Cambridge, MA: Harvard University Press.

Staudt, Kathleen A. and William G. Weaver. 1997. *Political Science and Feminisms: Integration or Transformation?* New York: Twayne.

Sylvester, Christine. 1994. *Feminist Theory and International Relations in a Post-Modern Era*. New York: Cambridge University Press.

Tetreault, Mary Ann, ed. 1994. *Women and Revolution in Africa, Asia, and the New World*. Columbia: University of South Carolina Press.

Spaces for Feminism
in Geography

By LYNN A. STAEHELI and PATRICIA M. MARTIN

ABSTRACT: This article examines the ways in which spaces for feminism in geography have been constructed. As with most disciplines, the increased visibility of feminist approaches in geography is related to the status of women, so, in this article, the authors briefly review trends related to women's status. The status of women in the discipline reflects the masculinist orientation of the discipline and its traditional focus on exploration of far-off places. Feminist geographers' fundamental concern, however, is with the social construction of space and place and the ways gender is implicated in those constructions. The authors examine theoretical perspectives and empirical examples within feminist geography as they are used to understand the interrelations of space, place, and gender. The authors demonstrate the implications of this approach for feminist praxis in research and teaching.

Lynn A. Staeheli is an associate professor at the University of Colorado, Boulder. Her research interests include feminist perspectives on democracy and citizenship; community activism; public space; and transnational migration.

Patricia M. Martin is a Ph.D. student at the University of Colorado, Boulder. Her research interests include feminist perspectives on the construction and politics of identity; the politics of globalization; and democratization in Latin America.

I N 1992, Susan Hanson presented the presidential address to the Association of American Geographers. Hanson is a professor in one of the top-ranked departments of geography, is a member of the National Academy of Sciences, and is author of numerous books and articles. She is also a feminist, and her presidential address focused on the relations between feminism and geography and on the challenges posed by each to the other. She made two points. First, she argued that academic feminism would benefit from a firmer grounding in the material, real world. The approach taken by geographers to the study of the everyday world would reinvigorate academic feminism and reconnect it to the lives of women. Second, she argued that geographers needed to recognize the profound ways in which the world and our understandings of it are gendered.

The present article examines the ways in which Hanson's challenge has been addressed within the discipline of geography and in which spaces for feminism within the discipline have been constructed. In the first section of the article, we provide an overview of the demography of geography. As with most disciplines, the increased visibility of feminist approaches in geography is related to the status of women. We briefly review those trends. We suspect, however, that many readers will be somewhat puzzled by the possible role that feminism could play in geography, a discipline commonly associated either with the study of "the principal products of Peru" or with the *National Geographic Magazine*. Therefore, the second section of the

article provides a brief discussion of the academic discipline of geography. Geographers' fundamental concern is with the ways in which the world— the cities, towns, landscapes, places where we work, live, and play—is constructed. As Hanson clearly demonstrated in her address, gender is central to most of those processes. These first two sections will serve as a backdrop for the latter sections, in which we discuss the contribution that feminism makes to geography and that geography makes to feminism. In particular, we focus on the ways in which feminist geographers understand place and space and the implications of these understandings for confronting oppressive practices. The final substantive section of the article considers the implications of feminist geographic analysis for praxis as it involves fieldwork, activism, and teaching. We do not attempt either a comprehensive or a representative review of the literature within feminist geography in this article, as the literature is too vast and diverse (for excellent reviews, see Rose 1993; the journal *Gender, Place and Culture*; reports in *Progress in Human Geography*; Jones, Nast, and Roberts 1997; Women and Geography Study Group 1997; McDowell and Sharp 1997; Oberhauser et al. 2000). We hope, instead, that our analysis can be used as a framework for interpreting that literature.

PUTTING FEMINIST
GEOGRAPHY IN CONTEXT

Before proceeding to a discussion of the theory and practice of feminist geography, it is important to provide a bit of context. The development of feminist geography has been closely linked to the position of women in the discipline. This position has been structured by the intellectual history of the discipline, the paucity of women in the discipline until recently, and a dominant mode of research.

Geography gained prominence as a field of study during the ages of exploration (Livingstone 1992). Early geographic societies, such as the Royal Geographic Society (established in 1791) and the National Geographic Society (established in 1888), were founded to disseminate information and knowledge gathered by explorers. Bringing the world in its splendor to the general public was and remains the primary focus of those organizations. Geography was understood to be a discipline devoted to codification and systematization of knowledge created largely through fieldwork in places deemed remote and dangerous. With such a mission, it is not surprising that the academic discipline of geography was dominated by men. While some women did engage in exploration and there were women's societies, the knowledge produced by women was not incorporated into the more formal knowledge base of geography within universities (Domosh 1991). When women entered the academy, it was often in the area of geography education, either training teachers or working in teaching colleges (Monk 1998).

Geography in the twentieth century has been masculinist in its demographic composition and its approach to studying the world. In the United States, the situation began to change in the late 1960s as women broke through the disciplinary barriers and entered graduate schools in larger numbers. By 1990, women were often part of the staff of academic departments in major universities, but in junior positions. Also in the 1990s, the number of women entering graduate studies in geography increased (Oberhauser et al. 2000). As women moved through the academic pipeline, the number of women on the faculty has also grown. Today most Ph.D.-granting departments have more than one woman on staff, and they are often in senior positions. Within the Association of American Geographers, women play prominent roles on governing boards, and three women have served as president of the association. Women, and more particularly feminist women, are also in other key, gatekeeping positions in funding agencies and journals.

Not only are more women in the discipline, but also courses in gender and geography are frequent offerings at the undergraduate and graduate levels. Feminist geography is one of the largest and most quickly growing specialties within the discipline. A journal of feminist geography, *Gender, Place and Culture*, has been established. Feminist work is regularly funded by extramural agencies. Feminist geography is clearly part of the thick braid of geographic research called for by the women who struggled to make spaces for women and feminism within the discipline (for example, Monk and Hanson 1982). This is not to say that women do not face barriers within the discipline; rather, we wish to recognize—and celebrate—the advances made by women and feminism in geography.

WHAT DOES FEMINISM HAVE TO DO WITH STATE CAPITALS?

Geography is an intellectually diverse discipline in which scholars study a wide range of topics. The Association of American Geographers, the primary professional organization for the discipline, currently records over 7000 members who list specialties ranging from A (aging) to Z (zoogeography, the study of the spatial distribution of animals and animal habitats). In some universities, it is classified as a natural science; in others, it is a social science. An increasing number of geographers identify with the humanities and, in particular, with cultural studies. Within the same department, it is not unusual to find scholars who specialize in climatology, hydrology, human-environment interactions, economics, politics, culture, landscape, environmental processes, development, and gender. In addition, geographers often have strong links with more applied pursuits in planning and engineering; the increased importance of geographic information systems and visualization in problem solving is of particular salience here. Most feminist geographers describe themselves, however, as studying human geography or environment-society interactions.

Geographers typically rely on a synthetic approach to understanding the world. We try to understand the ways in which processes combine to shape the places in which we live and the ways in which places shape experience, opportunity, and meaning. Given the wide range of topics and processes that are examined within the discipline, geography is often described as inherently interdisciplinary. As will become clear later, it is often difficult to differentiate the work of geographers from that of sociologists, political scientists, and so on. What marks geography as a discipline, however, is a concern with the spatial organization of phenomena, the processes that organize the world spatially, and the implications of the spatial organization for particular issues and people. This approach is termed "the geographical imagination."

Doreen Massey (1995) explains the geographical imagination as being organized around two sets of questions: (1) questions about basic geography and its interpretation, meaning, or significance to various actors; and (2) questions about the individuals and social groups who have access to resources (as socially, economically, politically, and culturally defined) and the environment. Within this approach, feminist geographers pay particular attention to the gendered ways people come to learn about and interpret places (environmental cognition), the access women as individuals and as members of social groups have to places, and their ability to act in various ways within those places.

Grounding in the material world is central to the discipline of geography. As researchers, geographers are typically not content to remain in the realm of abstract theory or representations. But neither are we pure empiricists. Contemporary human geography is centrally concerned with abstract theories, representations, and processes as they are made material and the ways in which material relations shape abstractions, theories, representations, and processes. For example, we are concerned with the ways in which representations of neighborhoods on television or in government policy shape the cities that planners design and the lives of the women and families who live down the street (McDowell 1983). We are concerned as well with the people and neighborhoods that are left out of those representations: with the homeless (Ruddick 1996), with poor people (Gilbert 1998), with people of color (Pulido, Sidawi, and Vos 1996), with people who live in nontraditional families (Brown 1997), with the young (Valentine 1997), with elders (Laws 1994), and with women. The geographical imagination—its focus on how people understand places and on who has access to the resources within places—helps us understand the shape of the world in which we all live.

SPACES FOR FEMINIST
THEORY AND RESEARCH
IN GEOGRAPHY

In this section of the article, we examine the contributions of specifically feminist geographical imaginations to both geography and feminism. We begin with a discussion of the conceptualization of space and place employed by feminist geographers. This conceptualization is predicated on a dynamic and fluid understanding of space and place that is absent from some uses of these terms as deployed in feminist and cultural studies. We then provide examples that feminist geographers have used to explore the processes of identity formation and the marking of space and places that convey meaning and shape social and political action.

The social construction of space and place

Feminist geographers have noted the ways in which spatial metaphors, such as "position," "location," "margins," and "mapping," have gained currency in feminism and cultural studies (see Smith and Katz 1993). Grounding metaphors can reinforce attempts to be more reflexive in the conduct of fieldwork and the kinds of knowledge we produce. Spatial metaphors are used to make what is unfamiliar familiar through comparison. Thus abstract ideas of social standing, or social location, can be related to ideas of location on a map or in space. Metaphors such as "borders," "location," and "mapping" can be used to explain, for example, abstract arguments about relative relationships of identity and power between social subjects. Spatial metaphors are often used in this way because they draw on an idea of space that is familiar and commonsensical. Herein lies the problem, because this taken-for-granted idea of space is often static.

Just as most feminists (and indeed, most social scientists) would argue that social positions and identities are fluid and are constructed in and through social relations, geographers argue that space is also constructed in and through social relations that are equally fluid. The spaces and places in which we live are not fixed and they are not natural. For example, the borders and boundaries that exist between social subjects—such as between men and women—are not given but rather contradictory, shifting, and constructed through gendered relationships of power. The borders and boundaries that exist between places—at global, regional, national, and subnational scales—are similarly constructed. Places and spaces are constructed in the landscape through the accretion of activities, built forms, experiences, and conflict through time. And through time, places and spaces change. For example, a gentrified area of the city is the product of changing sets of behaviors and practices—behaviors, practices, and experiences that led to the initial development of the place as part of a city, to its deterioration, and to reinvestment. As Bondi (1991) demonstrates, the changes involved in gentrification reflect dynamic and contested ideas about gender roles, family norms, and sexuality. At the core of human geography, then, is an attempt to understand the social production of space. This means that we examine the ways in which spaces and places are produced in and through economic, political, and social structures and through the actions of individuals and social agents as they negotiate their everyday lives. Within this theoretical frame, feminist geographers argue that space and the places in which we live are every bit as much a social construction as is gender and that these constructions must be seen as fluid and interacting.

It is important to highlight a distinction between *place* and *space*. At its most basic level, the concept of place highlights the uniqueness of particular locations such as Denver, Southeast Asia, or the suburbs. For geographers, the concept of place also includes the symbols and elements of the landscape—its semiotics—through which such uniqueness is understood and expressed, and the degree of attachment or alienation that individuals might experience in relationship to particular places. Geographers conceive of places as being contested, multiple, layered, subject to shifting and porous boundaries, and constructed in relationship to systems of power, including economic relations, racialization, ethnicity, and gender. For example, Jane Jacobs (1998) has examined the controversies about public art in the business district of the city of Melbourne. One project, the Another View Walking Trail, was intended to foster a national goal of Aboriginal and non-Aboriginal reconciliation. Installations along the trail included memorials of hangings and other violent events suffered by Aboriginals that are intended to expose the oppression and pain of colonialism and racism and to recognize difference in public places. Jacobs demonstrates that some of the installations have provoked strong response, with opponents arguing they were either inaccurate representations or inappropriate in a place intended for reconciliation. As a result, some planned installations were not included in the final trail.

Geographers also recognize that places are connected through flows and networks (such as flows of capital or kinship networks) that change over time and that vary for different social groups. We use the term "space" to refer to the broader network of relations and processes that connect places with each other (Massey 1994). The conditions found within households, communities, and neighborhoods are directly related to national policies and to broader patterns of global economic development and underdevelopment. Joni Seager's *State of Women in the World Atlas* (1997) provides a visual sense of these connections and the spaces of opportunity for women that operate in and through those connections. In other examples, feminist geographers have demonstrated the ways in which development policies (such as the structural adjustment policies initiated by the International Monetary Fund and the World Bank) connect the lives of urban and rural women in developing countries with the lives of women in the developed world. These connections may be constructed in a variety of ways in which women may play more or less active roles. Among others, Victoria Lawson (1998) analyzes the role of women's migratory practices in the development of particular industries in Latin America,

as well as the dependence of source areas on the remittances that women send to their families. These practices shape the space economy of the region. Brenda Yeoh and Katie Willis (1999) examine the ways in which regional development policy in Singapore relies on a particular vision of families and women's roles within them. In these examples and others, gender ideologies and the practices of women and men are central to the ways in which spaces are constructed. These processes and practices are dynamic and fluid; they are constantly re-created and re-formed, even as the spaces they construct are changed and transformed.

Feminist geographers, then, have a particular interest in understanding how place and space interact with the construction, practice, and politics of gender. Reflecting this, feminist geographers have not only expanded the sites of research to include locations such as the home (see Domosh 1998), neighborhoods (for example, Clark 1994), and communities (for example, Moore-Milroy and Wismer 1994). They have also demonstrated how global processes, such as geopolitics and the world economy, intersect with constructions of gender (Sharp 1996). The result is a rich body of feminist geographic literature that aims to integrate the metaphorical and material uses of space and place. Two examples of research in feminist geography demonstrate this point.

Richa Nagar (1997) examines the interrelations between place and space as they shape the politics of Hindu communal organizations in Dar es Salaam. She demonstrates that broader spatial processes such as colonization, decolonization, international and national migration, and Tanzanian postcolonial nationalism created a set of circumstances that shaped and reshaped the South Asian community in Dar es Salaam. The South Asian community displayed trends toward both greater unification and greater fracturing in response to such broader temporal and spatial pressures. Particular communal, public locations in Dar es Salaam including temples and caste-based and non-caste-based community centers figured both symbolically and materially in such community negotiations. Place identity and its material inscription into the landscape influence, therefore, definitions of community and social identity. Such research exemplifies feminist geographers' concerns with how social identities, including gender, and the social production of space are mutually constituted in particular sites and places.

Feminist geographers are also concerned with the ways the relations between individuals, society, and the natural environment are implicated in the mutual construction of place and women's lives. Feminists working within the environment-society tradition explore the uncertain and shifting boundaries between human societies and the natural environment; in so doing, they highlight changing patterns of extraction, production, use, and value of natural resources, as these are shaped by social and political practices, including the construction of gender. The work of Judith Carney (1996) provides a key example of this

approach. She argues that interactions with the natural environment through natural resource use is a central way in which gendered identities throughout the world are produced, maintained, contested, and renegotiated. Carney demonstrates that as agricultural production in Gambia became integrated into the world economy in the nineteenth century, the spatial and gendered division of agricultural labor became increasingly segmented. Male agriculture focused on upland commercial peanut production for export, which increased demands on women's production of household subsistence rice in lowland areas, such that rice became identified as a female crop, and women kept any cash from sale of the crop. As colonial and development policies shifted to emphasize rice production, women began to produce a bigger surplus. That surplus, however, became the basis for a gendered set of struggles over crop ownership in which women were denied access to the value of crops they traditionally produced. Carney demonstrates, therefore, that the meaning and value of landscapes and places continuously interact with the dynamics of gender and development policy. Landscape and place are the terrain for the struggle over legal, political, and economic rights. By intervening in these struggles, the process of development can be highly disruptive precisely because of the implicit geographical imagination it carries. Similarly, as sustainable development projects are encouraged by development agencies, new dynamics are introduced into gendered relations of power. In grounding their analyses of these dynamics in specific spaces and places, feminist geographers have demonstrated how the use of space, place, and the environment is articulated with the dynamics of unequal gender relations.

The foregoing examples emphasize the significance of place and space to the lives of women. In the following subsection, we examine the social construction of space and place as they frame key questions or issues in feminist geography. These issues involve processes of identity formation for people and for places and the marking of spaces as public and private. In examining these issues, we are also concerned with the ways in which identity and the coding of spaces shape the actions of social subjects.

The mutual constructions of place and gender

Massey (1994) argues that "construction of subjectivities . . . is a specifically feminist project" (8). As a research agenda, this claim resonates with hooks's assertion (1987) that feminism and feminist research should represent a political stance against all forms of oppression, including oppression based on class, race, ethnicity, sexuality, and gender. Because place is a location where systems of power intersect, feminist geographers have a particular stake in investigating the role of place in the construction of identity. Feminist geographers evaluate place not only in terms of gender relations but also in terms of its interactions with class, ethnicity, sexuality, and race.

Westwood and Radcliffe (1993) present an example of such a feminist approach to the study of place. In their introduction to an edited volume about women and popular protest in Latin America, they make problematic the very concept of Latin America as a clearly bounded region with a distinct identity, arguing that Latin America represents a European imagined geography that was produced through discourses of the New World. The representations that resulted from this imagination mask the diversity of populations, perspectives, and realities in Latin America. To some degree, the representations have been internalized, and they are maintained by racist ideologies and cultural representations that have been adopted within Latin America. Such racialized representations of place clearly affect and interact with gender and ethnic social identities, in terms of both how social subjects in Latin America position themselves and how they continue to be represented. Interpreting gender relations and the politics of gender in Latin America requires, therefore, an understanding of how the context of place identity within Latin America provides a particular lens through which diverse groups of men and women see themselves and are seen. In later work in Ecuador, for example, Radcliffe (1998) interviewed women who moved from the Andean regions to the more urbanized coastal plain. To the extent that these women became integrated into the dominant social structure in the regions to which they moved and experienced a degree of social mobility, they began to describe themselves as white rather than black and to assume new gender roles in their households. In this case, a change in place context also involved changing social locations, with dramatic implications for women's self-identity.

Feminist geographers often look to symbols representing places to understand how the construction of gender interacts with the construction of places. The construction of nations and national identities provides one of the most salient examples of place making in the world today. Yet, as Sharp (1996) argues, the construction of nations in relationship to representations of gender has remained largely uninvestigated. On a visual level, an idealized female figure is often used to represent the nation (Nash 1994), and women are seen therefore as literally embodying the nation. By extension, reproduction through childbearing becomes women's national role, and issues related to family planning, sexual orientation, sexual violence, and war are frequently cast in national terms. The nation-as-woman equation constructs women either as passive or as objects of veneration and purity, whereas masculine roles are often cast as actively protecting the feminine nation. The horrors of recent wars—in which rape of women and children both is a tactic of the military and is used to generate support for international intervention—suggest the continuing salience of images of women in need of protection from the state.

The relations between identity and place are clearly not unidirectional, and feminist geographers have explored the mutual construction of place identity and subjectivity. One way this has been accomplished is through research on the making of colonial places and its impacts on women's subjectivity. A collection edited by Blunt and Rose (1995) demonstrates that the construction of colonial and colonized identities occurred through very specific interpretations of places. Blunt (1994), for example, examines the landscape depictions found in the writings of Mary Kingsley, a nineteenth-century female British explorer of West Africa. Despite a general contrast with male-generated travel writing of the time, Blunt highlights a great deal of ambivalence in Kingsley's writing. Such ambivalence demonstrates how Kingsley's subject position was located both within and outside of the masculine and imperialist visions of West Africa and how both her identity and the identity of the place or region were mutually constructed. Importantly, Kingsley expressed her subjectivity in relationship to the landscape and people there.

Constructions of place and identity have political content as well. Ideas of publicity and privacy have been central to feminism as a rallying call ("the personal is political") and as concepts involved in the social construction of gender. In much feminist theory, ideas of a public sphere involve an assumption that public acts are committed by public agents in public places. Feminist geographers, however, have argued that we can enrich these theories through the recognition that publicity and privacy are multifaceted or multidimensional. Thus it is possible to conceptualize public actions in private spaces and private acts in public spaces. Added to this could be questions of identity—whether political agents see themselves acting as public or private agents in different spaces. For example, one of the first women to serve on the City Council in Boulder, Colorado, got her start in politics in the 1950s when several men encouraged her to run for office. They believed that the woman's image as a mother and housewife would mask her environmental politics. Here the complicated relationships between public and private are clear. This woman took skills learned in the ostensibly private spaces of the home to activate her political vision in the public sphere of municipal politics. Although some assumed that this woman's identification with the private space of the home meant she could be manipulated, her position within her home provided a basis for her understanding of public issues. Most significantly, she used the discourses of publicity and privacy in a set of strategic (and sometimes opportunistic) choices about where to locate her activism to achieve political and public ends (Staeheli 1996).

The interest that feminist geographers have in understanding the social construction of space, place, and identity has very clear implications for the ways we locate the field of our work. It shapes our understanding of the field as a site of research, teaching, and praxis generally. We turn to these issues in the next section of the article.

LOCATING THE FIELDS OF PRAXIS

Reflecting the legacy of geography's "sternly practical" origins in the process of exploring, mapping, and colonizing the globe (Livingstone 1992), fieldwork and bringing the field home through teaching and lectures have long been thought to be key components of the discipline and its praxis. Influenced by standpoint feminism and feminist philosophers of science (McDowell 1996; Rose 1997), feminist geographers have closely scrutinized the political implications found within the process of doing fieldwork. The production of knowledge is neither objective nor innocent but, rather, underpinned by sets of power relations. Thus the researcher's acts of locating the field, placing boundaries around the field, positioning oneself in relation to the field, and interpreting voices from the field become immanently political processes. These issues are not unique to feminist geography, but they take on particular significance given the discipline's field orientation and the praxis of many feminist geographers.

Rather than thinking of the field as a typically bounded place where the researcher is a clearly displaced, outside, dispassionately objective observer, feminist geographers have argued for destabilizing the boundaries. The blurring of boundaries is meant in both a concrete and metaphorical manner. In a concrete sense, this has meant "bringing the 'field' *home*" (Gilbert 1994). Katz (1994), for example, has conducted comparative research about the marginalization of children in the Sudan and New York City (her home). For Katz, such an approach prevents thinking of field sites as "vessel(s) for holding cultural attributes" (68). Instead, the broader social, political, economic, and cultural processes that go into structuring particular places as different as rural Sudan and New York City can be highlighted. Kobayashi (1994) has also brought the field home through her study of Japanese Canadian communities, communities with which she self-identifies. For Kobayashi, bringing the field home has represented a concerted attempt to destabilize the institutionalized boundaries between academic research and political engagement.

From a feminist perspective, blurring the boundaries of the field also means clearly acknowledging the problematic relationships between the researcher and the object of study (the researched places or people). This requires a recognition that the dynamics of the power relationships that structure the researcher-researched relationship can never be unveiled completely. Drawing on poststructuralist feminist theory, Rose (1997) contends, for example, that subjectivities are not transparent and cannot fully be made so. One of the most difficult challenges that comes out of this realization for feminist geographers is that there will continue to be tension, ambiguities, and uncertainties in the relationship between the researcher and the researched, particularly when the distribution of power in the relationship is highly unequal. The disjunctures that continue to arise within such research settings should not be ignored but, rather, should be seen as creating situations of "in-betweenness" (Katz 1994). In effect, the researcher is cognizant of her role in actively re-creating difference.

Indeed, while much of feminist geography has been inspired by the hope that research can be a process that might transform existing patterns of oppression and inequality into something better, feminist geographers have also recognized the extreme difficulties of such a normative goal. Katz (1994), for example, discusses the difficulty of publishing applied or policy work. As she states, "We have theories about theory and practice, but practice takes a beating in the high stakes of academia" (71). Kobayashi (1994), furthermore, confronts the degree to which naturalized and essentialized understandings of the world persist both in the field and in interpretations of the field. Finally, Staeheli and Lawson (1994) call for the continued recognition of the privileged position of many researchers within the Western academy. Acknowledging such privilege is a partial step in enacting a feminist politics of social change.

Another field that is of particular importance to feminist geographers within the academy is the classroom. In this field, a central goal is to create an environment in which the voices of all people can be expressed and respected. While this concern is shared by feminists, it is a particular issue for geography, given the masculinist orientation and history of the discipline described previously. Women have often felt excluded from some portions of the discipline, notably within the subfields of physical geography (Dumayne-Peaty and Wellens 1998; Maguire 1998). In response to this experience, feminist pedagogy within geography has focused on the development of teaching styles that highlight the value of multipositionality in approaching subjects and creating environments and teaching strategies that draw all voices into class discussions (Nairn 1997; Maguire 1998).

Recognizing the challenge of fully acknowledging difference has been central to the efforts to build a feminist pedagogy within the discipline of geography. In the classroom, feminist geographers recognize that difference can appear through several means: as instructors discuss places and relationships that may be different from what students have previously experienced; as students negotiate differences between themselves; and as students and instructors negotiate their subject positions. For example, Kim England (1999) describes her efforts to discuss sexuality and the ways in which spaces are constructed as heterosexual. In attempting to address these issues in undergraduate geography classes, she must negotiate the resistance that some students feel to the idea that some places may be identified as places for heterosexuals exclusively (for example, residential suburban neighborhoods) and the likelihood that some students may be offended (either by the discussion of sexuality or by comments made about sexuality). Finally, she negotiates her own relationship to sexualized spaces when she discloses her sexuality in the context of teaching. This presents difficult pedagogical terrain, and one that is often avoided. Such discussions take on particular significance, however, as relations within classrooms are overlaid with power. Yet discussing difference—in all its dimensions—has been an affirmative and empowering praxis in the field of the classroom (Bell and Valentine 1995).

Exposing the social construction of places, genders, and knowledge within these arenas (research, publication, the discipline) is central to feminist geographic praxis. Feminist geographers participate in a social activity, and it is critical that this activity be directed toward a transformation of the oppressive relations that construct difference, in all its forms. Engaging in this activity requires a self-reflexive analysis of the relationships, experiences, and places that shape oppression. It also requires an understanding of the multiple sites of praxis for feminist geographers—the classroom, the academy, the communities with which we identify, and the communities we study—and what can be achieved in each (Staeheli and Lawson 1994). Feminist geographers have labored hard on this project, but it remains incomplete.

CONCLUSION

The spaces for feminism in geography are being constructed through the efforts of women and men throughout the discipline. The numbers of women in the discipline are growing, and an exciting body of feminist research, teaching, and praxis has developed. Barriers to feminist geographers clearly persist, most notably in the idea that feminist research pertains to and should be engaged only by women. In other words, the broader theoretical, methodological, and pedagogical implications of feminism for geography are not always recognized across the discipline. This, however, provides only further impetus to geographers who identify with feminism to continue to expose the construction and experience of gender relations in space and place. Feminist geographers' interest in grounding spatial metaphors, therefore, derives from a clear concern with bridging the lived experience of people across the globe with the more abstract theories that frame our understanding of the social world. Such an agenda is of value for both its approach to theory and its normative goals of fighting oppressive practices and spaces.

References

Bell, David and Gill Valentine. 1995. *Mapping Desire: Geographies of Sexuality.* New York: Routledge.

Blunt, Alison. 1994. Mapping Authorship and Authority: Reading Mary Kingsley's Landscape Descriptions. In *Writing Women and Space: Colonial and Postcolonial Geographies,* ed. Alison Blunt and Gillian Rose. New York: Guilford Press.

Blunt, Alison and Gillian Rose. 1995. *Writing Women and Space: Colonial and Postcolonial Geographies.* New York: Guilford Press.

Bondi, Liz. 1991. Gender Divisions and Gentrification: A Critique. *Transactions of the Institute of British Geographers* 16(2):190-98.

Brown, Michael. 1997. *RePlacing Citizenship: AIDS Activism and Radical Democracy.* New York: Guilford Press.

Carney, Judith. 1996. Converting the Wetlands, Engendering the Environment. In *Liberation Ecologies: Environment, Development and Social Movements,* ed. Richard Peet and Michael Watts. New York: Routledge.

Clark, Helene. 1994. Taking up Space: Redefining Political Legitimacy in New York City. *Environment and Planning A* 26:937-55.

Domosh, Mona. 1991. Toward a Feminist Historiography of Geography. *Transactions of the Institute of British Geographers* 16(4):94-104.

———. 1998. Geography and Gender: Home, Again? *Progress in Human Geography* 22(2):276-82.

Dumayne-Peaty, Lisa and Jane Wellens. 1998. Gender and Physical Geography in the United Kingdom. *Area* 30(3):197-206.

England, Kim. 1999. Sexing Geography, Teaching Sexualities. *Journal of Geography in Higher Education* 23(1): 94-101.

Gilbert, Melissa. 1994. The Politics of Location: Doing Feminist Fieldwork at "Home." *Professional Geographer* 46(1):90-96.

———. 1998. "Race," Space, and Power: The Survival Strategies of Working Poor Women. *Annals of the Association of American Geographers* 88(4):595-621.

Hanson, Susan. 1992. Presidential Address: Geography and Feminism: Worlds in Collision? *Annals of the As-*

sociation of American Geographers 82(4):569-86.

hooks, bell. 1987. Feminism: A Movement to End Sexist Oppression. In *Feminism and Equality*, ed. Anne Phillips. New York: New York University Press.

Jacobs, Jane. 1998. Staging Difference: Aestheticization and the Politics of Difference in Contemporary Cities. In *Cities of Difference*, ed. Ruth Fincher and Jane Jacobs. New York: Guilford Press.

Jones, John Paul, III, Heidi J. Nast, and Susan M. Roberts, eds. 1997. *Thresholds in Feminist Geography: Difference, Methodology, Representation*. Lanham, MD: Rowman & Littlefield.

Katz, Cindi. 1994. Playing the Field: Questions of Fieldwork in Geography. *Professional Geographer* 46(1):67-72.

Kobayashi, Audrey. 1994. Coloring the Field: Gender, "Race," and the Politics of Fieldwork. *Professional Geographer* 46(1):73-80.

Laws, Glenda. 1994. Aging, Contested Meanings and the Built Environment. *Environment and Planning A* 26(11): 1787-802.

Lawson, Victoria. 1998. Hierarchical Households and Gendered Migration in Latin America: Feminist Extensions to Migration Research. *Progress in Human Geography* 22(1):39-53.

Livingstone, David. 1992. *The Geographical Tradition*. Cambridge, MA: Blackwell.

Maguire, Sarah. 1998. Gender Differences in Attitudes to Undergraduate Fieldwork. *Area* 30(3):207-14.

Massey, Doreen. 1994. *Space, Place and Gender*. Minneapolis: University of Minnesota Press.

———. 1995. Imagining Worlds. In *Geographical Worlds*, ed. John Allen and Doreen Massey. New York: Oxford University Press.

McDowell, Linda. 1983. Towards an Understanding of the Gender Division of Urban Space. *Environment and Planning D: Society and Space* 1(1):59-72.

———. 1996. Spatializing Feminism. In *BodySpace*, ed. Nancy Duncan. New York: Routledge.

McDowell, Linda and Joanne Sharp, eds. 1997. *Space, Gender, Knowledge: Feminist Readings*. New York: Arnold.

Monk, Janice. 1998. The Women Were Always Welcome at Clark. *Economic Geography* 74 (extra issue):14-30.

Monk, Janice and Susan Hanson. 1982. On Not Excluding Half of the Human in Human Geography. *Professional Geographer* 34(1):11-23.

Moore-Milroy, Beth and Susan Wismer. 1994. Communities, Work and Public/ Private Sphere Models. *Gender, Place and Culture* 1(1):71-90.

Nagar, Richa. 1997. The Making of Hindu Communal Organizations, Places and Identities in Postcolonial Dar es Salaam. *Environment and Planning D: Society and Space* 15:707-30.

Nairn, Karen. 1997. Hearing from Quiet Students: The Politics of Silence and Voice in Geography Classrooms. In *Thresholds in Feminist Geography: Difference, Methodology, Representation*, ed. John Paul Jones III, Heidi J. Nast, and Susan M. Roberts. Lanham, MD: Rowman & Littlefield.

Nash, Catherine. 1994. Remapping the Body/Land: New Cartogrophies of Identity, Gender and Landscape in Ireland. In *Writing Women and Space: Colonial and Postcolonial Geographies*, ed. Alison Blunt and Gillian Rose. New York: Guilford Press.

Oberhauser, Ann, Donna Rubinoff, Karen De Bres, Susan Mains, and Cindy Pope. 2000. Geographic Perspectives on Women Specialty Group. In *Geography in America at the Dawn of the*

21st Century, ed. Gary Gaile and Cort Wilmott. New York: Oxford University Press.

Pulido, Laura, S. Sidawi, and R.O. Vos. 1996. An Archaeology of Environmental Racism in Los Angeles. *Urban Geography* 17(5):419-39.

Radcliffe, Sarah. 1998. "Now I've Made Myself White": Gender, Migration, and Identity in Ecuador. Paper presented at the annual conference of the Royal Geographical Society–Institute of British Geographers, 8 Jan., Guilford, United Kingdom.

Rose, Gillian. 1993. *Feminism and Geography*. Cambridge: Polity Press.

———. 1997. Situating Knowledges: Positionality, Reflexivities and Other Tactics. *Progress in Human Geography* 21(3):305-20.

Ruddick, Susan. 1996. *Young and Homeless in Hollywood*. New York: Routledge.

Seager, Joni. 1997. *The State of Women in the World Atlas*. New York: Penguin.

Sharp, Joanne. 1996. Gendering Nationhood. In *BodySpace*, ed. Nancy Duncan. New York: Routledge.

Smith, Neil and Cindi Katz. 1993. Grounding Metaphor: Towards a Spatialized Politics. In *Place and the Politics of Identity*, ed. Michael Keith and Steve Pile. New York: Routledge.

Staeheli, Lynn. 1996. Publicity, Privacy, and Women's Political Action. *Environment and Planning D: Society and Space* 14:601-19.

Staeheli, Lynn and Victoria Lawson. 1994. A Discussion of "Women in the Field": The Politics of Feminist Fieldwork. *Professional Geographer* 46(1):96-102.

Valentine, Gill. 1997. "Oh Yes I Can." "Oh No You Can't": Children and Parents' Understandings of Kids' Competence to Negotiate Public Space Safely. *Antipode* 29(1):65-89.

Westwood, Sallie and Sarah Radcliffe. 1993. Gender, Racism and the Politics of Identities in Latin America. In *"Viva" Women and Popular Protest in Latin America*, ed. Sarah Radcliffe and Sallie Westwood. New York: Routledge.

Women and Geography Study Group. 1997. *Feminist Geographies*. Essex, UK: Longman Press.

Yeoh, Brenda and Katie Willis. 1999. "Heart" and "Wing," Nation and Diaspora: Gendered Discourses in Singapore's Regionalisation Process. *Gender, Place and Culture* 6(4):355-72.

ANNALS, *AAPSS*, **571**, September 2000

Feminist Media Criticism and Feminist Media Practices

By S. CRAIG WATKINS and RANA A. EMERSON

ABSTRACT: This article explores four thematic areas in feminist media criticism. First, it considers how gender informs norms and values that pattern industry production practices and conventions. Next, it explores how feminist criticism has influenced one of the emergent areas in media scholarship: reception studies. This particular subgenre of media studies examines how audiences actively engage the mediascape around them. Third, the focus shifts to the rising influence of black feminist criticism, which has identified many of the tensions within feminism and also has pointed toward new modes of media criticism and practice. Fourth, the article examines how feminism has informed the study of masculinity. The final section of the article identifies and briefly discusses two areas that will forge new directions in feminist media studies: the burgeoning sex industry and globalization.

S. Craig Watkins teaches in the Departments of Radio-Television-Film and Sociology at the University of Texas at Austin and is the author of Representing: Hip Hop Culture and the Production of Black Cinema *(1998).*

Rana A. Emerson is a doctoral candidate in the Department of Sociology at the University of Texas at Austin. Her research interests include the sociology of mass media and popular culture, race, and gender and sexuality.

FEMINISM has had a considerable effect on the field of media studies. In addition to influencing how journalists, scholars, and consumers of media read and think about gender, feminism has also influenced the images, narratives, and genre forms produced in the media culture industry.

The present article centers on two broad areas of the feminist enterprise: media studies and practice. Feminists have established a body of reading strategies, analytical frameworks, and theoretical models for better understanding the crucial role that media perform in the reproduction of gender inequality. For example, feminism helps cultivate a society that is more cognizant of the social and political implications of gender role stereotyping in popular media discourse. Still, we also recognize that feminist politics have never been simply about criticism but fundamentally about effecting social change. Therefore, at various points in this article, we also focus on how feminist practices labor to create counternarratives and counterrepresentations that contest male regimes of cultural production and empower women to use media for their own interests and pleasure. In other words, we examine the efforts of feminists to carry out their own distinct forms of political intervention.

Feminist media criticism and practice began as a challenge to the culture industry's misrepresentations of women. Throughout the 1960s and 1970s, popular media culture came under increasing attack as a particularly pernicious site of gender inequality. Feminists charged, for instance, that gender role stereotyping in television and film normalized the dominant cultural values and customs that legitimate male domination of women. As the second wave of feminism was hitting its stride in the early 1970s, therefore, many participants in the movement turned to the field of popular media as a prominent, even preferred site of social and political struggle.

Throughout the 1970s, several studies analyzed popular media depictions of women, often with strikingly similar results (Dominick and Rauch 1972; McNeil 1974). The studies found that women tended to be depicted in subordinate roles (for example, housewives, secretaries), whereas men were often portrayed in roles of authority (for example, household breadwinners, professionally employed). Furthermore, the studies reported that images of women were more likely to be set in the domestic sphere, whereas workplace and other public settings were more likely characterized as male spaces. Moreover, advertising on television typically targeted women only in relation to purchasing household products and appliances (such as detergent, refrigerators) that reinforced their homemaker status or cosmetics designed to make them more attractive to men.

Feminist analysis of the dominant news media organizations revealed that issues salient in the lives of women—employment and wage discrimination, spousal abuse, child care—were generally marginalized, if not ignored outright. Conversely, the issues most likely to be designated as newsworthy—the economy, electoral politics, crime—typically involved male authority figures. Analysts of news media consistently reported that men were far more likely than women to be selected as media commentators and sources (Zeidenberg 1990). One such study concluded, "Men in our culture not only control news discourse but are authorized to know more than women" (Reeves and Campbell 1994, 65). In addition, as radical feminist groups began to employ dramatic forms of protest in order to highlight gender inequality, many media organizations tended to either vilify or trivialize the feminist movement (Gans 1979; Gitlin 1980; Douglas 1994). For example, news media organizations would focus on sensationalized images of "bra burners" rather than the issues that drove women to dramatize their protest politics.

It is within this context that various incarnations of a feminist-inspired media criticism and practice began to develop. While media criticism has been especially prominent in academic circles, more direct forms of intervention have been situated within the media industry. Even though these two forms of feminist intervention seem unrelated, in truth, a symbiotic relationship has emerged such that an instance of one can inform the other. In other words, feminist media criticism identifies some of the salient issues, themes, and conflicts that require a more direct challenge on the part of media practitioners. Similarly, as feminist media workers struggle to redefine the gendered norms and customs of the media industry, they enrich the development of feminist theory and media studies.

In this article, we explore some of the major currents in feminist media criticism today. Due to space limitations, we highlight four specific topical areas where media and feminist studies intersect. First, we consider how gender informs the industrial processes and production logic that shape network television. In this section, we discuss some of the gender norms and values that penetrate and pattern industry production practices and conventions. Next, we explore how feminist criticism has influenced one of the emergent areas of media scholarship: reception studies. This particular subgenre of media studies examines how audiences actively engage the mediascape around them. Third, we turn our focus to the rising influence of black feminist criticism, which has identified many of the tensions within feminism and also has pointed toward new modes of media criticism and practice. Finally, we look at how feminism has informed the study of not only femininity but masculinity, too.

FEMINIST CRITICISM AND THE MEDIA INDUSTRY

Any serious feminist analysis of the media industry must devote considerable attention to the organizational milieu in which media products are created. Since the late 1970s, network television has been in a constant state of flux due to social, technological, and industry change.

For example, increasing patterns of female labor force participation have redefined when and how women watch television and the degree to which they are identified as a niche market (Santi 1979, 61). Additionally, technological innovations like cable television, the VCR, and the personal computer vie fiercely with conventional sources of home entertainment. As the industry has been forced to reinvent itself in the face of constant change, its programming strategies and practices have changed also.

Network television, like its cable competitor, has shifted almost exclusively to the narrowcast philosophy of programming, meaning that executives now design programs to capture specific viewer demographics. Much of network television programming targets white, middle-class men and women in order to attract the greatest advertising revenue. Because women constitute the largest share of television viewers, they have emerged as an especially coveted demographic. As feminist values and beliefs have become more broadly disseminated, the televisual representations of women have become more varied, too. Whereas the dominant television image of women before the 1970s was the happy homemaker, current female roles include a greater range of paid professionals (for example, lawyers, judges, police).

Although the images of women have undergone some changes, the organizational structure and culture of the television industry have proved much more difficult to alter. In fact, the very foundation of television programming is shaped by gendered assumptions, values, and beliefs. Gender structures the time and space coordinates that determine network programming schedules (for example, daytime, prime time, and late night), genre forms (for example, soap operas, cop shows, situation comedies), and character types (for example, dumb blondes, male hunks). Although image-based studies and content analysis illuminate specific patterns in media representations of women, they fail to examine the organizations that produce media content.

Take, for example, Julie D'Acci's study (1994) of the popular television show *Cagney & Lacey*. The initial conceptualization of the program challenged conventional codes of femininity insofar as it featured two female lead characters in a traditionally male-oriented genre, the cop show. In addition to marking the characters with feminist sensibilities, the initial episodes of *Cagney & Lacey* pivoted around dramatic issues and situations—violence, antagonistic commanding officers, and action sequences—that typify the cop show genre. Many of the key scenes were set in the workplace or some other public sphere, and it was not unusual for the two female leads to forcefully apprehend criminals.

D'Acci notes, however, that as the show's producers and writers struggled to maintain viable ratings in the face of competing programs that offered more traditional gender portrayals of women, *Cagney & Lacey* shifted from a cop show to a more traditionally defined woman's program. As a result, the show underwent a major overhaul. Among many other things, the topical issues featured in the show became more exploitative and sensational (such as rape, spousal abuse, pornography); the characters more stereotypically feminine (for example, in terms of their hairstyle or clothing); and the settings for scenes more domestic (many scenes were set in the home). She also notes that the very tone of the show changed as the producers sought less action-oriented sequences (considered too masculine) and more dialogue between the characters as a way to highlight their emotional side and personal lives (such as their romantic relationships).

The peculiar journey of *Cagney & Lacey* is not distinct but, rather, exemplifies the profound ways in which gender ideology shapes television production practices. More generally, the show demonstrates how representations of women are governed by genre conventions, competitive constraints, and audience familiarity with and presumed affinity for stereotypical codes of femininity.

Equally important, programs like *Cagney & Lacey* demonstrate how elements of feminist discourse have successfully pierced the corridors of network television. Still, the industry's appropriation of feminism has been selective. Despite a polyphony of voices, ideas, and perspectives that make up a very multifaceted and multilayered feminist movement, television writers and executives customarily appropriate elements of only the liberal feminist tradition to inform their creation of feminist-inflected shows, characters, and

narrative situations. But, as critics within the feminist movement argue, because the liberal tradition is defined mostly by white, middle-class women, it often fails to acknowledge the race and class differences between women. Popular programs like *The Mary Tyler Moore Show* and *Ally McBeal*, reflecting liberal feminist ideals, highlight issues like equal pay, occupational mobility, and protection against sexual harassment. Although these issues are important to all women, these shows tend to reflect racial and class biases insofar as they ignore topics like the problem of jobs that pay inadequate wages and the specific stereotypes and forms of discrimination encountered by poor women and women of color.

The limited employment of women in decision-making roles is a key element in understanding how gender inequality is woven into the media industry. In their study of gender stratification in the film industry, Denise and William Bielby found that, as the screenwriting profession has become more prestigious and lucrative, it has also transitioned from a female- to male-dominated occupation (Bielby and Bielby 1996). During the silent film era, women dominated the screenwriting profession. However, the introduction of sound and other technological, social, and economic innovations led to the industry's transformation toward male domination. Bielby and Bielby write that "as filmmaking became more industrialized and rationalized, men dominated key roles in corporate channels of production, distribution, and exhibition"

(252). Eventually, screenwriting underwent a process of masculinization, suggesting that it became not only male dominated but also more likely to reward those individuals who expressed masculine sensibilities in popular genres like action-adventure and science fiction.

MEDIA RECEPTION

The systematic study of media reception is recent. While the rise of cultural and media studies was quite proficient in raising questions regarding what Stuart Hall (1977) terms the "ideological effect" of the media, questions regarding how individuals receive and use media remained largely underprobed. Feminist media criticism began to develop important frameworks for studying audiences and their media reception practices.

Feminist film criticism employed the psychoanalytic theory of Sigmund Freud and his follower Jacques Lacan in order to demonstrate how the camera presumes a male viewer and positions the audience in an inherently masculine manner. In her groundbreaking essay, "Visual Pleasures and Narrative Cinema" (1975), Laura Mulvey introduced the notion of the male gaze in feminist film theory. Although her work focused on the cinema, its implications for media reception studies were far broader. Because this gendered gaze privileged the point of view of men, the very process of watching a film was constructed as an essentially male activity. According to this perspective, the masculine gaze so thoroughly shapes the film-viewing experience that it socializes women into identification and compliance with the very patriarchal values and ideologies that reproduce their marginalized status.

Indeed, many of the earliest theories of media reception assumed that receivers of media content were passive victims, rendered subservient to both the medium and its message. Stuart Hall's influential essay, "Encoding/Decoding" (1980), however, marked an important theoretical shift insofar as it posited that receivers of media are actively involved in the construction of meaning. As researchers sought to more effectively understand the complex process of media reception, the notion of the active female receiver of media came into greater view. In other words, rather than assuming that women internalized images of gender inequality and objectification, this theoretical break compelled media analysts to contemplate the creative ways women engage images of gender subordination.

As the area of media reception continues to flourish, researchers are exploring the different ways in which media have become a central feature of everyday life. Feminists today argue that watching television and films, listening to music, reading the newspaper, and surfing the Internet have the potential to both reproduce and contest gender inequality. As a result of feminist scholarship, we better understand how women selectively use media to make sense of and inform their own lived experiences.

A recent example of such feminist scholarship is Andrea Press and

Elizabeth Cole's ethnographic study (1999) of the ways in which women of different class, religious, racial, and ethnic backgrounds respond to and interpret the discourse surrounding the abortion debate in broadcast television movies and shows centered on the topic. The study's most important discovery reveals that the complicated nature of women's opinions on the abortion issue is not accounted for by the for-or-against dichotomy that dominates activist and academic notions of the debate. Press and Cole argue, consequently, that such dichotomous notions of public opinion do not accurately represent the ambivalences regarding abortion that emerge in women's everyday life, of which television viewing and media reception are integral parts.

Like Press and Cole's work, some of the most noteworthy feminist audience studies focus on how television viewing is a gendered practice. Several researchers explore and illuminate the ways in which television and other forms of media function as a site within which the gender order of the household is both contested and reinforced (Seiter 1989; Modleski 1982; Radway 1984; Brunsdon, D'Acci, and Spigel 1997). One of the most interesting findings suggests that gender hierarchies in the family determine television-viewing patterns. In homes where male control is the norm, gender inequality is a significant influence on the choice of programs to be viewed. The practice of television watching tends to be gender segregated, with mom and kids unable to watch their favorite shows if they conflict with dad's football game or cop show. In this way, gender inequality in the family serves to restrict the spaces available for women to use the media (Ang 1996).

However, this restriction does not mean that women are excluded from media use altogether. Feminist media criticism investigates the strategic ways girls and women use the media in their everyday lives in order to cultivate personal space, negotiate the broader social issues they face, derive pleasure, and bring their own lived experiences to media consumption. Most compellingly, feminist perspectives on media reception have revealed the ways in which women appropriate the media as a site of meaning construction, actively engaging and, occasionally, contesting images and themes of gender domination. This theme is exemplified in Jane Shattuc's work (1997) on the genre of the daytime television talk show in the 1980s and 1990s. Shattuc argues that this genre provides a space for women to explore in a public forum women's issues that are relegated to the private sphere of the home.

Additionally, the desire for nontraditional media images of women sometimes stimulates collective action. Women viewers have organized national letter-writing campaigns in order to urge television networks to continue broadcasting shows that feature feminist themes, such as *Designing Women* in the 1980s and *My So-Called Life* in the 1990s, which were threatened by cancellation from the prime-time schedule. These organized initiatives illustrate how girls and women may actively struggle against the sexism and male bias that pervades television programming and often marginalizes the female point of view.

The female-dominated communities that spring up around various sites of media are another example of how women actively engage the popular media terrain. For instance, many young women gathered for "*Melrose Place* nights"—viewing parties at bars, nightclubs, and other hangouts in the mid-1990s. Camille Bacon-Smith's ethnography (1992) of women's participation in television "fandom" culture shows how communities that have developed around television shows like *Star Trek* serve not only as sites for women's collective creative expression but also as spaces for subversive acts of rebellion against dominant society's norms of women's behavior.

The Internet is also a site for the development of female communities. The Internet enables large discussion groups to form in relation to a wide range of issues. One Internet discussion group, for example, has formed to debate the soap opera *The Young and the Restless*. In between discussing hairstyles, outfits, and seemingly ridiculous plot twists, the predominantly female subscribers of the list-server frequently criticize the submissive and passive behavior of female characters on the show and ridicule the often hypermasculinized, dominating actions of male characters. Instead of merely accepting the representations of gender relations depicted in the soap opera, the participants in the e-mail discussion bring their own experiences to their viewing. Laura Stempel

Mumford (1995), for example, describes how women reinterpret and appropriate the dominant ideological meanings of daytime soaps and thus find pleasure and enjoyment in viewing them.

In England, Angela McRobbie (1991, 1994) explores how adolescent girls are active participants in the making of popular media culture. McRobbie accurately notes that the scholarly analysis of how youths use style, music, language, and other cultural forms to engage in practices of meaning making, identity formation, and cultural resistance typically focus on young men. Yet girls create and enthusiastically consume a vast popular culture universe—fashion, popular music, dance, and teen magazines—that is distinct and relatively unexplored. Lisa Lewis's work (1990) on the fans of female rock stars in the 1980s (such as Madonna, Pat Benatar, Tina Turner, and Cyndi Lauper) demonstrates how girls create cultural spaces to construct new modes of expression and identity politics that transgress conventional gender norms and stereotypes.

Although many of these forms of mass consumption may not be called "feminist" by a strict, political definition of the term, they nevertheless reflect sensibilities and practices that are designed to empower women. Instead of supporting the notion that women are mere receptacles for the ideologies disseminated through the media, studies show that media reception is a gendered social practice that can be enabling rather than constraining, empowering rather than oppressive, and active rather than passive.

THE BLACK
FEMINIST CHALLENGE

Black feminists have transformed several fields of academic study and popular discourse, including media studies. These scholars have focused on how media culture and the feminist criticism of it reproduce the continued domination of black, Latina, and Asian women by rendering invisible the intersection of race, class, and gender in their everyday lives. Black feminist criticism forged open space to consider the particular ways black women are represented in public discourse.

For example, Patricia Hill Collins (1991) uses the concept "controlling images" to discuss the politics that shape representations of black women. According to Collins, the images of black women reflect the interlocking processes of race, class, and gender oppression. Images like the mammy (such as "Aunt Jemima"), the jezebel (the highly sexualized black woman), and the welfare mother have become staple icons in the popular mediascape, finding routine expression not only in popular media culture but also in the arena of social policy discourse.

Black feminist criticism also considers how nonwhite women appropriate the sphere of popular media culture to document their own experiences and express distinct, often counterhegemonic, worldviews. For many black women, independent or avant-garde cinema is an especially important space of cultural production. Although the work of filmmakers like Julie Dash, Euzhan Palcy,

Kasi Lemmons, and Darnell Martin goes largely unnoticed, their cinematic visions reflect a desire for alternative representations of black womanhood. *Just Another Girl on the IRT*, directed by Leslie Harris, provided a young black woman's perspective on urban life, a theme whose cinematic treatment was dominated by stories told from the point of view of young black men.

Similar representational strategies of black female cultural producers are apparent in the production of popular music. Angela Davis (1998) discusses the ways in which black women performers utilized the blues as a public space to comment on the social conditions of racism and sexism faced by black women in everyday life. In the same way, black female rhythm and blues singers influenced the popular and commercial trajectory of postwar-era popular American music (Ward 1998). Even though the burgeoning hip-hop scene is typically viewed as a male-dominated terrain of cultural production, young black women have always participated in the evolution of hip-hop culture as rappers (or MCs), DJs, graffiti artists, and less often as B-girls (or breakdancers) (Guevara 1996; Rose 1994).

Several feminist media critics have explored the construction of gender and sex relations in music videos (Kaplan 1987; Rose 1994; Stockbridge 1987). Rana Emerson (1999) argues that black female performers, through music video, address the complex experiences that young black women deal with in society on a day-to-day basis. She maintains that black women use music video to counter and revise dominant and oppressive notions of black female sexuality.

Although black women are usually cast in a limited range of roles—dancers, models, sex objects, and love interests—some black women performers who have achieved greater creative independence in the music industry use their music videos to express self-determination, strength, and independence. Erykah Badu, Missy "Misdemeanor" Elliot, and Lauryn Hill, all of whom write and produce their own music and often direct their videos, comment, in their work, on the state of male-female relations, efforts to be economically self-sufficient, and the everyday world inhabited by young black women.

Furthermore, Emerson (1999) contends that black women recognize that music services not only male pleasures and desires but female pleasures and desires, too. For example, in the video *Red Light Special* of the rhythm and blues trio TLC, T-Boz, Left-Eye, and Chilli play a game of strip poker with a group of buff-bodied men, who end up as the scantily clad objects of female desire. Instead of constructing a world filtered through a male gaze, the black female performers construct modes of spectatorship that presume female viewers and privilege female-oriented narratives.

Black feminist readings of the gender and sexual politics in black popular culture are especially notable. Bell hooks and Jacquie Jones, for example, examine how forms of black popular culture routinely reproduce controlling images of black femininity (hooks 1992; Jones 1991). Two of the most vibrant spheres of black cultural production—rap music and black cinema—have generated intense debates regarding the possibilities and problems associated with the commodification of black popular culture (see, for example, Rose 1994; Gray 1995; Watkins 1998). Whereas many analysts view rap music and black cinematic discourse as formations of cultural resistance, black feminists note that hegemonic ideas about gender inform the most popular and most commercially viable aspects of the black culture industry (Lubiano 1991).

For example, the most popular subgenres in the brief history of rap music—message and gangsta—privilege male agency and pleasure. Although themes related to black protest, nationalism, and self-empowerment are prevalent in message rap (Decker 1989; Kelley 1994), the thrust of this subgenre is hypermasculine insofar as it imagines black political empowerment as a primarily male enterprise. Gangsta rap has been heavily criticized for its misogynistic depictions of women that include demeaning language and acts of violence. Some black feminists note, however, that these and other subgenres of rap music have always been multilayered expressions of youth discourse and, at times, generative of self-criticism, parody, and social critique (Kelley 1994; Rose 1994).

Although analysts examine the expressive forms, styles, and exuberance that characterize rap music, few note how the production sites in which this form of popular music is produced privilege male producers over their female counterparts. The technological innovations crucial to the production of rap music—digitization, multitrack recording devices, sampling machines, turntables, and video—are largely controlled by men. Consequently, the most important site in rap music—the studio—is constructed as a masculine space, thus limiting, though not negating, the ability of young female cultural producers to assert their creative agency and independence in the production of rap music.

Moreover, as black American cinema has achieved a certain degree of popularity and commercial viability, the emergence of a mostly male-directed black cinematic enterprise raises serious questions regarding black representational politics. Much like the field of rap music, black filmmaking has emerged as a critical space for black cultural production. Popular filmmaker Spike Lee, for example, challenges the racialized practices of the film industry, both the misrepresentation of black Americans and the institutional barriers that restrict black employment opportunities in the industry. Yet, as Lee has appropriated the arena of popular film to engage hegemonic ideas about blackness, his interrogation of dominant gender ideologies is less vigorous. Much like the dominant filmmaking practices he routinely assails, Lee's cinematic imagination is intensely masculine insofar as it typically privileges males as the primary source of narrative agency, employs female characters to introduce sexual

tension, and positions spectators from the perspective of a male gaze (Lubiano 1991; Watkins 1998).

The rise of a vibrant black feminist perspective has broadened the terms of feminist discourse and media criticism. It has brought attention to issues of representation surrounding not only black women in media but also other women, including Asian and Latina Americans. Consequently, this particular tradition of feminist discourse contributes to the struggle to create a more diverse and empowering mediascape for women.

REPRESENTING THE MALE BODY

Much as the study of race (long perceived as the study of blacks, Latinos, and Asians) has led to a more focused interrogation of whiteness, the study of femininity highlights the importance of examining the social construction of masculinity, too. The dominant representations of masculinity vary by industry and genre. For example, television genres such as the cop or detective show, dramatic serial, and broadcast sports programs present men in formulaic gender roles and predictable narrative situations. In cinema, the action-adventure or gangster genre are also predicated on familiar codes of masculinity: strength, violence, and individualism. In television news, men are often cast in the anchor role, thus marking them as the authority figures in the dissemination of news and information.

The action-adventure genre has become a staple in U.S. cinema. This particular genre is predicated on a

Hollywood star system in which the white, heterosexual male has become the chief global icon representing a complex system of ideological meanings and values. Critics contend that the action-adventure genre not only transmits values that reinforce notions of male dominance but also animates discourses about national, racial, and military supremacy (Jeffords 1994).

But if the cinema is a primary site of hegemonic masculinity, the fashion and the advertising industries circulate alternative, if not counter-hegemonic notions of masculinity. In her discussion of visual presentations of the male body, Susan Bordo (1999) writes, "It was male clothing designers who went south and violated really powerful taboos—not just against the explicit depiction of penises and male bottoms but against the admission of all sorts of forbidden 'feminine' qualities into mainstream conceptions of manliness" (168). For example, ads for Calvin Klein products—cologne, blue jeans—depict men in provocative poses that sexualize the male body. The queering, or feminization, of male representations reflects the degree to which ideas about masculinity are constantly in flux, shifting in correspondence with emergent discourses about gender and sexuality.

Differences also proliferate within popular constructions of masculinity. Inevitably, representations of masculinity intersect with changing ideas about race and class. The coding of masculinity in broadcast sports is a prominent example. Research suggests that sports broadcasts employ different rhetorical and visual strategies in their representation of black and white male athletes. Commonsense ideas about racial biology and difference inform the language that sports commentators use in their description of athletes (Hoberman 1997). For example, commentators frequently portray white athletes as intelligent ("he is a heady ball player"), contemplative ("he studies his opponent's weaknesses"), or hard working ("his work ethic is exemplary"). Conversely, black athletes are typically described along a different axis, usually in relation to their physical bodies ("he is big and strong"), genetic constitution ("his dad was a great athlete"), or athletic attributes ("he is a quick jumper"). Although these rhetorical strategies are commonplace, they nonetheless reveal the extent to which pernicious ideas about racial "otherness" permeate society and the sports broadcasting industry.

Furthermore, the visual strategies employed in sports broadcast media canonize particular images of black masculinity. Because blacks dominate many of the sports that receive extensive television coverage—basketball, football, track—the spectacle of black athletes in motion reinforces commonsense ideas and popular myths about black bodies. The use of technological innovations like slow motion, camera close-ups, and instant replay not only fetishizes the black male body but also reinforces and popularizes the belief that blacks are genetically predisposed to succeed in certain areas (athletics) and fail in others (academics). Interrogation of such media strategies as well as masculinity enhances our understanding of how gender differences are culturally constructed rather than naturally produced.

CONCLUSION

The primary aim of this article has been to highlight some of the major developments that shape feminist media criticism and practice. Although we focused primarily on the television and film industries, we recognize that feminist scholarship includes analysis of other media spheres, too. For example, because broadcast radio represents the first electronic form of mass media and popular culture, its role in shaping the genres (for example, family sitcom, detective show) and gender role types (for example, housewife, male-breadwinner) on which television and film representations were established cannot be overlooked (Hilmes 1997).

Today, the field of feminist media criticism is a thriving enterprise. Although several emergent areas—youth culture, postfeminism, women-owned media, and women's athletics—promise to forge new directions in feminist media studies, we briefly highlight two areas that will certainly shape that future: the burgeoning sex industry and globalization.

Perhaps no issue reflects the tensions within and about feminism more than pornography. While women's attitudes regarding pornography vary considerably, two contingencies of feminist discourse shape the debate. Feminists who oppose pornography argue that it reinforces male supremacy, objectifies women, and reproduces gender inequality (MacKinnon and Dworkin 1997). Most important, the movement against pornography contends that the issue is not sex but, rather, power and the civil rights of women.

There is, however, a divide within feminism that also generates concern about efforts to outlaw sex-oriented media. From this view, at issue are the First Amendment and personal freedom. Feminists who oppose the anti-pornography movement argue that state control of any form of expression, sexual or otherwise, invites the erosion of free speech as well as many of the gains the women's and gay and lesbian movements have struggled for (Strosser 1995). The debate illustrates how feminism has never been a monolithic movement but one driven by different interests, values, and politics.

Feminist media criticism of pornography will intensify if only because of the growth of sex-oriented media. Two technological innovations—the VCR and the Internet—have revolutionized the business of pornography, transforming a once-marginal enterprise into a vibrant industry. In addition to the social and political implications of sex-oriented media, feminist media criticism must also address the economic and technological factors that drive the industry. Prestige films such as *Boogie Nights*, on-line sex-related products, and the rise of adult film production companies that employ quasi-Hollywood production and marketing techniques reduce some of the stigma that once tainted pornography.

Moreover, the movement of AT&T into the phone sex industry (originally through 900 numbers) and the development of pay-per-view by Time Warner and Cablevision mean that some of the most powerful media companies in the United States are now selling sex (Schlosser 1997).

Finally, the trend toward globalization will be crucial in the evolution of feminist media criticism. Globalization has a profound influence on the nature and ideological content of media around the world. Because corporations like Disney and Time Warner are such formidable players in the global economy, the United States exerts a disproportionate influence on how audiences receive and incorporate media in their everyday lives. For example, researchers at Harvard Medical School have found that the introduction of U.S. television to the island of Fiji is correlated (although not definitively linked) with a rise in eating disorders and body-image consciousness among teenage Fijian girls (Goode 1999; Reynolds 1999). This finding is especially intriguing because Fijian culture has traditionally valued healthful eating and a more voluptuous female body shape than the idealized images of femininity popularized in the United States.

Another prominent area related to globalization and media criticism is communication in developing countries. Feminists studying this area of communication investigate how the dominance of U.S. media colors representations of developing countries while patterning the formation of foreign policy. Jo Ellen Fair's work (1996) reveals that images of African women in Western media culture are informed by American conceptions of African American women and fail to consider the particular experiences of African women. In her study of U.S. media depictions of famine in the Horn of Africa, Fair demonstrates how Western media draw from blaming-the-victim notions of African American women and, consequently, depict African woman as culpable for widespread poverty.

Feminist scholars such as Fair, H. Leslie Steeves, Bella Mody, Johannes Bauer, and Joseph Straubhaur foreground how the globalization of media influences the lives of women in Third World countries by perpetuating hegemonic ideologies of these women. In addition, these researchers highlight the role that global media play in international communications, in development policy, and as instruments to benefit Third World women in the development process (Steeves 1993; Mody, Bauer, and Straubhaur 1995). This area of scholarship animates the need for feminist scholarship to speak to and engage the concerns of non-Western women.

References

Ang, Ien. 1996. *Living Room Wars*. New York: Routledge.

Bacon-Smith, Camille. 1992. *Enterprising Women: Television Fandom and the Creation of Popular Myth*. Philadelphia: University of Pennsylvania Press.

Bielby, Denise D. and William T. Bielby. 1996. Women and Men in Film: Gender Inequality Among Writers in a Culture Industry. *Gender & Society* 10:248-70.

Bordo, Susan. 1999. *The Male Body: A New Look at Men in Public and in Private*. New York: Farrar, Straus & Giroux.

Brunsdon, Charlotte, Julie D'Acci, and Lynn Spigel. 1997. *Feminist Television Criticism*. Oxford: Clarendon Press.

Collins, Patricia Hill. 1991. *Black Feminist Thought*. New York: Routledge.

D'Acci, Julie. 1994. *Defining Women*. Chapel Hill: University of North Carolina Press.

Davis, Angela. 1998. *Blues Legacies and Black Feminism*. New York: Pantheon.

Decker, Jeffrey Louis. 1989. The State of Rap: Time and Place in Hip Hop Nationalism. *Social Text* 34:53-84.

Dominick, Joseph and Gail Rauch. 1972. The Image of Women in Network Television Commercials. *Journal of Broadcasting* 16(3):759-65.

Douglas, Susan. 1994. *Where the Girls Are*. New York: Times Books.

Emerson, Rana A. 1999. From Object to Subject: Negotiating Black Womanhood in Music Video. Master's thesis, University of Texas at Austin.

Fair, Jo Ellen. 1996. The Body Politic, the Bodies of Women, and the Politics of U.S. Television Coverage of Famine in the Horn of Africa. *Journalism and Mass Communication Monographs* 158:1-26.

Gans, Herbert. 1979. *Deciding What's News*. New York: Pantheon Books

Gitlin, Todd. 1980. *The Whole World Is Watching*. Berkeley: University of California Press.

Goode, Erica. 1999. Study Finds TV Alters Fiji Girls' View of Body. *New York Times*, 20 May.

Gray, Herman. 1995. *Watching Race: Television and the Struggle for "Blackness."* Minneapolis: University of Minnesota Press.

Guevara, Nancy. 1996. Women Writin' Rappin' Breakin'. In *Droppin' Science: Critical Essays on Rap Music and Hip Hop Culture*, ed. William Eric Perkins. Philadelphia: Temple University Press.

Hall, Stuart. 1977. Culture, the Media, and the "Ideological Effect." In *Mass Communication and Society*, ed. James Curran et al. Beverly Hills, CA: Sage.

———. 1980. Encoding/Decoding. In *Culture, Media, Language*, ed. Stuart Hall et al. London: Hutchinson.

Hilmes, Michele. 1997. *Radio Voices*. Minneapolis: University of Minnesota Press.

Hoberman, John. 1997. *Darwin's Athletes: How Sport Has Damaged Black America and Preserved the Myth of Race*. Boston: Houghton Mifflin.

hooks, bell. 1992. *Black Looks: Race and Representation*. Boston: South End Press.

Jeffords, Susan. 1994. *Hard Bodies: Hollywood Masculinity in the Reagan Era*. New Brunswick, NJ: Rutgers University Press.

Jones, Jacquie. 1991. The New Ghetto Aesthetic. *Wide Angle* 13(3-4):32-44.

Kaplan, E. Ann. 1987. *Rocking Around the Clock: Music Television, Postmodernism and Consumer Culture*. New York: Methuen.

Kelley, Robin D. G. 1994. Kickin' Reality, Kickin' Ballistics: Gangsta Rap and Postindustrial Los Angeles. In *Race Rebels: Culture, Politics, and the Black Working Class*. New York: Free Press.

Lewis, Lisa. 1990. *Gender Politics and MTV*. Philadelphia: Temple University Press.

Lubiano, Wahneema. 1991. But Compared to What? Reading Realism, Representation, and Essentialism in School Daze, Do the Right Thing, and the Spike Lee Discourse. *Black American Literature Forum* 25(2):253-82.

MacKinnon, Catharine and Andrea Dworkin, eds. 1997. *In Harm's Way: The Pornography Civil Rights Hear-*

ings. Cambridge, MA: Harvard University Press.

McNeil, Jean. 1974. Feminism, Femininity, and the Television Series: A Content Analysis. *Journal of Broadcasting* 19:259-69.

McRobbie, Angela. 1991. *Feminism and Youth Culture: From "Jackie" to "Just Seventeen."* Boston: Unwin Hyman.

———. 1994. *Postmodernism and Popular Culture*. New York: Routledge.

Modleski, Tania. 1982. *Loving with a Vengeance: Mass-Produced Fantasies for Women*. Hamden, CT: Archon Books.

Mody, Bella, Johannes M. Bauer, and Joseph D. Straubhaur. 1995. *Telecommunications Politics: Ownership and Control of the Information Highway in Developing Countries*. Hillsdale, NJ: Lawrence Erlbaum.

Mulvey, Laura. 1975. Visual Pleasures and Narrative Cinema. *Screen* 16(3): 6-18.

Mumford, Laura Stempel. 1995. *Love and Ideology in the Afternoon: Soap Opera, Women, and Television Genre*. Bloomington: Indiana University Press.

Press, Andrea L. and Elizabeth R. Cole. 1999. *Speaking of Abortion: Television and Authority in the Lives of Women*. Chicago: University of Chicago Press.

Radway, Janice. 1984. *Reading the Romance*. Chapel Hill: University of North Carolina Press.

Reeves, Jimmie and Richard Campbell. 1994. *Cracked Coverage: Television News, Reaganism, and the Journalistic Crusade Against Cocaine Use*. Durham, NC: Duke University Press.

Reynolds, Tom. 1999. Sharp Rise in Disordered Eating in Fiji Follows Arrival of Western TV. *Focus: News from Harvard Medical, Dental and Public Health Schools*, 28 May.

Rose, Tricia. 1994. *Black Noise: Rap Music and Black Culture in Contempo-rary America*. Hanover, NH: Wesleyan University Press.

Santi, Tina. 1979. The New Woman Market Is Here: How Do You Market to Her? *Advertising Age*, 18 June, 61.

Schlosser, Eric. 1997. The Business of Pornography. *U.S. News & World Report*, 10 Feb.

Seiter, Ellen. 1989. *Remote Control: Television, Audiences, and Cultural Power*. New York: Routledge.

Shattuc, Jane. 1997. *The Talking Cure: TV Talk Shows and Women*. New York: Routledge.

Steeves, H. Leslie. 1993. Creating Imagined Communities: Development Communication and the Challenge of Feminism. *Journal of Communication* 43(3):218-40.

Stockbridge, Sally. 1987. Music Video: Questions of Performance, Pleasure and Address. *Continuum: The Australian Journal of Media and Culture* 1(2). Available at http://kali.murdoch. edu.au/~cntinuum/1.2/stockbrigde.html. Accessed 2 Apr. 1997.

Strosser, Nadine. 1995. *Defending Pornography: Free Speech, Sex, and the Fight for Women's Rights*. New York: Scribner.

Ward, Brian. 1998. *Just My Soul Responding: Rhythm and Blues, Black Consciousness, and Race Relations*. Berkeley: University of California Press.

Watkins, S. Craig. 1998. *Representing: Hip Hop Culture and the Production of Black Cinema*. Chicago: University of Chicago Press.

Zeidenberg, Leonard. 1990. Watchdog Group Gives Poor Marks to Nightline, MacNeil/Lehrer: Fairness and Accuracy in Reporting Criticizes Both Shows Mainly for Their Predominantly White, Male Conservative Guest Lists. *Broadcasting* 118(22): 68-69.

ANNALS, *AAPSS*, **571**, September 2000

Feminism at Work

By AMY S. WHARTON

ABSTRACT: This article examines the contributions of feminist scholarship to the study of work, occupations, and organizations. Three themes in the literature are explored: (1) characteristics of housework and so-called women's work more generally; (2) economic inequality between men and women; and (3) structural and institutional bases of gender in the workplace. Feminist activists have shaped the direction of feminist scholarship on these themes, and this scholarship in turn has influenced feminist activists' strategies and orientations. The article concludes with a discussion of future challenges for feminist research on work.

Amy S. Wharton is associate professor of sociology at Washington State University. Her areas of research interest include gender, stratification, and work organizations. She is the editor of Working in America *(1998). She has published articles in several journals, including* Work and Occupations; Academy of Management Review; Gender & Society; *and* Social Problems.

F EMINISM and the societal changes it reflected and inspired have transformed the landscape of the social sciences. Although this transformation has occurred to some extent in all social science disciplines, feminism's impact on the social sciences has been uneven. In general, feminism's impact seems to be greater in disciplines with larger percentages of women and people of color—such as anthropology and sociology—as compared to those that are more male and white, such as economics and political science. Of course, a discipline's gender, racial, and ethnic composition may be as much a consequence of feminism's impact as a cause of that impact. Regardless of which came first, however, changes in social science scholarship have been accompanied by changes in the people who produce this scholarship.

This article examines the contributions of feminist scholarship to the study of work, occupations, and organizations. I focus primarily but not exclusively on sociology and use a broad definition of what counts as feminist scholarship. For the purposes of this article, it includes theory and research aimed at uncovering and reducing gender inequalities in the workplace. Feminist scholarship on work has evolved considerably over the past few decades. This evolution corresponds to some extent to developments in feminism as a social movement. Feminist activists have shaped the direction of feminist scholarship on work, and this scholarship in turn has influenced feminist activists' strategies and orientations.

Although feminist scholarship on work is vast, certain themes have received particular attention over the years. Each theme can be linked to a distinct set of feminist political goals. In this article, I discuss three key themes in feminist scholarship and activism, and I trace the evolution of each theme over time. The emergence of each theme loosely corresponds to a different historical era, though these themes are better understood as intellectual genres rather than stages in a chronological sequence. The study of housework and so-called women's work more generally composes the first theme I discuss. Economic issues, such as the gender wage gap, are central to the second theme. The third theme encompasses research on the structural and institutional bases of gender in the workplace. In the final section of the article, I discuss current developments and the future of feminist scholarship on work.

WOMEN'S WORK, DOMESTIC LABOR, AND THE WORK OF CAREGIVING

One of the most important expressions of the feminist movement in colleges and universities in the 1960s and 1970s was its critique of academic disciplines, like sociology and other social sciences, for ignoring women. Research on work, occupations, and organizations was singled out as being especially inattentive to women. Documenting women's experiences in the paid labor force was seen as one way to compensate for their previous neglect and an emphasis on men. This research on women's work focused on a range of occupations. Women in female-dominated clerical and service jobs, such as beautician, waitress, and office worker, for example, were the subject of Louise Kapp Howe's *Pink Collar Workers* (1977). During the 1970s, the vast majority of employed women worked in these types of jobs. Several edited collections, such as one by Stromberg and Harkness (1978), took a somewhat broader view, focusing on issues for women employed in a range of settings, from clerical and service to professional. The occupation-specific focus of these studies was consistent with a tradition of older sociological work on occupations.

The literature on women's work did not entirely ignore theoretical questions and issues of work structure and organization, but, like the sociology of occupations more generally, these were not central concerns. This growing literature on women's work had other omissions as well. There was relatively little discussion of women of color, while professional women received attention disproportionate to their share of the labor force. In addition, as noted previously, while various writers described problems faced by women working in particular settings, there was little systematic focus on work structure and organization or on gender inequality as a pervasive feature of work.

Because most sociological research on work focused on paid work, unpaid work done by women in the home received virtually no attention. Indeed, sociologists rarely treated households as places of work, viewing them instead as realms of "expressive activity" in the tradition of sociologist Talcott Parsons. Feminist scholars attempted to show that housework could be understood in the same terms as paid work. However, while work done in the home provided useful goods and services, it was unrecognized and undervalued.

Oakley's book *The Sociology of Housework* (1974) was among the first products of this new scholarship. She concluded that housework could be understood in the same terms as paid work: "Women define housework as labour, akin to that demanded by any job situation. Their observations tie in closely with many findings of the sociology of work; the aspects of housework that are cited as satisfying or dissatisfying have their parallels in the factory or office world" (41). The homemakers Oakley interviewed, however, did not see themselves as an oppressed group and were unsympathetic to feminism. Consistent with the consciousness-raising agenda of the feminist movement at this time, Oakley explored ways to increase homemakers' awareness of their oppression. "The 'deconditioned' housewife," she observed, "is thus a potential revolutionary" (197).

Marxist feminists also attended to these sorts of questions. As Secombe (1974) noted, mainstream sociologists and economists were not the only ones who had ignored the work of housewives. In what became known as the "domestic labor debates," Marxist feminist scholars sought to increase the recognition given homemakers by Marxist theorists by showing how homemakers were—like their working-class husbands—exploited by capital (Secombe 1974; Beechey 1976). This debate had both a scholarly and political agenda; Marxist feminists challenged male-dominated notions of the working class and sought to uncover the potential political power of housewives.

Feminist scholarship on housework and homemakers called attention to the productive, but unpaid, work performed in the home, and it also highlighted the precarious economic position of full-time housewives. Although wages for housework did not become a major feminist demand, feminist efforts to calculate the economic value of homemaking showed that women in this occupation worked long hours and performed services that would command a substantial wage in the paid labor market (Bergmann 1986). Because homemakers are unpaid, however, their contributions to the household are unrecognized. This becomes particularly problematic when divorce occurs or when the husband dies or becomes disabled. Feminist economists like Bergmann (1986) and Sawhill (1983) showed how current policies designed to protect wage earners, such as Social Security, offer little protection to displaced full-time homemakers.

Caregiving as a feminist issue

Women continue to perform most household work, and feminist activists and scholars continue to explore this issue. The traditional feminist approach to housework—treating it as an occupation—has given way to new orientations, however. Compare this quote from DeVault's book, *Feed-*

ing the Family (1991), to the earlier quote from Oakley:

The women I talked with referred to their activity as something other than "work" in any conventional sense, as activity embedded in family relations. . . . Though they recognize that they work at feeding, and that the work includes many repetitive, mechanical tasks, their language reveals an unlabeled dimension of caring as well: some speak of their efforts as "love," while others talk about caring for children as not quite a job, but as "something different." (10)

DeVault (1991) is one of a growing number of feminist scholars throughout the social sciences interested in understanding caregiving. In contrast to Parsons, who separated the instrumental from the affective, and in contrast to early feminists, who focused only on the instrumental aspects of household work and caring, current feminist scholarship unites these two strands: caregiving is both an instrumental and an expressive activity. This approach can also be seen in studies of emotional labor and other forms of caring work done for pay (Hochschild 1983; Steinberg and Figart 1999).

WAGE INEQUALITY AND
GENDER SEGREGATION

Simpson (1989) describes the 1970s and 1980s as a time when sociologists interested in work abandoned more traditional sociological concerns and embraced an economic approach to work-related issues. In Simpson's view, this shift was marked by a move away from "the behavior of flesh-and-blood workers at the level of the face-to-face work group" toward a more macrostructural, economic approach (564). Simpson's description of this change could also apply to feminist scholarship on work during the same era. Feminist scholarship began to more systematically attend to structural and economic issues, and attention shifted from women's work to issues of gender and gender inequality. Feminist interest in these issues was also motivated by changes occurring in women's lives. Rising divorce rates meant that more women were working for pay to support themselves and their children. Economic independence proved difficult, however, as most women worked in low-paying, predominantly female clerical and service jobs.

Explaining the gender wage gap

Economists have devoted considerable attention to understanding what determines the worth of jobs and why some jobs pay more than others. For the most part, these scholars have emphasized the role of human capital in wage determination. Human capital refers to the portfolio of skills that workers acquire through various kinds of investments in education, training, or experience. Applied to the gender wage gap, human capital theory implies that women earn less than men because of differences in the kind and amount of human capital each has accumulated.

Feminist scholars were skeptical that this provided a complete understanding of the gender wage gap, and they critiqued economic arguments for overlooking the many ways in which social factors shape wage setting and wage inequality (for example, England and Farkas 1986; Steinberg and Haignere 1987). In addition, feminist researchers have suggested that "institutional" or structural factors, as well as individual-level factors, contribute to the gender wage gap (Roos and Gatta 1999). By focusing on these issues, feminist scholars helped broaden the study of gender inequality and the gender wage gap from a narrow focus on individuals' human capital to a concern with social structural and institutional factors. On a more general level, feminists' interest in understanding women's earnings and work experiences has contributed to a more accurate view of labor markets. Researchers who focus only on men—especially white men— tend to "exaggerate the extent to which labor market processes are meritocratic" (Reskin and Charles 1999, 384).

During the last few decades, feminist research on the wage gap has proliferated. Women's lower earnings relative to men's has become, as Roos and Gatta (1999) observe, "a social truism" (95). Moreover, researchers' understanding of how the gender-based wage inequality occurs, how it has changed over time, and its variations between women and between men has become increasingly complex and nuanced. Two major themes in this work illustrate recent developments.

First, research on the gender wage gap has become increasingly attentive to issues of race and ethnicity (Browne 1999; Kilbourne, England, and Beron 1994; Tomaskovic-Devey

1993). As Reskin and Charles (1999) note, the historical tendency has been a "balkanization of research on ascriptive bases of inequality" (380). Studies of the gender wage gap, in particular, have often ignored racial and ethnic variations among women and men. Not only does this produce potentially inaccurate results, but it also has hindered efforts to understand the forces generating and maintaining wage inequality. A second, emerging theme in recent studies of the gender wage gap are attempts to relate gender-based wage inequality to wage inequality more generally. Wage inequality in the United States has increased in recent decades—a pattern that reflects industrial and occupational restructuring, changing labor force demographics, globalization, and political trends (Morris and Western 1999). This widening inequality reflects not only earnings differences between women and men but also differences between women and between men (Mishel, Bernstein, and Schmitt 1999). As researchers now realize, a narrow focus on the gender wage gap misses these broader patterns of inequality.

The gender segregation of occupations and jobs

Gender segregation is an entrenched and pervasive feature of the industrial workplace. Women make up almost half of the paid labor force, but women and men are employed in different occupations, firms, and jobs. Although occupational segregation has declined over the twentieth century (with most of the decline occurring in the 1970s),

its persistence in the face of so many other changes both inside and outside the workplace has inspired a tremendous amount of feminist research.

One line of research on segregation involves large-scale, quantitative studies of occupational segregation in the labor force as a whole. These studies document trends in segregation over time and identify factors associated with changes in segregation levels. Recent findings suggest that the declines in occupational segregation that took place in the 1970s appeared to level off in the 1990s (Jacobs 1999). Other researchers have examined segregation cross-nationally, looking for clues as to the economic, political, and cultural factors that produce gender segregation and inequality.

This literature on occupational segregation has been supplemented in recent years by research at other levels of analysis. Bielby and Baron (1984), for example, moved segregation research from the occupation to the job and firm levels of analysis; they showed that job segregation within firms was considerably higher than segregation at the occupational level. Tomaskovic-Devey (1993) also found extremely high levels of job segregation by gender in his study of North Carolina firms. Even if occupations appear gender integrated, these studies demonstrate that women and men rarely work together, holding the same job in the same firm. A second extension of segregation research moves it in a more macro direction by focusing on labor markets—rather than jobs or occupations. Cotter et al. (1997) show that occupational integration at the local labor market level improves earnings for all women in that labor market, regardless of the gender composition of a woman's own occupation.

Links to feminist activism: Affirmative action and pay equity

Feminist research on gender segregation and the gender wage gap has always been more than an academic pursuit; it has also been used to advance efforts to reduce gender inequality in earnings and to improve women's position in the workforce. These two goals are closely connected; women's concentration in lower-paying predominantly female jobs and their exclusion from higher-paying jobs held mostly by men both help explain the gender wage gap. Improvement in women's labor market situation, then, requires that women have greater access to higher-paying male jobs or that the wages for predominantly female jobs increase. These are not mutually exclusive objectives, and feminist research provides evidence supportive of both strategies.

Affirmative action, which grew out of Title VII of the 1964 Civil Rights Act and was later elaborated through numerous executive orders, focuses on improving women's and minorities' access to jobs from which they have been excluded. This policy thus aims to break down gender and racial segregation by moving women and minorities into jobs traditionally held by men and whites. Recent studies evaluating the effectiveness of affirmative action policies and programs suggest that they have been relatively successful (Reskin 1998). Although these programs have become politically unpopular, affirmative action does seem to improve women's and minorities' access to higher-paying jobs held disproportionately by men and whites.

Despite this success, most feminist scholars believe that affirmative action alone is insufficient for eliminating discrimination and increasing women's wages (England 1992). The vast majority of women work in predominantly female jobs, and affirmative action is unlikely to ever completely remedy this situation. As a result, feminist scholars and women workers have attempted to improve the pay of predominantly female jobs by compensating these jobs at wages equivalent to comparable jobs held by men. The pay equity (or comparable worth) movement uses job evaluation methods to determine the relative worth of jobs. Job evaluation is a strategy for determining how pay is assigned to jobs and thereby to justify (or critique) relative pay rates. Employers use job evaluation as a tool to decide how to compensate different jobs, and feminists use it to demonstrate gender bias in wage setting.

Job evaluation techniques have been used in several state and local settings, including Washington, Oregon, New York State, and the city of San Jose, California (Acker 1989; Steinberg and Haignere 1987; Blum 1991). In all these cases, this technique was proposed as a way to correct perceived gender biases in the ways in which wages were attached to jobs. Most notably, job evaluation showed that jobs evaluated as comparable in terms of their skill requirements, working conditions, and the like were often compensated at different levels depending upon their sex composition. Predominantly female jobs tended to be devalued relative to jobs of comparable skill filled by men. These results called into question the notion that wages were set according to gender-neutral processes and instead revealed an important source of gender bias. In fact, as England (1992) notes, "if a single job evaluation plan is used to set pay throughout a firm or government, *it nearly always gives women's jobs higher wages relative to men's than most employers pay*" (205; emphasis in original). Feminist scholars and labor organizations often cooperated in their efforts to use job evaluation as a means of identifying and correcting gender bias in wage setting.

GENDERED JOBS, ORGANIZATIONS,
AND WORK ACTIVITIES

Rosabeth Moss Kanter's 1977 classic, *Men and Women of the Corporation*, reshaped feminist scholarship on work and gender. Kanter argued that many differences between women's and men's work-related behaviors and attitudes that previous researchers had attributed to gender could be better understood as being due to women's and men's different structural positions in organizations. Although some of Kanter's claims have been widely criticized, her contention that much gender-related behavior on the job stems from how work is organized rather than the characteristics of workers has gained wide acceptance among feminists.

Kanter's claims about the effects of group composition are among her most important, though intensely debated, contributions to feminist understandings of work. These claims rest on the proposition that, "as proportions shift, so do social experiences" (Kanter 1977, 207). Kanter was particularly interested in "skewed groups," in which one social type is numerically dominant and the other constitutes a very small numerical minority (for example, 15 percent or less). Her focus on this type of group stemmed from the fact that this is likely to be the situation experienced by newcomers to a social setting. Members of the numerical minority in skewed groups are called tokens. Kanter argued that relations between tokens and dominants in skewed groups worked to the tokens' disadvantage, and she attributed these negative dynamics to social structural factors. The relative proportions of different social types—not the particular gender, race, ethnic background, and so forth, of group members—were to blame for the effects of tokenism.

For two decades, feminists have been debating Kanter's claims. Most now agree with Williams (1998) that, while Kanter's search for a structural explanation for gender-related behavior was an important contribution, she was "wrong about tokenism" (141). As Williams's research (1989) shows, gender does matter when considering the consequences of tokenism: women who enter predominantly male jobs and work settings typically encounter much more resistance and hostility from their male coworkers than do men who enter predominantly female jobs and work settings.

Konrad, Winter, and Gutek (1992) refer to Kanter's perspective (1977) as a "generic" approach and contrast it with an "institutional" orientation. Though not specifically directed to feminist scholarship, this distinction captures an important difference between feminist approaches to the workplace: Kanter argued that gender differences in the workplace were really manifestations of something else—the effects of social structure. Institutionalists, by contrast, suggest that gender is embodied in social structures and other forms of social organization. Hence, aspects of the workplace that are conventionally treated as genderless or gender neutral in fact are expressions of gender. This latter view represents a gendered institutions perspective.

Gendered institutions

Institutions are those features of social life that seem so regular, so ongoing, and so permanent that they are often accepted as just "the way things are." Because highly institutionalized social arrangements require relatively little effort to sustain them, it is much more difficult to alter something that is highly institutionalized than it is to perpetuate it. The concept of a gendered institution is consistent with these ideas. In her 1992 article on this theme, Acker contends that many of the institutions that constitute the "rules of the game" in American society—and, indeed, most societies—embody aspects of gender. As Acker defines it, to say that an institution is gendered means

that gender is present in the processes, practices, images, and ideologies, and distributions of power in the various sectors of social life. Taken as more or less functioning wholes, the institutional structures of the United States and other societies are organized along the lines of gender.... [These institutions] have been historically developed by men, currently dominated by men, and symbolically interpreted from the standpoint of men in leading positions, both in the present and historically. (567)

This way of thinking about gender directs us to the organization, structure, and practices of social institutions, such as the workplace, and it calls attention to the ways in which these entrenched, powerful, and relatively taken-for-granted aspects of the social order produce and reproduce gender distinctions and inequality.

Drawing on the notion of gendered institutions, feminists suggest that the structures and practices of work organizations are gendered at all levels. As Steinberg (1992) notes, "Masculine values are at the foundation of informal and formal organizational structures.... Images of masculinity and assumptions about the gendered division of labor organize institutional practices and expectations about work performance" (576). As an example of this line of argument, some research has focused on how cultural beliefs about gender infuse people's understandings of jobs, occupations, and particular work activities. By establishing certain work roles, jobs, and occupations as appropriate for one gender and off-limits to another, these cultural beliefs establish the "way things are" or a set of commonsense understandings of who should engage in what type of work.

That jobs dominated by a particular gender come to be seen as most appropriate for that gender may seem unproblematic and inevitable, but this association is produced through a complex process of social construction. As Reskin and Roos (1990) note, virtually any occupation can be understood as being more appropriate for one sex or another "because most jobs contain both stereotypical male and stereotypical female elements" (51). Nursing, for example, requires workers to be skilled in the use of complex medical technologies. Emphasizing the caring aspects of this occupation, however, allows it to be cast as an occupation particularly appropriate for women. Most jobs and occupations contain enough different kinds of characteristics that they can be construed as appropriate for either women or men.

The gendering of work can also be seen in gender-integrated positions or in jobs that contain a minority of the other gender, and it applies to jobs held by men as well as those that are predominantly female. As a growing literature on work and masculinity has shown, many predominantly male jobs implicitly and explicitly require incumbents to display traditionally masculine behaviors, such as aggressiveness. Maier (1999) argues that managerial practices and organizational cultures—not merely specific jobs—embody a "corporate masculinity" that privileges individualism, competitiveness, and technical rationality (71).

In some situations, the work tasks may be gendered as feminine, but the worker performing them is male. Hall's study (1993) of table servers offers a useful example of these arrangements. Styles of table service are laden with gender meanings. A familial style of service, which Hall labels "waitressing," has been historically associated with women working in coffee shops and family restaurants. By contrast, "waitering" is a more formal style, usually associated with male servers in high-prestige restaurants. Hall suggests that even in sex-integrated restaurants, "work roles, job tasks, and service styles" continue to be gendered, such that "waitering"—whether performed by women or men—is more highly valued by employers and customers than is "waitressing" (343).

The gendering of work also shapes the relations between jobs, especially hierarchical relations. In his writings on bureaucracy, the classical sociologist Max Weber provided one of the definitive sociological understandings of work hierarchies. For Weber, bureaucratic work arrangements were necessarily hierarchical and involved specialization, a fixed division of labor, and meritocratic rules and regulations (Weber 1946). Feminists have inserted gender into these arguments in two important respects. First, some argue that gender is an aspect of bureaucracy itself; that is, gender is embedded in this formal system of organization (Ferguson 1984). In *The Feminist Case Against Bureaucracy*, Ferguson suggests that, as a hierarchical system, bureaucracy perpetuates the interests of the powerful over the powerless. In this respect, it is a metaphor for the dominance of men over women. By rewarding character traits such as "impression management, need to please, conformity, identification with the organization, dependency and so forth," bureaucracies "feminize" those at the bottom of the hierarchy while concentrating power at the top (116).

While Ferguson (1984) suggests that bureaucracy itself is gendered, more recent work suggests that gendering is more central to the informal social relations of workplace hierarchies. For example, Pierce (1995) explored the relations between lawyers (mostly male) and paralegals, predominantly female. Although the lawyers and paralegals she studied engaged in some of the same kinds of tasks (for example, legal research and writing) and were very interdependent in many respects, the relations between these positions were highly gendered. As Pierce states, "Structurally, paralegal positions are specifically designed for women to support high-status men, and the content of paralegal work is consistent with our cultural conceptions of appropriate behavior for traditional wives and mothers" (86). Paralegals thus are expected to defer to and serve lawyers, who in turn rely on paralegals to perform this caretaking labor.

Links to feminist activism:
Gender on the job

Research deriving from a structural or institutional perspective on gender has been especially useful in feminists' efforts to improve women's and men's lives inside work organizations. Kanter's recognition (1977) that the relative power and opportunity of individuals and groups at work can be altered by redesigning organizational structures has inspired some efforts in this direction. In addition, recent years have seen an infusion of feminist scholarship into organizational research. Some of this research has its roots in Kanter's work, as it explores how the demographic composition of work groups shapes interaction and behavior (Chemers, Oskamp, and Costanzo 1995; Ruderman, Hughes-James, and Jackson 1996). An important finding to emerge from this research is that differences between people—such as those deriving from gender or race—are not always salient in the workplace. While sex category is probably more salient in more situations than many other attributes of a person, organizational research suggests that it is not always an important factor in workplace social relations. Understanding when and why gender (or race or some other characteristic) matters and for what outcomes are important tasks facing feminist scholars studying organizations.

Research informed by a gendered institutions perspective has helped feminists identify and combat the "glass ceiling" (U.S. Department of Labor 1991). The metaphor of the glass ceiling speaks to the powerful, yet invisible, forces that prevent women and minorities from reaching the highest levels of organizations. Research addressing how gender is built into job requirements, work activities and hierarchies, and cultural beliefs about job worth has identified the more subtle factors that maintain gender and racial inequality in organizations. This research also contributes to efforts to combat sexual harassment at work and to understand how sexuality as well as gender is embedded in work organizations.

Feminist scholarship in the tradition of a gendered institutions perspective has also addressed issues of gender inequality and the pay gap. For example, while early pay equity research relied on job evaluation to identify gender bias, recent studies suggest that job evaluation methods themselves contain their own sources of bias (Acker 1989; England 1992). Bias in job evaluation occurs when predominantly female, "nurturant" jobs are given fewer points than they merit, while predominantly male jobs are given a boost in ranking. An example cited by England (1992) illustrates the point: "Attendants at dog pounds and parking lots (usually men) were rated more highly than nursery school teachers, and zookeepers more highly than day care workers" (199). Researchers question whether it is possible to objectively measure the worth of jobs.

RETHINKING GENDER AND A LOOK TOWARD THE FUTURE

One of the ongoing and most significant contributions of feminist scholarship has been its intensive examination of the concept of gender. This examination has produced a conceptual shift over time in how gender is understood. Early feminist scholars treated gender as an attribute of individuals; gender was a role people acquired through socialization, and it was carried into workplaces (or to schools or families), where it was then expressed in people's behaviors and beliefs. Because gender was treated as a property of people, the possibility that institutions or features of the social context could play a role in the reproduction of gender distinctions and inequalities was overlooked. Although some contemporary feminist scholars continue to view gender solely as an aspect of the person, most believe that gender is a multifaceted system of practices and relations that operates at all levels of the social world (Ridgeway and Smith-Lovin 1999; Hawkesworth 1997).

This more multilayered view of gender can be seen in many areas of feminist research, but it has been most powerfully put to use in research on the workplace. Its impact can be most clearly seen in feminist scholars' move away from unidimensional explanations of workplace phenomena. As England (1999) observes, "Simple 'it's all this' stories [about gender] are usually wrong" (3). Pierce's study of gender in contemporary law firms (1995), which draws on psychoanalytic theories of gender identity, as well as more structural approaches to gender, provides an example of this more multilayered approach. Another example can be found in Ridgeway and Smith-Lovin's conception of the "gender system" (1999). Ridgeway (1997) uses this approach to explain how interactions at work help sustain gender inequality. Although feminist scholarship—including scholarship on work—has not been immune from attempts to enforce disciplinary, methodological, and theoretical boundaries, feminists interested in workplace issues have generally been more concerned with reducing workplace inequality than perpetuating narrow intellectual agendas.

The broadening of feminist conceptions of gender has increased the reach of feminist scholarship and expanded its influence on the social sciences. Treating gender strictly as an individual-level characteristic limits our ability to examine how gender distinctions and inequality are produced at other levels of the social order. A gendered institutions approach makes clear, however, that social structure, institutions, and interaction cannot be understood without taking gender into account. Applied to the workplace, this implies that work and the social practices that compose it are organized in ways that create and reproduce gender distinctions and inequalities. Hence, as feminist scholars have addressed issues raised by a gendered institutions approach, they have helped to reframe understandings of fundamental social processes, including the social processes that organize the workplace.

While these developments are promising, even more could be done. Feminist scholars as a whole have become increasingly concerned with the relations between gender and other bases of distinction and stratification, such as age, race or ethnicity, sexual orientation, and social class. A growing literature challenges the notion that women (or men) represent a homogeneous category, whose members have common interests and experiences. Theory and research seeking to describe the intersections between race, class, and gender, in particular, have proliferated, and there is increasing attention to these questions among those interested in the workplace. However, with some exceptions, feminist scholars' attention to the links between race, class, and gender has been largely confined to qualitative research focusing on specific occupations and work settings (for example, Romero 1992; Collins 1997). In the years ahead, it will be important for feminist scholars to more systematically address how other forms of social differentiation besides gender are constructed and maintained in the workplace. Doing this requires that we overcome the balkanization of the literatures on racial, gender, and other forms of inequality referred to earlier (Reskin and Charles 1999, 380) and begin to focus on "organizational systems of inequality" (Nelson and Bridges 1999, 5).

CONCLUSION

As we prepare to enter the twenty-first century, we live in an increasingly capitalist world economy in which most women are employed for pay and perform the bulk of child care and domestic labor. Feminist research on work and workers is as relevant to women's lives (as well as the lives of men and children) as ever, and feminist scholarship on these topics has become increasingly mainstream in the social sciences (and sociology, in particular). Ironically, however, this integration has occurred just as feminist scholarship as a whole has shifted its center of gravity away from the study of economic inequality and large-scale structures like the workplace to issues of personal politics and identity. This suggests that relations between feminism and the social sciences are likely to remain—as they have been in the past—somewhat contested. Fortunately, however, this has not prevented new generations of feminist scholars from taking up the important tasks of understanding and dismantling gender, racial, and class inequality at work.

References

Acker, Joan. 1989. *Doing Comparable Worth: Gender, Class, and Pay Equity*. Philadelphia: Temple University Press.

———. 1992. Gendered Institutions. *Contemporary Sociology* 21:565-69.

Beechey, Veronica. 1976. Some Notes on Female Wage Labour in Capitalist Production. *Capital and Class* 3:43-66.

Bergmann, Barbara. 1986. *The Economic Emergence of Women*. New York: Basic Books.

Bielby, William T. and James N. Baron. 1984. A Woman's Place Is with Other Women: Sex Segregation Within Organizations. In *Sex Segregation in the Workplace*, ed. B. F. Reskin. Washington, DC: National Academy Press.

Blum, Linda M. 1991. *Between Feminism and Labor: The Significance of the Comparable Worth Movement*. Berkeley: University of California Press.

Browne, Irene, ed. 1999. *Latinas and African-American Women at Work*. New York: Russell Sage Foundation.

Chemers, Martin M., Stuart Oskamp, and Mark A. Costanzo. 1995. *Diversity in Organizations*. Thousand Oaks, CA: Sage.

Collins, Sharon M. 1997. *Black Corporate Executives: The Making and Breaking of a Black Middle Class*. Philadelphia: Temple University Press.

Cotter, David A., JoAnn DeFiore, Joan M. Hermsen, Brenda Marsteller Kowalewski, and Reeve Vanneman. 1997. All Women Benefit: The Macro-Level Effect of Occupational Integration. *American Sociological Review* 62:714-34.

DeVault, Marjorie L. 1991. *Feeding the Family: The Social Organization of Caring as Gendered Work*. Chicago: University of Chicago Press.

England, Paula. 1992. *Comparable Worth: Theories and Evidence*. New York: Aldine de Gruyter.

———. 1999. Thoughts on What We Know and Don't Know About Gender. *Sex and Gender News* Nov.: 3-4.

England, Paula and George Farkas. 1986. *Households, Employment, and Gender: A Social, Economic and Demographic View*. New York: Aldine de Gruyter.

Ferguson, Kathy E. 1984. *The Feminist Case Against Bureaucracy*. Philadelphia: Temple University Press.

Hall, Elaine J. 1993. Waitering/ Waitressing: Engendering the Work of Table Servers. *Gender & Society* 7:329-46.

Hawkesworth, Mary. 1997. Confounding Gender. *Signs* 22:649-85.

Hochschild, Arlie Russell. 1983. *The Managed Heart: The Commercialization of Human Feeling*. Berkeley: University of California Press.

Howe, Louise Kapp. 1977. *Pink Collar Workers*. New York: Avon Books.

Jacobs, Jerry A. 1999. The Sex Segregation of Occupations: Prospects for the 21st Century. In *Handbook of Gender and Work*, ed. G. N. Powell. Thousand Oaks, CA: Sage.

Kanter, Rosabeth Moss. 1977. *Men and Women of the Corporation*. New York: Basic Books.

Kilbourne, Barbara S., Paula England, and Kurt Beron. 1994. Effects of Individual, Occupational, and Industrial Characteristics on Earnings: Intersections of Race and Gender. *Social Forces* 72:1149-76.

Konrad, Alison M., Susan Winter, and Barbara A. Gutek. 1992. Diversity in Work Group Sex Composition. *Research in the Sociology of Organizations* 10:115-40.

Maier, Mark. 1999. On the Gendered Substructure of Organization: Dimensions and Dilemmas of Corporate Masculinity. In *Handbook of Gender and Work*, ed. G. N. Powell. Thousand Oaks, CA: Sage.

Mishel, Lawrence, Jared Bernstein, and John Schmitt. 1999. *The State of Working America, 1998-99*. Ithaca, NY: ILR Press.

Morris, Martina and Bruce Western. 1999. Inequality in Earnings at the Close of the Twentieth Century. *Annual Review of Sociology* 25:623-57.

Nelson, Robert L. and William P. Bridges. 1999. *Legalizing Gender Inequality*. New York: Cambridge University Press.

Oakley, Ann. 1974. *The Sociology of Housework*. New York: Pantheon Books.

Pierce, Jennifer. 1995. *Gender Trials: Emotional Lives in Contemporary Law Firms*. Berkeley: University of California Press.

Reskin, Barbara F. 1998. *The Realities of Affirmative Action in Employment*. Washington, DC: American Sociological Association.

Reskin, Barbara F. and Camille Z. Charles. 1999. Now You See 'Em, Now You Don't: Race, Ethnicity, and Gender in Labor Market Research. In *Latinas and African-American Women at Work*, ed. I. Brown. New York: Russell Sage Foundation.

Reskin, Barbara F. and Patricia A. Roos. 1990. *Job Queues, Gender Queues: Explaining Women's Inroads into Male Occupations*. Philadelphia: Temple University Press.

Ridgeway, Cecelia L. 1997. Interaction and the Conservation of Gender Inequality. *American Sociological Review* 62:218-35.

Ridgeway, Cecelia L. and Lynn Smith-Lovin. 1999. The Gender System and Interaction. *Annual Review of Sociology* 25:191-216.

Romero, Mary. 1992. *Maid in the U.S.A.* New York: Routledge.

Roos, Patricia A. and Mary Lizabeth Gatta. 1999. The Gender Gap in Earnings: Trends, Explanations, and Prospects. In *Handbook of Gender and Work*, ed. G. N. Powell. Thousand Oaks, CA: Sage.

Ruderman, Marian N., Martha W. Hughes-James, and Susan E. Jackson, eds. 1996. *Selected Research on Work Team Diversity*. Washington, DC: American Psychological Association; Greensboro, NC: Center for Creative Leadership.

Sawhill, Isabel V. 1983. Developing Normative Standards for Child Support Payments. In *The Parental Child Sup-*

port Obligation, ed. J. Cassetty. Lexington, MA: Lexington Books.

Secombe, Wally. 1974. The Housewife and Her Labour Under Capitalism. New Left Review 83:3-24.

Simpson, Ida Harper. 1989. The Sociology of Work: Where Have the Workers Gone? Social Forces 67:563-81.

Steinberg, Ronnie J. 1992. Gender on the Agenda: Male Advantage in Organizations. Contemporary Sociology 21:576-81.

Steinberg, Ronnie J. and Deborah M. Figart. 1999. Emotional Labor Since The Managed Heart. The Annals of the American Academy of Political and Social Science 561:8-26.

Steinberg, Ronnie J. and Lois Haignere. 1987. Equitable Compensation: Methodological Criteria for Comparable Worth. In Ingredients for Women's Employment Policy, ed. C. Bose and G. Spitze. Albany: State University of New York Press.

Stromberg, Ann H. and Shirley Harkness, eds. 1978. Women Working: Theories and Facts in Perspective. Palo Alto, CA: Mayfield Press.

Tomaskovic-Devey, Donald. 1993. Gender and Racial Inequality at Work. Ithaca, NY: ILR Press.

U.S. Department of Labor. 1991. A Report on the Glass Ceiling Initiative. Washington, DC: Department of Labor.

Weber, Max. 1946. Bureaucracy. In From Max Weber: Essays in Sociology, ed. H. H. Gerth and C. Wright Mills. New York: Oxford University Press.

Williams, Christine L. 1989. Gender Differences at Work. Berkeley: University of California Press.

———. 1998. What's Gender Got to Do with It? In Required Reading: Sociology's Most Influential Books, ed. D. Clawson. Amherst: University of Massachusetts Press.

ANNALS, *AAPSS*, **571**, September 2000

Feminism in Psychology:
Revolution or Evolution?

By JUDITH WORELL

ABSTRACT: This article discusses the major contributions of feminism to the discipline of psychology in the areas of theory, research, and practice. Among the most important of these innovations are the introduction of the psychology of girls and women as legitimate topics of study; naming and exploring important issues in the lives of women; reconstructing research methods and priorities to study women in the context of their lived experiences; integrating multiple diversities into all areas of the discipline; developing innovative approaches to therapeutic practice; transforming institutions toward being more inclusive and collaborative; and advocating for social action and public policies that benefit the health and well-being of both women and men. Although feminist scholarship and practice have permeated substantive areas of the discipline in both subtle and visible ways, many sectors of psychology remain wary of perspectives that are openly feminist. Feminist psychology remains active, however, and will continue to insist on the visibility of women in all its sectors and practices and on a discipline that values and promotes equality and social justice for all.

Judith Worell is a licensed clinical psychologist and professor emeritus in the Department of Educational and Counseling Psychology at the University of Kentucky. She is author or editor of eight books and past editor of the Psychology of Women Quarterly, *a journal of research. She is past president of the Kentucky Psychological Association, the Southeastern Psychological Association, the Society for the Psychology of Women, and the Clinical Psychology of Women section of the American Psychological Association.*

I N this article, I discuss the extent to which the feminist movement has altered the focus and direction of psychology as a discipline and the major contributions of feminism to psychological theory, research, and practice. Feminist psychologists have opened doors to the opportunities for a revised discipline by asking new questions, naming new problems, challenging research priorities, giving voice to the invisible woman, revising applied practice (the practice of psychology in clinical and other settings), and applying research findings to public advocacy.

The introduction of feminist scholarship and research to the field of psychology has been relatively recent. Feminist psychologists generally endorse a common core of principles, but we are also confronted by controversies that divide and challenge us. Challenge comes also from mainstream psychology, which has been alternately accommodating, ambivalent, or clearly inhospitable. The story of the feminist movement itself has reflected struggle and dissension, but the movement has achieved and retained its positive outlook by resolving conflict through consensus and constructive action toward personal and social change. Feminist psychologists follow a similar path. The feminist revolution in psychology has not overturned the profession, but the evolving influence of feminism continues. I conclude that the impact of feminism on the future of psychology will be significant and robust.

EARLY BEGINNINGS

Psychology is dedicated to the study of human development, cognition, and behavior within a diversity of environments. It is a young discipline, established as an institution in 1892 with the inception of the American Psychological Association. From its infancy, psychology quickly established its territory as that of an objective, quantitative, empirical, and value-free science. The researcher, as an unbiased observer, conducted carefully controlled laboratory experiments and remained distanced from the subjects of study. Although many early studies were conducted with animals, the goals of research were generally to understand and predict human behavior. The outcomes were conceived as universal truths or laws that would apply to a wide range of individuals across situations and time.

Interest in applying psychological principles to the amelioration of human distress and misery developed after traumatic experiences during World War II drove veterans to seek relief from their pain and confusion. Since then, the field of psychology has experienced expansive growth across a range of basic and applied areas, including, among others, neurological, cognitive, developmental, personality, social, organizational, clinical, and counseling psychology. Paradoxically, the introduction of applied practices to the field of psychology has both enriched and divided the discipline.

ENTER FEMINISM

The roots of feminist psychology were nourished in the soil of the wider feminist movement. As a broad interdisciplinary movement, feminism has aimed to achieve equality and justice for all women. To this end, three specific goals have provided a common denominator across the social sciences: (1) to understand the imbalances of power and privilege for women in all societies; (2) to challenge the disadvantaged status of women in both public and private arenas; and (3) to advocate on behalf of and empower girls and women of diverse social, national, and ethnic identities. Among contemporary social reform movements, feminism is especially notable for its appeal to groups both within the scientific, academic, and professional communities as well as in the general public.

Psychology
acknowledges feminism

We can date our psychological origins about 30 years ago to Naomi Weisstein's classic dictum, "Psychology constructs the female" (1968), in which she declared that psychology had neglected and omitted women from its corpus of knowledge. Since then, in a relatively brief period of time, feminist psychologists have made their presence known through multiple efforts to revise and reconstruct the discipline. An overriding goal for feminist psychology has been to uncover, reshape, rename, and transform the face of its parent discipline and its connection to the real lives of girls and women everywhere (Worell and Johnson 1997). As a corollary to this goal, when the lives of women are liberated and transformed, men will also be freed from the bonds of their gendered lives.

Transformations in psychology have taken place on many fronts. In the early 1970s, feminist psychologists questioned the androcentric bias of psychological knowledge, which they believed reflected a male model of reality. They pointed out that researchers and the people they studied were predominantly male; the topics they studied, such as aggression and achievement, reflected male concerns; and the results of research based on male samples were assumed to apply also to women (Crawford and Marecek 1989). When women were studied, they were evaluated according to a male standard, so that women's personality and behavior were seen as deviant or deficient in comparison. For example, early research that focused on sex differences claimed that in comparison to men, women were less motivated to achieve, less assertive, and less proficient in science and mathematics. These presumed deficiencies were then seen as stereotypes of all women and were used to deny women entry or advancement in male-dominated employment settings.

Feminist psychologists began to challenge this androcentric perspective by illuminating how commonly held sex role or gender stereotypes were biased against women. In a landmark study on gender stereotyping by psychotherapists, Inge Broverman and her colleagues

(1970) reported wide differences in stereotypes of the healthy woman or man. Men were more likely to be seen (by both women and men) as more independent, aggressive, direct, unemotional, competent, and dominant. Men were also viewed as more similar than women to the "healthy person." In contrast, women were more likely to be seen as warm, expressive, and sensitive, as well as emotional and childlike. These researchers concluded that therapists subscribed to a double standard, by defining mental health in terms of an androcentric model. Phyllis Chesler (1972) then proposed that women are "driven crazy" by men and male therapists as a means of maintaining patriarchal power and control. Studies such as these were early precursors to feminist models of counseling and psychotherapy with girls and women (cf. Worell and Remer 1992).

In contrast to these stereotypes, Sandra Bem's research (1974) on gender stereotyping found that many women and men possessed an equal balance of both feminine and masculine characteristics, which she labeled "psychological androgyny." Bem further proposed that androgyny is the ideal model of mental health, in which both women and men could be flexible in their sex role characteristics, displaying a range of characteristics appropriate to the situations in which they found themselves. Thus women could be assertive or compliant, powerful or compassionate, depending on the circumstances. The concept of androgyny as a model for ideal adjustment was attractive for a while as a viable alternative to prior conceptions that women and men exist as polar opposites.

Androgyny eventually came under attack, however, as just another way to maintain cultural stereotypes that differentiate women from men. That is, it defined certain personality traits as stereotypic for either women or men, thus perpetuating the myth that the two are indeed quite different from each other. Additionally, the androgyny model was conceived in a narrow frame that omits many aspects of behavior and personality that are not defined by these two groups of traits. Although androgyny no longer maintains its popular appeal in psychology (Worell 1978), Bem's research was an important marker for the challenges to sex-difference research, most of which tends to portray women as deficient in comparison to men.

These early studies provided the impetus for a burgeoning field of research and scholarship on women and the multiple meanings of gender. In succeeding years, feminist psychologists have contributed to innovative approaches in theory development and measurement (Brabeck and Brown 1997); research method and content (Grossman et al. 1997; Worell and Etaugh 1994); and the inclusion of those overlooked women who have contributed to the development of the discipline (Scarborough and Furamoto 1987). Some of the areas in which feminist psychologists have produced transformations include constructions of ethical behavior (Rave and Larson 1995), curriculum development and pedagogy (Kimmel and Worell 1997), violence toward women (Koss et al. 1994), women's sexuality (Wyatt and Riederle 1994), and our understandings of women's mental health and well-being (Rosewater and Walker 1985; Worell and Remer 1992). We have also influenced conceptions of effective management and leadership (Eagley and Johnson 1990) and the structure and functioning of our professional organizations (Mednick and Urbanski 1991). The new psychology of men and masculinity was born from and fueled by the energy and insights of the feminist movement.

Although this list of feminist contributions appears substantial, our influence remains limited within each domain. Further, many areas resist change. Among these are forensic psychology (the relationship between psychology and the law), mainstream social psychology, communication and social processes, the psychology of personality, and processes in child development. The barriers remain where the term "feminism" defines the scope or process of research. However, when feminist psychologists use feminist process or content without using the label, we are often more successful in transmitting our message.

The wave of interest and commitment to a new psychology of women and gender was followed by the establishment of feminist organizations and scholarly journals. The Division of the Psychology of Women (now the Society for the Psychology of Women) was admitted to the American Psychological Association in 1973, and its flagship journal, *Psychology of Women Quarterly*, was launched in 1975. During the same period, other scholarly journals appeared that focused on feminist issues, and research on women and gender began to be accepted into the mainstream journals in psychology. However, the specialized journals on women, gender, and feminism continue to provide the major outlets for feminist writing and research. It is clear that psychology's acknowledgment of feminism remains cautious and that feminist scholarship tends to be kept at the margins.

Feminist psychology embraces diversity

Perhaps most important, feminist psychology has become more diverse and more inclusive. In moving beyond simplistic questions about sex differences, we have begun to acknowledge and explore the diversity of perspectives among women that intersect with gender (Greene and Sanchez-Hucles 1997; Landrine 1995). For many of us, some of these issues, such as race, ethnicity, sexual orientation, social class, or ablism, supersede and take precedence over those inequities created by gender. For lesbian and bisexual women, sexual orientation may predominate in their experiences. Lillian Comas-Diaz (1991) has called for "an integrative feminist psychology . . . that embraces cultural, ethnic, and social class pluralism" (607). We have only begun to open our eyes and our research efforts to the lives and experiences of diverse groups of women who have remained largely voiceless and invisible. In doing so, we expand our vision and enrich both our science and our practice.

*Feminist psychology
  remains at the margins*

On the other hand, feminist influences have also been restricted to specific areas of the discipline and have not visibly influenced most traditional theorizing and research practices. Although some innovations created by feminist psychology have been integrated into mainstream practice, there is limited recognition of their identity as feminist in origin. What are now believed by many psychologists to be correct or ethical practices had their origins in feminist activism. Examples of feminist-promoted practices include encouraging career exploration and planning for women, forbidding sexual intimacy between therapists and clients, and recognizing rape as an act of aggression rather than of sexuality.

One of the paradoxes for feminist psychologists, therefore, is how to bring about feminist transformations in a discipline that chooses to ignore but also to selectively assimilate its beliefs and practices. The major polemics center on whether feminist psychology is "real science" or "only politics." Although feminist psychologists agree that their science is frequently political (infused with values about justice and equality), they point out that all science is predicated on a set of values. A major issue between feminist and traditional science in psychology is the extent to which these values are visible and articulated or hidden and couched in the language of objectivity.

The resolution of issues such as remaining at the margin or moving to the center of the discipline is complicated by our diversity of interests and goals and by our plurality of identities and priorities. In psychology, as in all the social sciences, feminists subscribe to a wide range of beliefs. Despite media statements that attribute a unilateral position to "the feminists," we do not speak with one voice. As feminist psychologists, we also participate in a wide range of activities—as educators, researchers, health providers, administrators, entrepreneurs, authors, and community leaders—and we subscribe to many goals. Integration into mainstream psychology may be more important in some roles, for some issues, and for some psychologists than for others.

OPENING DOORS

Despite the ambivalence of their parent discipline, feminist psychologists have had major influences in many spheres. Among these are (1) opening innovative areas of research by asking new questions; (2) naming and renaming the problems; (3) challenging research methods and priorities; (4) revising approaches to therapeutic practice; (5) integrating multiple diversities; (6) applying research to public advocacy and legislative policies; and (7) transforming programs and institutions to render them more collaborative and woman friendly. I provide a few examples of these contributions in the following sections.

Asking new questions

The questions and hypotheses that drive the research process both frame the issues and determine our fund of knowledge. By asking questions about the lives of women that were never before considered, feminist psychologists have illuminated the hidden experiences and gender asymmetries that remained submerged and unexplored. For example, instead of asking about the effects of broken homes or the loss of masculinity of fatherless boys, feminist psychologists began to ask about the health and well-being of single mothers (Worell 1988). By reframing the research question to address the well-being of single parents, the focus moved to those environmental variables that affected their lives and their parenting opportunities, including poverty, isolation, and lack of social support.

In a similar vein, research on spouse abuse has been reframed from the question of "Why doesn't she just leave?" to those such as "Why do some men beat their wives and partners?" or "What are the barriers that keep her from leaving?" The new questions redirect focus from a woman's internal pathology (is she just masochistic, gaining pleasure from being hurt?) to the pathology of the system that keeps women imprisoned by fear and lack of resources. The questions raised by feminist psychologists have opened up entire areas of new research and knowledge about the lives of women and families. For the issues of single motherhood and spouse abuse, feminist research has been the source of public policies to intervene, remediate, and legislate.

Naming and renaming the problems

Until a problem or event is given a name or title, it remains unidentified and devoid of research. Although women have been exposed to sexual assault for centuries, feminists have shown that naming the problem exposes it to public examination. Two examples here are date rape (Koss et al. 1994) and sexual harassment (Fitzgerald 1993), neither of which existed until recently because no one had given them a name. At the present time, both of these topics have received extensive research attention, exposing the problems and documenting their prevalence. Feminist research on rape and sexual harassment again resulted in public demands for education, legislation, and prevention. Feminist psychologists have developed rape-prevention programs for presentation in schools and have lobbied for health services and legal resources to assist sexually assaulted girls and women.

Challenging research priorities

As in other social sciences, feminists in psychology introduced a whole new paradigm for conducting research. They challenged the notion that all research is objective and value free, declaring that personal and political values enter into all scholarly efforts. By changing the questions asked, by including girls and women as research participants, by including research subjects as participants in a collaborative enterprise, and by turning to qualitative methods that assessed women's lived experiences, feminists mined new territories in women's lives.

Although quantitative approaches to data collection remain strong in psychological research, the inclusion of qualitative methods enabled researchers to explore the individual experiences of women within the context of their lives. In contrast, traditional laboratory research tends to view the person outside of her community and cultural context and thus may ignore important variables that affect her responding. The debate in psychology around quantitative versus qualitative research is no longer an active one, however, as both approaches are recognized as relevant to the questions we ask. Of particular importance in feminist research, as in all feminist principles, is the ethic of social policy and advocacy for the well-being of women and families. Thus research is directed toward identifying, examining, and remediating social injustices and status inequities.

Revising therapeutic practice

The introduction of a new subfield of feminist therapy and counseling was a direct response to the sexism and bias that characterized both Freudian psychoanalysis and other more traditional therapies (Worell 1980). At the base of these theories were practices that assumed that the lives and experiences of men (the dominant male culture) and of middle-class heterosexual white women provided the standards for normal and desirable human behavior.

Feminist therapy grew from the earlier consciousness-raising groups that characterized the revised women's movement. In consciousness raising, small groups of women gathered informally to explore their lives and to identify their commonalities through an analysis of women's oppression and their subservient place in society. Discussions in consciousness-raising groups led to the theme that "the personal is political." This theme implies that women's personal distress is embedded in inequalities in the political, economic, legal, and social structures of society that disempower all women (Worell 2000).

Feminist therapists typically view women's symptoms as their best attempts at coping with pathological situations, rather than as reflecting pathology within the woman. Feminist therapists explore women's distress from the following perspectives:

1.   Attention is directed to the external sources of women's problems as well as women's internal conflicts. This position locates women's pathology in a social and political context.

2.   Power imbalances are acknowledged and egalitarian relationships are encouraged both within and outside of therapy. This position acknowledges women's lower social status with respect to men, as well as the power imbalances for minority women.

3.   Personal and social identities—with respect to gender, race, ethnicity, sexual orientation, social class, ablism, nationality, and so forth—are honored and explored.

4. By valuing women's perspectives, feminist therapists validate women's lived experiences, identify personal strengths, encourage self-care as well as caring for others, and encourage women to value themselves and one another (Enns 1997; Worell and Remer 1992).

The tenets of feminist therapy may be articulated differently across therapists who have particular training backgrounds and theoretical preferences. However, research on feminist, as compared to nonfeminist, therapists has clearly demonstrated that, as a group, they are more likely to adhere to the principles previously listed (Chandler et al. 1999). As a result, women (and some men) have received the kind of therapeutic experiences that are more likely to lead to personal and social empowerment. The goals of empowerment therapies are intended not only to alleviate symptoms of distress but also to strengthen individual well-being and the ability to cope in future stress situations with effective interpersonal and problem-solving skills.

*Applying research
to public advocacy*

Traditional psychology has tended to function within the ivory tower. That is, research was conducted for its own value as basic information about human behavior and the human condition. In contrast, feminist psychologists have promoted the principle of social activism and advocacy for underrepresented groups. Within this perspective, research that is socially relevant to the lives of

women and families is highly valued, in part because it is more likely to translate into policies that benefit women and that remedy injustices. Socially relevant psychological research has been effective in advocating for women's abortion rights, freedom from marital rape, financial support following divorce, programs to intervene with eating disorders, the rights of gay and lesbian parents, initiatives for funding women's health concerns, and many more issues of similar importance to women's well-being. In this advocacy role, feminist psychology has been influential in moving mainstream psychology toward adopting an activist stance.

CONTINUING CONTROVERSIES

Both established and innovative factions within any discipline are subject to ideological conflicts and internal disagreements. Within feminist psychology, at least three areas of concern elicit continuing dialogue and dissent: feminist psychology versus the psychology of women; essentialism versus social construction views; and the question of the appropriate locus of women's subordination and oppression, be it gender or the many other locations of women's personal and group identities.

*Feminist psychology versus
the psychology of women*

Many psychologists research and write about women and women's issues without identifying themselves as feminist. Although the issues may be surface or substantive, the division is real and has some direct implications. Taken to its extreme, the psychology of women could include popular women's magazines that offer advice on how to keep one's man or the pop psychology books that opine on why men hate women. In a more reasonable vein, the psychology of women implies the study of women, not men, and its focus avoids a blueprint for the inclusion of values, visions of science, or guideposts for activism. The study of women implies a focus on gender as difference (women from men), and the variations that exist between diverse groups of women become blurred or invisible.

Further, stripped of its feminist value orientation and activist stance, the psychology of women is little different from traditional psychology, with the addition of women as topics of study. Divested of its inclusive and activist positions, the study of women as targets remains static and stabilizes the field with entrenched positions that isolate the individual from her social and political contexts.

Identification with feminist psychology, in contrast, may place the researcher or scholar at risk of isolation, lower status in the academic community, exclusion from mainstream journals, and marginalization within her own profession (Worell 1994). For some psychologists, the risk seems too great. But a recent study of 77 randomly selected feminist psychology professors across a range of colleges and universities found that feminism was protective for them in the face of academic gender discrimination.

"Rather than making it hard for women to swim in academic waters, feminism seemed to serve as a life raft for many professors" (Klonis et al. 1997, 333). Although 97 percent of these women said they had experienced gender discrimination, they found that feminism provided them with the tools to defend against the negative effects of such discrimination. Over half of the respondents said that their feminist commitment helped them to frame the issues and to join with others to combat the problems. Thus they may have been better equipped to recognize that negative social judgments were a function of sexism rather than of their own shortcomings. These considerations of how feminism will impede or assist in one's career confront each scholar who desires to pursue a profession in either the psychology of women or feminist psychology.

Essentialism versus social constructionism

Two distinct and contrasting views permeate the feminist community. On the one hand, those who subscribe to an essentialist view take the position that women's development is uniquely different from that of men, resulting in women's being intrinsically more caring and relational than men. Women are not only different from men; they are much better human beings than men because women care for others rather than being invested only in themselves (Gilligan 1982). These qualities enable women to achieve greater mutuality and intimacy in relationships.

A social construction view of gender, in contrast, takes the position that the true natures of women and men are unknowable. The characteristics that we attribute to females and males are not intrinsic to the individual and determined by biological sex but are socially and situationally created. Differences across females and males are socially constructed categories that function to maintain female-male dichotomies and unequal power relations (Hare-Mustin and Marecek 1988). These social categories then become internalized as gendered self-concepts that organize both individual life activities and goals and the expectations of those with whom we interact.

The contrast between these two views of gendered relations is observed most clearly in their applications to practice. Some feminist therapists, for example, adhere to an essentialist position, while most gender researchers adopt a social construction point of view. However, a new area of research, evolutionary psychology, has adopted an essentialist position as well. Evolutionary theorists declare that differences between women and men are based on principals of survival of the fittest, such that male dominance and female relationship concerns are biologically determined. Needless to add, feminist psychologists do not take kindly to this position.

Gender versus diversity in women's oppression

The third major controversy in current feminist psychology involves the appropriate location of women's oppression. Feminist psychology was originally developed by white middle-class psychologists and is believed by some factions to reflect the privileged majority perspective that gender is the major site of unequal power relations. During the first two decades of feminist scholarship in psychology, women's subordination was attributed to patriarchy, or male-dominated social structures. The generic woman was compared to the generic man, with little distinction being attributed to social locations other than gender.

The feminist position of women of color was particularly influential in bringing into focus the diversity among women. In assuming the ethic of universal sisterhood, early feminists ignored the differing life experiences of women from diverse ethnic, racial, national, and multicultural backgrounds (Comas-Diaz and Greene 1994). The insistence of multicultural feminism on attention to the diversity of women's experiences spurred new areas of scholarship and research on the pluralism in women's social and personal identities. The issue of white privilege entered the dialogue and provided another dimension of discourse; the discussion of which group constitutes the real minority became prominent. For many women of color, the dichotomy of gender as female-male presented them with conflicting loyalties in which solidarity with their racial or ethnic group often takes priority over gender. Being asked to view men as the source of women's oppression denied their sense of loyalty to their community and support networks. On the other hand, "women of color are exposed to oppression not only within the dominant group, but also experience sexism and oppression within their own ethnic and racial communities as well" (Comas-Diaz and Greene 1994, 5). Thus issues of equity and power imbalance do not necessarily disappear within minority communities.

These multiple considerations of the social location of women's oppression also lead to research on discrimination based on physical appearance; ablism or disability; and social class and the situation of poor women and their families. However, there remains an undercurrent of disagreement across the community of feminist psychologists concerning which of these presumed disadvantages are most oppressive to women.

THE FUTURE OF FEMINIST PSYCHOLOGY

Where is feminist psychology headed in the next decade and beyond? The issues discussed in this article will probably not disappear. Feminist psychologists will continue their internal dialogue and differences with respect to theory, research, and appropriate modes of practice. Mainstream psychology may not be eager to welcome the dissident voices that challenge its supremacy. I believe that controversy and conflict concerning many issues have the potential to open new avenues of scholarship and research. Although many of us experience this conflict as painful, it can also lead to constructive alternatives and innovative approaches. However, feminist scholarship has permeated substantive areas of psychological research and knowledge. Feminist activism has promoted new structures within psychological associations, a substantive increase in the number of women in governance and leadership in the field, and scholarly publications that enrich and expand our psychological perspectives.

The creation of new structures within organized psychology that focus on women has affected the field in multiple ways. Institutionalized groups within psychology devoted to women's concerns have been successful in making women's issues visible and thus in attracting more women to join and become active in such groups. Within these groups, women have developed a network of support, a group of colleagues with whom to conduct research, and an advocacy group with which to lobby for resources and political strength. Within the American Psychological Association, which has a membership of over 160,000, the Society for the Psychology of Women is now the fifth-largest in membership of the 55 divisions of the organization. Women's groups within the American Psychological Association have lobbied for research resources, have promoted agendas and policies that focus on women's health and well-being, and have promoted the election of women to outstanding leadership positions. The incoming president of this organization, Norine Johnson, is a feminist psychologist whose leadership agenda will certainly reflect her feminist commitment. Likewise, feminist psychologists have achieved important leadership positions in university psychology departments and as presidents and provosts of leading universities. Although these very visible individuals may not publicly promote their feminist beliefs, their policies and actions reflect their commitment.

As feminist scholars, we envision a discipline that is open to change, that values and promotes equality and social justice across groups and individuals, and that is active in its insistence on public advocacy for the well-being of both women and men from all groups. It is too early in this process to determine whether we have witnessed a revolution in the field or the evolution of a new field of psychology that integrates the principles of feminism into all of its core functioning. We do know that feminist psychologists have opened doors that will not easily be closed.

References

Bem, Sandra. 1974. The Measurement of Psychological Androgyny. *Journal of Personality and Social Psychology* 42:155-62.

Brabeck, Mary and Laura Brown. 1997. Feminist Theory and Psychological Practice. In *Shaping the Future of Feminist Psychology: Education, Research, and Practice*, ed. Judith Worell and Norine Johnson. Washington, DC: American Psychological Association.

Broverman, Inge K., D. Broverman, F. E. Clarkson, P. S. Rosenkrantz, and S. R. Vogel. 1970. Sex-Role Stereotypes and Clinical Judgments of Mental Health. *Journal of Consulting and Clinical Psychology* 34:1-7.

Chandler, Redonna, J. Worell, D. Johnson, and A. Blount. 1999. Measuring Short and Long-Term Outcomes of Feminist Therapy. Paper presented at the annual meeting of the American Psychological Association, Aug., Boston.

Chesler, Phyllis. 1972. *Women and Madness*. New York: Doubleday.

Comas-Diaz, Lillian. 1991. Feminism and Diversity in Psychology: The Case of Women of Color. *Psychology of Women Quarterly* 15:594-610.

Comas-Diaz, Lillian and Beverly Greene, eds. 1994. *Women of Color: Integrating Ethnic and Gender Identities in Psychotherapy*. New York: Guilford.

Crawford, Mary and Jean Marecek. 1989. Psychology Constructs the Female. *Psychology of Women Quarterly* 13:147-66.

Eagley, Alice H. and B. T. Johnson. 1990. Gender and Leadership: A Meta-Analysis. *Psychological Bulletin* 108:233-56.

Enns, Carolyn Zerbe. 1997. *Feminist Theories and Feminist Psychotherapies: Origins, Themes, and Variations*. New York: Harrington Park.

Fitzgerald, Louise F. 1993. *The Last Great Secret: The Sexual Harassment of Women in the Workplace and Academia*. Washington, DC: Federation of Behavioral, Cognitive, and Psychological Sciences.

Gilligan, Carol. 1982. *In a Different Voice: Psychological Theory and Women's Development*. Cambridge, MA: Harvard University Press.

Greene, Beverly and Janice Sanchez-Hucles. 1997. Diversity: Advancing an Inclusive Feminist Psychology. In *Shaping the Future of Feminist Psychology: Education, Research, and Practice*, ed. Judith Worell and Norine Johnson. Washington, DC: American Psychological Association.

Grossman, Frances K., L. Gilbert, N. P. Genero, S. E. Hawes, J. S. Hyde, and J. Marecek. 1997. Feminist Research: Practice and Problems. In *Shaping the Future of Feminist Psychology: Educa-*

tion, Research, and Practice, ed. Judith Worell and Norine Johnson. Washington, DC: American Psychological Association.

Hare-Mustin, Rachel T. and Jean Marecek. 1988. The Meaning of Difference: Gender Theory, Post-Modernism, and Psychology. *American Psychologist* 43:3-16.

Kimmel, Ellen and Judith Worell. 1997. Preaching What We Practice: Principles and Strategies of Feminist Pedagogy. In *Shaping the Future of Feminist Psychology: Education, Research, and Practice*, ed. Judith Worell and Norine Johnson. Washington, DC: American Psychological Association.

Klonis, Suzanne, J. Endo, F. Crosby, and J. Worell. 1997. Feminism as Life Raft. *Psychology of Women Quarterly* 21:333-46.

Koss, Mary P., L. A. Goodman, A. Browne, L. F. Fitzgerald, G. P. Keita, and N. F. Russo. 1994. *No Safe Haven: Male Violence Against Women at Home, at Work, and in the Community*. Washington, DC: American Psychological Association.

Landrine, Hope, ed. 1995. *Bringing Cultural Diversity to Feminist Psychology: Theory, Research, and Practice*. Washington, DC: American Psychological Association.

Mednick, Martha T. and Laura L. Urbanski. 1991. The Origins and Activities of APA's Division of the Psychology of Women. *Psychology of Women Quarterly* 15:651-64.

Rave, Elizabeth J. and Carolyn C. Larson, eds. 1995. *Ethical Decision Making in Therapy: Feminist Perspectives*. New York: Guilford.

Rosewater, Lillian B. and Lenore Walker, eds. 1985. *Handbook of Feminist Therapy: Women's Issues in Psychotherapy*. New York: Springer.

Scarborough, Elizabeth and Laura Furamoto. 1987. *Untold Lives: The First Generation of American Women Psychologists*. New York: Columbia University Press.

Weisstein, Naomi. 1968. *Kinder, Kirche, Kuche as Scientific Law: Psychology Constructs the Female*. Boston: New England Free Press.

Worell, Judith. 1978. Sex Roles and Psychological Well-Being: Perspectives on Methodology. *Journal of Consulting and Clinical Psychology* 46:777-91.

———. 1980. New Directions in Counseling Women. *Personnel and Guidance Journal* 58:477-84.

———. 1988. Single Mothers: From Problems to Policies. *Women and Therapy* 7:3-14.

———. 1994. Feminist Publication: Academic Empowerment or Professional Liability? In *Gender and Academe: Feminist Pedagogy and Politics*, ed. S. M. Deats and L. T. Lenker. New York: Routledge & Kegan Paul.

———. 2000. Feminist Therapy. In *Encyclopedia of Psychology*, ed. Alan Kazdin. Washington, DC: American Psychological Association.

Worell, Judith and Claire Etaugh. 1994. Transforming Theory and Research with Women: Themes and Variations. *Psychology of Women Quarterly* 18:433-40.

Worell, Judith and Norine Johnson, eds. 1997. *Shaping the Future of Feminist Psychology: Education, Research, and Practice*. Washington, DC: American Psychological Association.

Worell, Judith and Pam Remer. 1992. *Feminist Perspectives in Therapy: An Empowerment Model for Women*. Chichester: John Wiley.

Wyatt, Gail and Monika H. Riederle. 1994. Reconceptualizing Issues That Affect Women's Sexual Decision-Making and Sexual Functioning. *Psychology of Women Quarterly* 18:11-26.

Report of the Board of Directors to the Members of the American Academy of Political and Social Science for the Year 1999

MEMBERSHIPS AND SUBSCRIPTIONS
AS OF DECEMBER 31

1989	4,903
1990	3,932
1991	4,378
1992	3,639
1993	3,472
1994	3,661
1995	3,455
1996	3,141
1997	3,124
1998	3,306
1999	2,671

PUBLICATIONS
NUMBER OF VOLUMES OF *THE ANNALS* PRINTED
(6 PER YEAR)

1989	40,269
1990	39,000
1991	37,246
1992	34,900
1993	31,000
1994	29,000
1995	28,200
1996	29,900
1997	29,909
1998	26,200
1999	26,187

FINANCES
SIZE OF SECURITIES PORTFOLIO
MARKET VALUE AS OF DECEMBER 31

1989	284,732
1990	139,451
1991	164,537
1992	150,560
1993	161,117
1994	124,644
1995	157,103
1996	180,754
1997	204,578
1998	227,067
1999	255,716

NUMBER OF VOLUMES OF *THE ANNALS* SOLD
(IN ADDITION TO MEMBERSHIPS
AND SUBSCRIPTIONS)

1989	4,802
1990	5,005
1991	3,766
1992	3,681
1993	3,538
1994	2,344
1995	2,449
1996	2,795
1997	2,372
1998	2,303
1999	2,567

STATEMENT OF ACTIVITIES FOR THE YEAR
ENDED DECEMBER 31, 1999

Revenues, gains, and other support

Royalty—Sage Publications	$225,232
Royalties and reprint permissions	746
Sales of review books	675
Rents	17,856
Grant income	9,999
Contributions	1,000
Interest income	8,630
Net gain (loss) from investments	6,900
Miscellaneous	(13,069)
Total revenues	261,296

Expenses and losses

Program	97,416
Administrative	93,956
Total expenses and losses	191,381
Change in net assets	69,915
Net assets—January 1	212,333
Net assets—December 31	282,248

Report of the Board of Directors

During 1999, the six volumes of THE ANNALS dealt with the following subjects:

January   *Emotional Labor in the Service Economy*, edited by Ronnie J. Steinberg, Professor and Director, Women's Studies Program at Vanderbilt University, Nashville, Tennessee, and Deborah M. Figart, Associate Professor, Richard Stockton College, Pomona, New Jersey

March   *The Evolving World of Work and Family: New Stakeholders, New Voices*, edited by Marcie Pitt-Catsouphes, Director, Center for Work & Family, Boston College, Chestnut Hill, Massachusetts, and Bradley K. Googins, Director, Center for Corporate Community Relations, Boston College, Chestnut Hill, Massachusetts

May   *The Silent Crisis in U.S. Child Care*, edited by Suzanne W. Helburn, Professor, University of Colorado, Denver

July   *Will the Juvenile Court System Survive?* edited by Ira M. Schwartz, Dean, School of Social Work, University of Pennsylvania, Philadelphia

September   *Civil Society and Democratization*, edited by Isidro Morales, Chairman, Department of International Relations and History, Universidad de las Américas–Puebla, Cholula, Mexico; Guillermo De Los Reyes, Ph.D. candidate, University of Pennsylvania, Philadelphia; and Paul Rich, Titular Professor of International Relations and History, Universidad de las Americas–Puebla, Cholula, Mexico, and Fellow, Hoover Institution, Stanford University, California

November   *The Social Diffusion of Ideas and Things*, edited by Paul Lopes, Assistant Professor and Director, Communications and Media Studies Program, Tufts University, Medford, Massachusetts, and Mary Durfee, Associate Professor, Michigan Technological University, Houghton

The publication program for 2000 includes the following volumes:

January   *School Violence*, edited by William G. Hinkle, Assistant Professor, Valparaiso University, Indiana, and Stuart Henry, Director, Interdisciplinary Studies Program, College of Lifelong Learning, Wayne State University, Detroit, Michigan

March   *The Study of African American Problems: W.E.B. Du Bois's Agenda, Then and Now*, edited by Elijah Anderson, Charles and William L. Day Professor of the Social Sciences, University of Pennsylvania, Philadelphia, and Tukufu Zuberi, Associate Professor and Director of African Studies, University of Pennsylvania, Philadelphia

May   *The African American Male in American Life and Thought*, edited by Jacob U. Gordon, Professor, University of Kansas, Lawrence

July   *Dimensions of Globalization*, edited by Louis Ferleger, Professor, Boston University, Massachusetts, and Jay R. Mandle, W. Bradford Wiley Professor of Economics, Colgate University, Hamilton, New York

September   *Feminist Views of the Social Sciences*, edited by Christine L. Williams, Professor, University of Texas, Austin

November   *Presidential Campaigns: Sins of Omission*, edited by Kathleen Hall Jamieson, Dean, Annenberg School for Communication, and Director, Annenberg Public Policy Center, University of Pennsylvania, Philadelphia, and Matthew Miller, syndicated columnist and Senior Fellow, Annenberg Public Policy Center, University of Pennsylvania, Philadelphia

During 1999, the Book Department published 132 reviews. The majority of these were written by professors, but reviewers also included university presidents, members of private and university-sponsored organizations, government and public officials, and business professionals. More than 426 books were listed in the Other Books section.

Two hundred forty-nine requests were granted to reprint material from THE ANNALS. These went to professors and other authors for use in books in preparation and to nonprofit organizations for educational purposes.

OFFICERS AND STAFF

The Board elected the following officer: Jaroslav Pelikan, President. It reelected the following officers: Frederick Heldring, Treasurer; Mary Ann Meyers, Secretary.

Respectfully submitted,
THE BOARD OF DIRECTORS

Elijah Anderson
Lynn A. Curtis
Frederick Heldring
Kathleen Hall Jamieson
Richard D. Lambert
Sara Miller McCune
Mary Ann Meyers
Jaroslav Pelikan
Lawrence W. Sherman

Philadelphia, Pennsylvania
28 October 1999

Book Department

INTERNATIONAL RELATIONS AND POLITICS

CALLAN, EAMONN. 1997. *Creating Citizens: Political Education and Liberal Democracy.* Pp. x, 262. Oxford: Clarendon Press. $29.95.

Callan argues that the common schools should be responsible for providing a politically cohesive citizenry within the context of a pluralistic liberal society, and he examines the virtues and policies required to advance this responsibility.

A school is common, according to Callan, if it welcomes students without regard to factors (such as race, social class, religion, or first language) that tend to polarize people within the body politic. A school that discriminates along these lines, whether supported by public funds or not, is a separate school. This distinction is most important given that one of the critical questions in many countries is whether public funds should be used to support separate schools.

In an important chapter, Callan allows for exceptional circumstances in which support for separate schools is acceptable educational policy, especially in the case of some endangered minority cultures. However, while sympathetic to some claims for public support for separate education—namely, those cases that can be justified as a necessary prelude to the development of liberal virtues—Callan is reluctant to accept claims for such support based on parental rights, arguing that there can be no right where the burden of duties placed on others is so great that it cannot be justified. He would not, however, disallow such support in those (few) cases where a strong common-good argument could be made in favor of it.

His conclusion here is reasonable, but his argument is difficult to follow because it short-circuits important considerations. Take the following reason for rejecting rights-based separate education: "Judgment about the duties a [claimed] right [to separate schooling] imposes must be conducted with a keen eye to . . . the wider context of human good and bad in general." Because he believes those duties would be so onerous, he allows that there is no such right. Having rested a right on the duties it creates and having determined that the judgment on whether something is a right will require an assessment of the human good and bad it creates, he rejects the right to a separate school. Yet on the next page he notes that successful arguments might be made not on the basis of rights but on the basis of "the collective pursuit of the common good." The murky distinction between "human good and bad" on the one hand and "collective pursuit of the common good" on the other weakens his argument.

The argument might have worked if Callan had elaborated the reasons why we tax some individuals to advance the education of other people's children. These reasons would include intergroup respect, economic growth, political stability, and individual autonomy. Schools that are publicly funded need to be accountable to public bodies and publicly defined standards of these goods. It is not only questionable whether many separate schools would adhere to all of these standards (such as intergroup respect and individual autonomy); it is also questionable whether separate schools would welcome accountability to publicly defined standards in these areas.

Callan might have also addressed the question of state regulation of separate schools that do not enjoy public support. Does the state have any role in regulating the content of instruction in these schools? How much autonomy should financial independence be allowed to buy? While it would have been useful for Callan to address these issues, these gaps should not be allowed to minimize the excellent contribution that Callan has made to both educational philosophy and political theory. His discussions of education and patriotism, of parental and child sovereignty, and of the different forms of classroom dialogue are all carefully argued, penetrating, and important. The book is must reading for all educational philosophers and for political theorists with an interest in educational issues.

WALTER FEINBERG

University of Illinois
Urbana

CANOVAN, MARGARET. 1996. *Nationhood and Political Theory*. Pp. vii, 159. Lyme, NH: Edward Elgar. $75.00.

Previously underrepresented in the discipline of political science, the study of ethnicity, nations, and nationalism has accelerated in the 1990s. Indeed, it "should actually be at the heart of the discipline," argues Margaret Canovan in this short, lucid volume in which she surveys recent work and presents an incisive argument of her own.

Nationalism is an area where extensive empirical and historical studies (usually inconclusive from an explanatory point of view) overlap with a rather thin and equally unsatisfactory body of normative theory: is the defense of nations, national borders, and national identities justifiable? Canovan is a theorist who presents one of the stronger defenses of nations in the recent literature. Her theme is "nationhood" rather than often-destructive "nationalism" or the often-scorned idea of "national self-determination," although the distinction here is more verbal than real. Nationhood, when it exists or can be achieved, constitutes a desirable or perhaps even necessary basis for stable states, and hence its protection through nationally oriented policies is warranted. Like other analysts, Canovan wrestles somewhat inconclusively with the problem of defining a nation. There is no single necessary or sufficient criterion, although she leans more toward a cultural and subjectivist conception, downplaying ethnicity (hence she takes the United States to be, unproblematically, a nation). She also rejects essentialist or naturalist theories; nations are artificial entities, politically constructed; their peculiarity, as Burke (she notes) grasped, is that they are artifices that, through habit and other factors, feel natural to the people who are members of them.

Much recent political philosophy, Canovan notes, has been concerned with debates about liberal democracy—with rights, freedom, and social justice. These concepts have been pursued in an abstract and universalistic manner; their attainment, however, requires the existence of stable, cohesive, and bounded political communities within which members are prepared to acknowledge special obligations to one another. Recent arguments about community, however, have been similarly abstract, frequently focusing on communal sources of the self and personal identity. Canovan refreshingly espouses a more realistic and more political approach: in the real world, she argues, it is nationhood that provides the necessary underlying cohesion and loyalties on which even liberal states must rest. The actual practice of rights, freedom, and social justice thus presupposes nationhood; and those who theorize about these matters should face up to this reality on pain of indulging in utopian exercises.

Nationhood not only offers the communal foundation for ethical projects; it also, writes Canovan with Arendtian overtones, generates power by organizing people for concerted action. As a self-proclaimed realist, Canovan thinks political theorists should recognize the "messily Machiavellian reality" of the world, including the realities of territorial conflicts and border controls that national politics involve. It is not just that people need power to defend themselves and their interests. Even "general humanitarian principles and projects presuppose a power base sustained by particular solidarity." Indeed, even liberal rights and justice require a basis in collective power (just as they were created historically by state power), although liberal philosophers do not always keep this point in view.

These are challenging claims that need to be attended to. A tentative suggestion, however, would be that Canovan's realism does not go far enough in dealing with the problems her position entails. She grants that the nations underlying contemporary Western liberal states were created in the past, often by state policies that would not pass muster with today's norms: liberals have "Machiavellian skeletons" in their closets. How then does one build nations today where they do not exist,

constrained as we are by liberal principles (human rights) and when people are mobilized for democracy? How does one achieve relatively benign nationhood without the excesses of nationalism? How does one promote viable nations without encouraging disintegrative subnational ethnic assertiveness? When she mentions such problems (in chapter 9), Canovan's tone seems pessimistic with respect to peoples who are not so fortunate as to have nationhood already.

FREDERICK G. WHELAN

University of Pittsburgh
Pennsylvania

CRUZ, JOSÉ E. 1998. *Identity and Power: Puerto Rican Politics and the Challenge of Ethnicity*. Pp. xiv, 278. Philadelphia: Temple University Press. $59.95. Paperbound, $22.95.

On the surface, this book might seem as though it were focused simply on a Latino population in a mid-sized city in a small Eastern state. That would be a pity because it is a most interesting study of ethnicity, politics, and the intricacies of how a relatively new population in an urban center strives to acquire political representation and—via that representation—a measure of political power. This is the type of story that I do not doubt has been played out in many cities across the nation, especially given the number of new immigrant groups. Moreover, this book, a revised dissertation, rests on 50 interviews conducted by the author, many with the key players in this four-decade evolution of the Puerto Ricans' political presence in Hartford, Connecticut.

The first principal issue centers on how a group develops a sense of ethnic identity and then employs that identity in a bid for political representation. A second concerns the impact of situational variables both within the ethnic community and within the larger societal context, including the political structure of the city government, the evolving economic characteristics of the city, and the presence of previously existing political organizations and potentially competing ethnic groups. A third involves the potentially divisive consequences of in-fighting and personality clashes within the ethnic group's emerging political forces. A fourth and perhaps most critical one—upon which rest the key theses of this book—is the distinction between identity politics and the actual mastery of political power once representation has been achieved. Cruz frequently distinguishes between the capability of a group to exercise political power and the actual feasibility of doing so given the contextual limitations (namely, the political realities). The fifth issue in this carefully crafted analysis is a conclusion not about lessons learned and a necessarily happy ending but about lessons not learned quickly enough by a group relatively new to democratic politics and the lost opportunities to deliver on promises made to the voters. Finally, acknowledged but not delved into is the remarkable number of women who played key roles in Hartford's first generation of Puerto Rican political activists.

Cruz traces the arrival of Puerto Ricans as temporary agricultural workers; the growth of their communities to the north and south of downtown Hartford at the same time that economic changes alter the employment situation and generate white flight; the significant history of organizational efforts by Puerto Ricans well antedating their actual political mobilization; the specific episodes that triggered political action, beginning with several riots in the summer and fall of 1969; the political fragmentation of the community and its inescapable reliance on the political brokering of the deputy mayor, Nicholas Carbone, during the 1970s; the emergence of leaders willing to challenge the status quo and the successful election of Puerto Ricans to the Hartford City Council; the instrumental role of the Puerto Rican Political Action Committee in helping a number of men and women to win elections (culminating in Yolanda Castillo's selection as majority leader of the City Council in 1992 and Eugenio Caro's as deputy mayor in 1994); and the failure of the political action committee to build upon its election successes by both maintaining the loyalty of those it helped elect and developing the essential coalition politics and mastery of policy implementation. Cruz concludes that identity politics are necessarily conditional and that mobilizing an ethnic community to political action is no guarantee that those elected will know how to deliver what the voters hoped to see forthcoming.

ELLIOTT R. BARKAN

California State University
San Bernardino

FIELD, LESTER L., JR. 1998. *Liberty, Dominion, and the Two Swords: On the Origins of Western Political Theology (180-398)*. Pp. xviii, 542. Notre Dame, IN: University of Notre Dame Press.

This extraordinarily well documented book traces the origins and development in the Latin-speaking Roman Empire in the West of the relationship of church and state from the appearance in 180 of the oldest surviving Latin Christian text, the *Acts of the Scilitan Martyrs*, to the last of the letters of Pope Siricius in 398. In particular, Field stresses the difference between the Latin West, which was dominated by apocalyptic dualism, and the Greek East, where Pauline monism prevailed. Freedom, as seen especially in martyrdom, meant complete submission to the dominion of the Church. Political authority consisted of two principles, symbolized by two swords, reducible only in the figure of Christ, who was both king and priest. What the Church had not rendered to Caesar when the emperor was outside the Church a Christian Caesar had to render to God, since Caesar could not serve two masters.

And yet, as Field is careful to note, there was definite continuity between the pagan empire and the Christian empire, so that "pious" Christian emperors continued to allow or even to request the Senate to deify their deceased predecessors. As late as the fifth century, there was no real difference between the laws regarding protection of private property drafted by Christian quaestors and those promulgated by pagans.

A theme running through this book is that unlike the pagan Roman empire and unlike the Christian Roman Empire in the East, with its Caesaropapistic identification of church and state, religion and state were separate concepts in the West, so that one major difference between Christianity and Judaism in the West, we may add, is that Christianity is the first religion in history that, at least in theory, does not have an intrinsic political dimension to it. On the other hand, it is surely significant that it was an emperor in the East, Constantine, who called the Council of Nicaea and who himself suggested the Creed's *homoousios* doctrine with regard to the relationship of God and Jesus.

Field notes that, as a corollary, the enormously influential Tertullian (ca. 200) states categorically that as a Christian he has "seceded from the people," that he cannot serve as a soldier or participate in the state, that his only care is that he should not care, and that his only business is with himself. Christians thus were to look upon themselves as foreigners in the world. In theory, at least, this would seem to support Gibbon's famous charge that Christianity was largely responsible for the fall of the Roman empire. The fact that Pope Damasus I (366-84) praised Christian soldiers who courted martyrdom by throwing away their arms would appear to support this conclusion. On the other hand, the survival of the empire in the East, we may suggest, may well be connected with the Caesaropapism that prevailed there. But, as Field notes, Tertullian himself alludes to a considerable Christian presence in the army; nevertheless, Field remarks that Christians from the East were more numerous in the army than those from the West, but, we may suggest, this was probably due to the fact that the population of the East generally was considerably greater than that of the West, and the number of Christians there was certainly greater.

Field insightfully notes that, in the Latin West, Christian liberty tended to be more legalistic, apocalyptic, and militant than its Greek counterpart, presumably, we may suggest, under the influence of the great jurists—Papinian, Paulus, Ulpian, and Modestinus—all of whom wrote in Latin in the third century during the formative years of the Patristic tradition. As for the doctrine of the two swords in the Latin West, Field appositely quotes Jerome: "Caesars' laws are one thing, Christ's another; Papinian orders one thing, our Paul another."

LOUIS H. FELDMAN

Yeshiva University
New York City

HERZOG, DON. 1998. *Poisoning the Minds of the Lower Orders.* Pp. xvi, 559. Princeton, NJ: Princeton University Press. $29.95.

Don Herzog has steeped himself in the literature, memoirs, and journals of the four decades following 1789 and has a gift for the telling quotation. Herzog also has some important points to make. Recently, interest has revived in theories of civil society and in the dialogic encounters alleged to occur therein. Although hardly responsible for all the crimes perpetrated in its name, Jürgen Habermas is the name most often associated with theories of civil society. No one who reads Herzog can look at Habermasian visions of eighteenth-century civil society quite so innocently as before.

Herzog is most interested in the social barriers to dialogue. He looks at the ways in which forces internal to civil society restrict or avoid dialogic encounters. Starting with another look at that key shaper of the modern conservative mind, Edmund Burke, Herzog shows the importance Burke placed on keeping the great majority of the population from thinking about politics. Better for them to accept patently false assumptions about the political order than to think for themselves. Those who portray Thomas Paine and Edmund Burke as engaged in a debate miss the point entirely. The very idea of a debate between an experienced political leader occupying a high place in the social hierarchy and an upstart staymaker outside the established political order was fundamentally antithetical to Burkean conservativism. Paine was answered with contempt, not with measured argument. The beauty of contempt was its unanswerability; efforts on the part of those held in contempt to respond were tainted by their very disrepute. Even the most eloquent response only validated the views of their condemners; women who articulately rejected subordination compounded their inferiority with aberrance and were scorned as "unfeminine."

The use of contempt to terminate dialogue is really Herzog's grand theme, and he illustrates how it was used, by political radicals as well as by conservatives, to justify the subordinate position of workers, blacks, women, and Jews in early-nineteenth-century England. Contempt took many forms, from the vicious (for example, an incitement to violence) to the amiable (such as a form of affectionate condescension). Hairdressers are examined as especially interesting objects of contempt. Herzog explores the coffeehouses and pubs in which artisanal radicals discussed politics and shows the significance of aristocratic and elitist commentators' claims that cafés and pubs were environments incapable of reasoned criticism. Thus the very institutions necessary to the articulation of dissent were used to discredit it.

Unfortunately, Herzog's break with Habermas is incomplete. His whole discussion takes place in that vague and amorphous medium, "Frankfurt School Time." He identifies his study as examining the English response to the French Revolution and ranging from 1789 to 1832 without much attention to distinguish the early 1790s from the first decade of the 1800s or the 1820s. According to Herzog, responding to a strangely timeless and undifferentiated entity, the French Revolution, was pretty much the focus of British political debate. The Terror, the Napoleonic Wars, the Industrial Revolution, Catholic Emancipation, and the Reform Bill appear but have little consequence for understanding Conservatives' or Radicals' responses. Herzog never considers whether some groups, such as dissenters or merchants, who won significant power in the period became less contemptible as a result.

Unfortunately, this book suffers from a lack systematic exposition and is far too long. The first and last chapters of the book are worth reading, and the chapters on groups held in particular contempt can be trolled for juicy quotations. In an effort to capture subtle distinctions, Herzog loses sight of the overall picture.

MICHAEL HANAGAN

New School for Social Research
New York City

SADOWSKI, YAHYA. 1998. *The Myth of Global Chaos*. Pp. xix, 267. Washington, DC: Brookings Institution Press. $28.95.

In this lively and thoughtful work, Yahya Sadowski, of the Johns Hopkins School of Advanced International Studies, takes on the prophets of global gloom who became so fashionable in the 1990s.

The book begins with a long and respectful, almost too respectful, exegesis of the views of the main chaos theorists. Among these are Robert Kaplan, whose *Balkan Ghosts* seems to have been used conveniently to excuse Western inaction in the former Yugoslavia by putting forth the attractively simplistic notion that the conflicts there were, after all, merely the continuation of ancient ethnic hatreds that would go on forever no matter what outsiders did. Sadowski also deals with Samuel Huntington's *Clash of Civilizations* thesis, which has inspired much comment and outrage but, he suggests, has had little policy consequence with its "West versus the rest" prescriptions. Also considered are various globalization gloomsters who postulate that the expansion of the international economy will disrupt traditions and bring on cultural disorientation, anomie, and violent resistance.

Sadowski applies some crude (or, in his term, "back of the envelope") statistical analyses to develop a different worldview. He finds that cultural conflicts did not become notably more frequent after the Cold War—there had been plenty before and most were not new but simply continuations of previous conflicts. Moreover, the lethality of such strife did not increase.

What seems to have changed in the early 1990s was that some of these conflicts became more visible because they no longer had to compete for attention with Cold War concerns and because some of them took place in Europe. Thus, to a substantial degree, he convincingly demonstrates, clashists and chaosites have been misguidedly generalizing from a special, and quite possibly temporary, phenomenon. Most notably, they have extrapolated from the various disasters in the former Yugoslavia, but these, Sadowski ably argues, have stemmed less from traditional ethnic quarrels than from the maneuverings of calculating (if often foolish) politicians, organized militaries, and booty-seeking thugs and criminals.

In grappling with this phenomenon, which, he thinks, hardly furnishes a strategic threat, Sadowski concludes that the world has become not more chaotic but more complex because the West could neglect local ethnic and cultural concerns during the Cold War to focus on the comparatively easily understood international ideological conflict. But, clearly, this should mean that the world has become less complex, not more so. In the old days, there were both local and Cold War problems to consider. Although local complexities may have been ignored, that scarcely means they did not exist.

To deal with these residual complexities, Sadowski puts quite a bit of hope on economic advancement since he finds that, although cultural strife is found about as much in developed countries as in poorer ones, it is less likely to turn violent in prosperous societies. In this he may be too much of a economic determinist and, to that degree, too much of a pessimist. The actions of leading politicians and police organizations seem to be most important in keeping ethnic and cultural conflict from erupting into major violence. Prosperous societies do seem to do better in this regard, but wealth is not necessarily required.

For example, because of sound political policies, ethnic violence has been avoided in Bulgaria even though that country is hardly more developed than Serbia or Bosnia. Moreover, far from being inevitable, as chaos theorists essentially suggest, the disasters in Yugoslavia could almost certainly have been avoided if politicians and police had behaved in a more sensible manner—as Sadowski himself notes. Putting it another way, it is entirely possible to imagine Bosnian-like chaos in prosperous Quebec or Northern Ireland if the Canadian or British authorities, like their Yugoslav counterparts, had attempted to deal with those cultural conflicts through murderous rampage rather than through patient policing and political accommodation.

Chaotic behavior is more nearly a conscious human creation than a cosmic necessity. This book helps greatly to put it in appropriate perspective.

JOHN MUELLER

University of Rochester
New York

WILLIAMS, MELISSA S. 1998. *Voice, Trust, and Memory: Marginalized Groups and the Failings of Liberal Representation*. Pp. vii, 321. Princeton, NJ: Princeton University Press. $35.00.

The American political system, for very practical reasons, is not a pure democracy but an indirect one. Americans participate in government by selecting others to make decisions for them. How the government actually represents and does the people's bidding is an important question. In addition to designing a government with limited powers, the framers of the Constitution sought to ensure government-by-the-people or popular sovereignty through elections. Because they granted only two-year terms to legislators in the House of Representatives, the latter could be quickly replaced if they failed to live up to constituent expectations. In addition to regularly scheduled elections, there was the presumption that elected officials could be trusted to represent the people because government would be drawn from the ranks of the people. A perfectly representative body would be similar to the general population in race, sex, ethnicity, occupation, religion, and other fundamental social characteristics. Through the possession of social characteristics similar to their constituents, representatives could be counted upon to share their political beliefs and interests.

As methods of preserving popular sovereignty, these propositions have their shortcomings. Winning an election to the U.S. House of Representatives now usually requires at least half a million dollars, and generally those who spend the most win most often. There are now scholars who worry that political equality and popular sovereignty have been undermined by the high cost of winning an election. Thus an entire field has emerged devoted to the question of how campaigns and money have affected the American political system. That the U.S. government is socially unrepresentative of the public, with members of the government being wealthier, older, whiter, and overwhelmingly male, however, is generally not considered problematic.

In *Voice, Trust, and Memory*, Melissa S. Williams of the University of Toronto argues that the chronic underrepresentation of historically oppressed groups as elected representatives in government is highly problematic. She demonstrates why democratic theory, which she calls "liberal representation," along with the constitutional safeguards that framers assumed would make government accountable to all of the people, has not produced fair representation for historically marginalized groups (groups she defines as having endured a history of state-supported discrimination). In the case of blacks, for example, she shows how legislators in a two-party system can simply ignore them without bearing any meaningful electoral costs. In addition, although Madison assumed that legislators would create just laws simply because they, too, must live under these laws, this safeguard fails for stigmatized groups whose interests the majority has defined as outside of the community's or whose interests truly diverge. Her analysis validates the longstanding claims by women suffragists that women are best represented by women because of their unique perspectives and experiences. Both through logic and through her case studies of blacks and women, Williams justifies her claim that fair representation must include self-representation in government for political minorities.

Williams is not the first political theorist to join the voting-rights activists in pushing for political reform to enhance the descriptive representation of U.S. minority groups. However, Williams makes the best theoretical case for descriptive representation for marginalized groups to achieve democratic equality. Her review of democratic theory is both exhaustive and masterful. But having established that a democratic system that excludes subordinate groups from self-representation is inherently flawed, how much descriptive representation is truly necessary for fairness? The Voting Rights Act of 1965 comes up for

renewal again in 2007, but as there are to date many female and minority legislators, few will find the case for new or continued political reform compelling. Indeed, as in the case of the extension of the franchise to minorities, the very presence of these minorities in government has strengthened the claims of the democratic theorists who, although they belatedly recognized the exclusion of blacks as a failure, continue to assert that our democratic culture is at bottom inclusive. (Robert Dahl once noted that democratic cultures show a great capacity for correcting their own failures.) Thus, while Williams establishes how fair representation must involve some form of descriptive representation for minority groups, she fails to take the next logical step and make the same strong theoretical case for the need for empowering minorities in government even as they have won descriptive representation.

KATHERINE TATE

University of California
Irvine

YOST, DAVID S. 1998. *NATO Transformed: The Alliance's New Roles in International Security.* Pp. xx, 450. Washington, DC: United States Institute of Peace Press. Paperbound, $19.95.

If one is looking for a comprehensive assessment of the North Atlantic Treaty Organization's post–Cold War evolution and search for a mission, David Yost's book is the perfect source. Examined in depth are the broad themes of collective security versus collective defense, Wilsonian idealism versus balance-of-power realpolitik, and tighter relations with the Central European states versus respect for the traditional security interests of Russia. Having read the book, I am reminded of the inherent contradictions in an alliance that was born 50 years ago in response to the Soviet threat and then left without its most effective unifying element when the West was "deprived of an enemy" some 40 years later. David Yost has amassed an impressive, meticulously detailed account of the recent history of NATO and the challenges that face the alliance today. *NATO Transformed* belongs on any reading list that includes questions of European security, humanitarian intervention, and the future of the transatlantic alliance.

In addition to the introduction and the conclusion, the book is divided into three major sections. The first briefly discusses the history of NATO from the origins of the Cold War through 1998. It is a useful summary of the major events of NATO's past and is particularly helpful in describing the important functions that the evolving alliance served beyond the initial military response to a threat from the East. The complex motivations for sustaining the alliance, albeit in a modified form, are explained here. The second and third major sections deal with the alliance's new post–Cold War roles: cooperation with former adversaries (particularly Russia) and crisis management and peace operations. The section on cooperation with former adversaries stresses the alliance's goal of trying to promote a stable, lasting peaceful order, with an interesting section on the similarities and differences between NATO and the interwar period's League of Nations. Regarding NATO's new functions of crisis management and peace operations, the book emphasizes the risk to the alliance's cohesion and to its traditional mission of collective defense, while cautiously supporting collective security operations that are backed by major

power consensus in "a coalition of the willing."

It is very difficult to review this book on its (substantial) merits alone, as its arguments and premises are cast about on the shifting sea of NATO's military action in Kosovo. The Kosovo conflict is likely to deepen divisions in Europe, reinforcing Russia's wariness of the West, leaving non-NATO regional states like Romania and Bulgaria without security guarantees, and even revealing cracks between America's Western allies. Thus the war in Kosovo makes Yost's book both compellingly relevant and regrettably outdated. There is an interesting discussion of the negotiations over Bosnia, with some prophetic statements about the implications for NATO of a failure of the Dayton accords, but the book stops on the threshold of the current conflict. The attractions and dangers of writing about an evolving situation are both apparent: we are provided with a rich and extremely valuable understanding of how the current NATO policy of bombing without a long-term coherent strategy came to be, while also frustratingly left without an analysis of an operation that tests the central NATO quandaries that the book so effectively lays out. This weakness cannot be blamed on the author, however; the exigencies of history have confounded many a diligent writer publishing on evolving issues. (Perhaps there is a reason why some staid British academics consider the study of anything since 1945 to be merely journalism.) In the end, the book gives the reader a wonderful tool for evaluating NATO's Kosovo policy; it is highly recommended for anyone, specialist or generalist, who wishes to understand and evaluate the current dilemmas of European security.

AUDREY KURTH CRONIN

University of Maryland
College Park

AFRICA, ASIA, AND
LATIN AMERICA

CASANOVAS, JOAN. 1998. *Bread or Bullets: Urban Labor and Spanish Colonialism in Cuba, 1850-1898*. Pp. xiii, 320. Pittsburgh, PA: University of Pittsburgh Press. $45.00. Paperbound, $19.95.

This book is a solid contribution to the small but growing work on Cuban labor history. It might seem from the extensive literature on Cuban revolutions that exile leadership and ideology were paramount in these crucial episodes. Casanovas's study of organized labor on the island in the second half of the twentieth century makes it clear that the urban base of the 1898 revolution was of material and ideological importance and that, to become so, it had to overcome tremendous difficulties.

Cuban labor for several centuries before 1898 had been riven by deep divisions: slave and free; peninsular and creole; urban and rural. These lines also cut across class divisions as the wealthy elite was both peninsular and creole. By the nineteenth century, however, creole political power was confined by Spanish colonialism. In that century, elements of the creole elite began to shift their allegiance away from Spain. At first, they sought to protect their status as slave owners by favoring annexation to the pre–Civil War United States. After 1865, when slavery was gone in the United States and in decline in Cuba, some of the creole elite moved toward a separatist or even independence position.

During this same period, however, the popular classes on the island (peasants, agricultural workers, urban workers) slowly made their way toward a far more radical kind of independence ideology. Following (but not copying) the development of anarchism in Spain, Cuban workers took advantage of the decline of slavery and the growing rift between peninsular and creole Spaniards to form a militant, cross-race, and cross-ethnic popular movement. This worker's movement had to overcome the oppressive conditions in the urban workplace created by the double burden of owner exploitation and colonial political control. Moreover, a long history of slavery and unfree labor on the island meant that the urban underclass had to free itself (in legal and economic terms) before it could address the issues of internal divisions of race and ethnicity and of workplace exploitation as wage laborers. Against all of these obstacles, Cuban workers managed to create social networks and organizations that gave them some degree of self-expression. By the 1890s, they had begun to use this power to support the small exile independence movement that from 1895 to 1898 brought to its knees a still-powerful Spanish rule. The last-minute entry of the United States into the struggle should not distract us from the long and arduous work of people in Cuba and in exile who made their weight felt in the struggle against class and colonial domination.

Joan Casanovas has given us an important counterpoint to the study of elites in the formation of the Cuban nation. The ideas and organizing abilities of prominent exile leaders like José Martí need to be understood, she contends, by recovering the context in which they did their work. The impact of class-based, anarchist ideas and means of organizing that heavily influenced the associations created by Cuban workers was a real force to which the exile nationalists (as well as the Spanish rulers) had to respond. Without support from urban workers, the movement for independence would have been narrower and weaker. The slow process of bringing underclass Afro-Cubans, Spanish Cubans, mixed-race Cubans, and other ethnic and racial minorities as well as women of all these groups into the political arena made the revolt of 1895 very different from any of those that preceded it. For the first time, an exile-led guerrilla army based in the countryside had allies in the urban centers. Though in a much less spectacular way than by the independence army, Spanish colonial rule by 1895 was challenged in the very urban centers that were presumed to be the bases of Spanish power on the island.

JULES R. BENJAMIN

Ithaca College
New York

LANGLEY, LESTER D. 1996. *The Americas in the Age of Revolution 1750-1850*. Pp. xvi, 374. New Haven, CT: Yale University Press. $35.00.

Midway through the bicentennial of the dramatic half century that witnessed the achievement of independence by most of the British, French, and Spanish colonies in the Americas, the revolutions that changed the course of Western history deserve renewed attention. Lester Langley's extended essay, *The Americas in the Age of Revolution*, probably should not be the first book consulted in this context, for it presumes a basic familiarity with the leading individuals and events of the period that can best be acquired elsewhere. Its unique viewpoint and thoughtful insights, however, make it an excellent option for those with a deeper interest in any and all of these conflicts and a desire for a more integrated perspective on the region. In contrast with a long historical and patriotic tendency to paint these events in epic terms by stressing the high ideals, unity of purpose, and clarity of the goals of their promoters and participants, Langley argues that the U.S., Haitian, and Latin American revolutions were fundamentally contradictory in nature, chaotic in expression, and complex in legacy.

In general terms, this work is an investigation into the impact of revolution on social organization. Organized as a comparative analysis, it explores the collapse of the great colonial empires in the Americas and the efforts to build viable nations upon their ruins within the context of developing liberal thought. Although revolution—its definition, characteristics, and consequences—is ostensibly his dominant theme, Langley refrains from generalizations and argues instead that these events do not fit any comprehensive model. Rather, he demonstrates quite convincingly the extent to which liberalism and its contradictions served as the shared philosophy of this particular revolutionary age. Not surprisingly, this perspective leads him to focus heavily on the issue of slavery and to highlight how race relations became the most vexing social problem for revolutionary elites who hoped to protect their privileges after independence but who could not achieve it without lower-class mobilization. In many respects, as Langley notes, the social unrest unleashed in a revolutionary environment among societies divided by color, caste, and class became the defining characteristic of the period. Once the movements began, no one could control their political or social outcomes.

This work takes great pains to examine each revolution on its own terms. Yet it also shows the extent to which each affected the others and uncovers important shared causes and themes. Langley deserves credit for addressing the often overlooked Caribbean context to the revolutionary period, although at times his account underplays the complexities of the Haitian situation. Similarly, the conflicts that raged across Latin America are not easily reduced to some 80 pages of direct analysis. The work is capped off by a valuable inquiry into the consequences of the revolutions that extends the discussion of the period deep into the nineteenth century, thereby providing a more balanced, long-term assessment. By 1850, the revolutionary legacies were striking in their contradictions: Haiti succeeded in abolishing slavery but fell under the rule of self-styled emperors and strongmen; the United States forged a broad-based democracy with significant social mobility yet retained slavery; and Latin America set up the framework of democratic institutions but descended into extreme social and political unrest. While the reasons for these differences are not answered conclusively at the end of this work, Langley has provided a solid interpretive base from which to ask the questions.

TIMOTHY HAWKINS

Tulane University
New Orleans
Louisiana

PASHA, MUSTAPHA KAMAL. 1998. *Colonial Political Economy: Recruitment and Underdevelopment in the Punjab.* Pp. xxii, 300. New York: Oxford University Press. $42.00.

Mustapha Kamal Pasha explicitly sets out to debunk the martial races theory put forward by the British colonial authority to justify the use of Punjabi soldiers as "the sword arm of the British-Indian empire." Implicitly, however, he is concerned with the damage done by the process that produced a Pakistani Army dominated by Punjabis, and his book becomes an indictment of British colonial policy for creating the Punjabi military establishment that has dominated Pakistan for much of its history.

Pasha's analysis reduces the theory of martial races from rationale to rationalization. He concedes that use of martial race was congruent with Punjabi notions of honor (*izzat*) and that the strategic

positioning of the Punjab across South Asia's historical invasion route produced military skills that were ably demonstrated by Punjabis contesting the British takeover in 1849. Within this historical context, military careers were obviously understood and attractive. However, only the groups that remained loyal to the British during the Great Revolt of 1857 made the list of martial races, while it was almost 30 years later that the idea of martial races became part of colonial rhetoric and policy. Given this timing, martial races theory becomes simply a rationalization for this part of the comprador class—Indians well paid for their loyalty to the Raj.

Rewards for support during the Great Revolt was all-India policy, but Pasha pursues the issue at the provincial level and finds that the success of that policy was greatly enhanced by the land settlement imposed on the Punjab at the same time. That land settlement pushed young Punjabis from the poorer, rain-fed areas into the military by requiring cash payment of taxes, by allowing sale of agricultural land, and by producing a system of credit for mortgaging land. That settlement, combined with a general lack of nonagricultural opportunities, made the secure cash income provided by military service particularly attractive for those peasants lacking irrigation. This system threatened all peasants outside the cash nexus but was particularly difficult for those in arid regions completely dependent on the erratic rains. As a result, Stephen P. Cohen recently reported, 75 percent of Pakistan's ex-servicemen come from five arid districts bordering Azad Kashmir (three in the Punjab and two in the North West Frontier Province).

Pasha then moves to the *tehsil* (subdistrict) level to demonstrate, using colonial records of land transfers, the dynamics of the transition after the land settlement. Those records reveal great turbulence for the period 1857-65, a turbulence that made military service particularly attractive in the *tehsil* studied.

Finally, *Colonial Political Economy* is an excellent monograph on military recruitment in colonial India, a process of major consequence across South Asia. However, as an indictment of colonial practice, Pasha's study seems dated after 50 years of Pakistani independence. Neither colonizer nor colonized is around to be punished, and it is time to lay their ghosts to rest and look more realistically at present policy options. Pasha's emphasis on colonial guilt leads him to overlook the positive side of military recruitment for the underprivileged. For example, his data suggest to this reader that a son (or daughter) in the military is still the best bet for families in the Punjab's underdeveloped districts. Even democratic reform of Pakistan would not change that pattern, so long as Pakistan requires an army. And, alas, the Pakistan (or the United States or the India) that does not require an army has yet to be imagined.

GLYNN WOOD

Monterey Institute of
International Studies
California

READER, IAN and GEORGE J. TANABE, JR. 1998. *Practically Religious: Worldly Benefits and the Common Religion of Japan.* Pp. xii, 303. Honolulu: University of Hawai'i Press. $45.00. Paperbound, $22.95.

Ian Reader and George Tanabe argue that rituals for obtaining practical assistance in overcoming the obstacles of everyday life constitute the common religion of Japan. It is a common religion in the sense that its rituals are open to people from all strata of society regardless of religious affiliation or lack thereof; it unites elites, priests, and ordinary people; and its affirmation of this-worldly success is the governing orientation of Japanese religion as a whole. Scholars and social observers heretofore have largely ignored the religion of this-worldly benefits because they have been misled by a false dichotomy between true religion (usually defined as doctrines of ethics and of other-worldly salvation), which is worthy of study, and so-called superstitions and magic, the widespread practice of which can only be deplored. Reader and Tanabe, however, reject this distinction between true and false religion while asserting that ritual practices for benefits constitute a true religion insofar as they address deeply felt social and psychological needs, they are extensively practiced, and they are deeply embedded in Japanese society. *Practically Religious* explores in exhaustive detail the varieties of rituals, their popularity, and their social roles to document how Japanese religion is marketed in ways analogous to a commercial enterprise and to occasionally suggest that the seeking of material benefits has to do with not merely materialistic desires but also spiritual aspirations that link the attainment of inner peace, benefits, and faith.

Practically Religious presents a welcome corrective to the standard descriptions of contemporary Japanese religion found in tourist guidebooks, school textbooks, reference works, and official Japanese government publications. The standard descriptions frequently confuse and confound casual observers and serious students alike by suggesting that religion has lost its relevance for modern Japanese, by dividing Japanese religion into distinct "isms" (such as Buddhism, Shintoism) or sects (for example, Pure Land versus Zen), and by overemphasizing the philosophical and other-worldly aspects of Buddhism. In this work, Reader and Tanabe attempt to bridge the methodological divide that too often separates social-science-based studies of contemporary religious practices from text-based studies of doctrines and institutional history to show that rituals for material benefits have a long and distinguished history in Buddhism, one that is justified doctrinally by scriptures dating back to Buddhism's development in India. Reader and Tanabe focus on established Buddhist institutions to show how the rituals for worldly benefit they offer remain relevant for modern Japanese and how those rituals transcend sectarian distinctions and provide a nexus for the worship of Shinto gods and Buddhist divinities.

Practically Religious is not without weaknesses. One might counterargue, as has Helen Hardacre, that rituals for practical benefits function less as the centerpiece of Japanese religion and more as its main entrance, which leads practitioners toward other, less material orientations. In an intriguing digression, Reader and Tanabe suggest that the syncretism of Buddhism and Shinto never occurred in the ways in which established academic explanations describe, but the authors fail to provide the kind of sustained argument and evidence that any revisionist interpretation of Shinto-Buddhist relations demands.

All quibbles aside, *Practically Religious* succeeds splendidly in its main goals. It not only illustrates how the often ignored and usually misunderstood desire for material welfare finds almost infinite expression in Japanese religion, but it also demonstrates that this is a phenomenon that must not be overlooked in any scholarly interpretation of Japanese culture, society, or religion, whether contemporary or historical. Reading this book will benefit anyone interested in better understanding Japan.

WILLIAM M. BODIFORD

University of California
Los Angeles

WARREN, KAY B. 1998. *Indigenous Movements and Their Critics: Pan-Maya Activism in Guatemala.* Pp. xxii, 288. Princeton, NJ: Princeton University Press. $60.00. Paperbound, $17.95.

As Kay Warren states, "This book portrays the ways in which Maya public intellectuals, as cultural nationalists and agents of globalization, have pursued projects for 'self-determination' in Guatemala's climate of chronic political uncertainty." *Indigenous Movements* charts the pan-Mayanist movement, which refers to those Maya organizing around cultural, linguistic, and educational rights. For social scientist readers, the book places pan-Mayanism in the theoretical frameworks of Wallace's "revitalization movements," Hobsbawm and Ranger's "invented traditions," Anderson's "imagined communities," and Alvarez, Dagnino, and Escobar's work in new social movements. Warren is firmly engaged in the new social movements discussion, but she finds that "pan-Mayanism fails to rest comfortably in any one of these social scientific literatures [and so] helps us characterize the limitations of each." She also examines the movement's many domestic and foreign critics. For anthropologists, the book is written as an experimental ethnography and addresses an unusual transnational, pluri-ethnic, multilocational community. Its reflexive account directly confronts the changing relationships between Mayas and foreign (Maya: *kaxlan*) anthropologists.

The book succeeds in these aims. It is a challenging read, experimental as noted, but tied together by Warren's career-long concern for narrative, narrative authority, and readings that cross the grain. The book provides critical background on a major indigenous movement and on community responses to a devastating war. The diverse chapters document the different locations of Maya activism that sustain the pan-Maya movement. These include Maya community activists, young Maya apprentice linguists, Maya public intellectuals, the transnational contexts of Maya exile writings, international indigenous conferences, United Nations accords, and foreign research. Inspired by documentaries, Warren develops a photo essay of the movement's actors, settings, and activities. These shifts in level are well framed by the introductory and concluding chapters.

Indigenous Movements focuses on the pan-Mayanist movement's resurgence, 1987 to 1996, after the genocidal civil war. But it also draws on Warren's long-term relations with Mayan activists, from her earliest work (1969-71) in San Andres Semetebaj and at the Proyecto Linguistico Francisco Marroquin (PLFM). The PLFM drew inspiration from the 1945 linguistic activism of Adrian Chavez and also served as an early base for the current pan-Mayanist movement.

Today, the movement faces many contradictions, which Warren explores. At first, it seems a straightforward effort to secure the rights of the country's Maya majority. However, the pan-Mayanist movement has resulted in the founding of various research and educational institutions (and also in the rising prominence of an activist Maya middle-class), rather than other Maya points of organization in the popular and revolutionary Left. Warren discusses the movement's "reverse Orientalism" in playing off Maya identities in opposition to Ladinos (Hispanic-identified peoples). Furthermore, its foremost theorist's promotion of "collective rights" has provoked tense confrontations. Will the Maya movement disrupt, perhaps violently, a fragile postwar movement to establish a vibrant civil democracy?

Warren avoids essentializing pre-Columbian patterns as "really" Maya but

is respectful of their importance to pan-Mayanists. She describes the dilemmas of Maya public intellectuals, many of whom try to maintain the local roots that often legitimate a Maya, while at the same time having to stitch together various jobs in regional, national, and international projects.

I would have liked more coverage of the movement's gender contradictions, particularly those that result in the silencing of Maya women's voices. Also deserving of more attention are the movement's roots in foreign Catholic and evangelical missionary linguistic projects. However, Warren's clear response to Maya critiques of foreign researchers will go a long way toward reclarifying that tense relationship. Warren changes the question of "Who speaks for whom?" into "Who speaks with whom?" which examines how relations are undertaken, sustained, and reciprocated. In conclusion, the book is a must read at this moment of international support for indigenous rights—and concern over heightened ethnic separatism.

ABIGAIL E. ADAMS

Central Connecticut State
  University
New Britain

EUROPE

BERGLUND, STEN and FRANK AAREBROT. 1997. *The Political History of Eastern Europe in the 20th Century: The Struggle Between Democracy and Dictatorship.* Pp. xi, 196. Lyme, NH: Edward Elgar. $70.00

This slender volume by two Scandinavian political scientists endeavors to analyze Eastern Europe's "current experiment in democracy" against the background of the region's political development since World War I, the better to formulate "the conditions necessary for the survival of democratic government." The subject matter is both timely and important. More's the pity that although their presentation is occasionally insightful, Berglund and Aarebrot's conclusions are conventional and their treatment of complex historical considerations far too facile.

The book's core chapters (chapters 2-5) are given over to uneven surveys of the interwar period, the years of the Communist takeover (1945-49, curiously labeled "the democratic or semi-democratic interlude"), the crumbling of the Soviet imperial monolith from the death of Stalin to the rise of Gorbachev, and "the Second Coming" of democracy from 1989-90 to mid-1995 (the juncture at which the authors ended their research). All this is framed by a first chapter, "The Heritage," a once-over-lightly sketch of the sociopolitical contours of the pre-1914 era in Eastern Europe, and a final chapter, "Prospects and Paradoxes," which repeats, often verbatim, points made in the preceding chapters. One of the more intriguing of these points involves the suggestion that by fostering a strong secular state together with socially inclusive political mobilization, Communist rulers may have inadvertently bequeathed to their successors key functional prerequisites for democracy. On the other hand, the authors recognize the negative legacy of "clientism, kinship and corruption." They might also have added the residual mystique of dictatorship set against the growing post-Communist experience of a bloated but enfeebled state. After alluding to various economic and sociological factors, the authors conclude on the lame note that "the prospects of the new democracies in Eastern Europe would seem to revolve around two factors: the success with which they resolve the transitional problems and the passage of time."

This study draws upon various conceptual frameworks advanced by such noted social scientists as Rokkan, Satori, and Lijphart. It also makes liberal use of survey research data, especially the 1990 Times-Mirror (London) survey, the Eurobarometer East series, and other data compiled by the European Commission's Integration Studies. Such are the theoretical and empirical touchstones of the authors' approach, one which, they note, "with its emphasis on conceptual schemes always leads to a certain loss of information." This, they believe, "is a price well worth paying in view of the theory building potential" of their approach. Alas, the study does not come close to realizing the vaunted promise of "theory building," but it is characterized by egregious lacunae of "information." The hype on the volume's dust jacket that "the book will be essential reading for students of Eastern Europe, comparative politics and European History" is unwarranted.

MELVIN CROAN

University of Wisconsin
Madison

UNITED STATES

ABEL, RICHARD L. 1998. *Speaking Respect, Respecting Speech*. Pp. x, 355. Chicago: University of Chicago Press. $30.00.

Freedom of expression is at the very center of what legal scholars most concern themselves with. It is, so to speak, the superego of the Constitution—not what the Constitution is about, but what it is necessary to believe the Constitution is about if one wants to think of the Constitution in capital letters. Mainstream legal scholarship accepts a notion that, ideally at least, the Constitution established a system of self-rule driven by the free and equal participation of citizens in public discourse and that public discourse will simultaneously balance and steer a social system that is free but unequal. The belief in the power of expression entails similar beliefs in the autonomy of the individual and the metaphysical freedom of thought. Unlike material conflicts, where winners take from losers, in the marketplace of ideas, more for one is more for all.

Richard Abel does not accept these premises. Following in a thriving tradition of critical thinking, he insists that people exist not as individuals but as members of groups and communities; that expression is not innocent of the laws of the material world; and that expressive goods are won in a zero-sum game. In *Speaking Respect, Respecting Speech*, he applies these and other critical insights to current controversies, provides an analysis of their common structure, critiques the standard positions, and offers a remedy. His analysis is cogent, although elliptical; his critiques are agreeable, although familiar; and his remedy is appealing, although superficial.

Abel begins by recounting three big controversies: the MacKinnon-Dworkin anti-pornography ordinance, the Skokie Nazi demonstration, and the *Satanic Verses* furor. The unifying aspect of all three, he insists, was a competition for respect. He theorizes this competition as typical of "status conflict," which he explains using Weber's notion of status groups and Joseph Gusfield's account of symbolic crusades. He acknowledges, of course, that other things are at stake—gender, class, race, ethnicity, and religion are not reducible to status—but it is status, or respect, that is the aspect of, say, the Rushdie affair that is amenable to discussion and action. The other aspects are not considered in the rest of the book.

Neither civil libertarianism nor state regulation offers a sufficient explanation or remedy for status conflicts. Civil libertarianism unrealistically denies the grim facts of expression—that it is ambiguous, power-ridden, already regulated by both the state and the private sector, and never autonomous. State regulation is equally unhelpful, failing to understand nuance, context, irony, and art in expression; relying on an unsupportable consequentialism for justification; and often ironically punishing victims more than offenders and valorizing offensive speech. Abel's recitation of the shortcomings of these two schools is quick and broad. Scholars will be able to fill in the longer theoretical arguments that Abel alludes to; adherents might judge his treatment superficial, however.

Of course, there is a third way, and this is Abel's remedy. Status conflicts can be resolved through apologies. Effective apologies arise when complaints are heard sympathetically and communities demand them; in these cases, a "structured conversation" between offender and victim results in a "ceremonial exchange of respect." Because respect is a zero-sum game, as Abel consistently reminds us, hard choices will arise. It is necessary to be partisan, to take sides. Ultimately, then, Abel characterizes his remedy as an extension of affirmative action to the arena of discussion—a positive social policy of encouraging complaint and apology on behalf of historically disfavored groups, not an extension of formal (neutral) procedures. One wonders, however, how his remedy really differs from the status quo.

This is a solidly researched argument. Abel writes in a staccato style, piling example upon example, and readers will find themselves confronted once again with all the greatest hits of the golden age of the political correctness debate. It makes for strenuous reading at times, but Abel has a good ear for the arresting sound bite.

Like law generally, though, Abel's book delights in the odd case. Some sections are virtual freak shows, drawn from the headlines of the past two decades. A question Abel does not raise about his material is its mediation. All of the stuff he talks about is gleaned from the news media—only matters that rise to the level of national media attention are considered here. He must, therefore, take this matter as a fair representation of politics on the ground. But this implies that a nonpoliticized process of representation has taken place, which is something he elsewhere dismisses. Or should this book have been written as media analysis rather than a legal analysis?

JOHN NERONE

University of Illinois
Urbana-Champaign

HAYNES, JOHN EARL and HARVEY KLEHR. 1999. *Venona: Decoding Soviet Espionage in America.* Pp. xiii, 487. New Haven, CT: Yale University Press. $30.00.

The National Security Agency's 1995 release of the Venona files, decoded intercepts of Soviet KGB traffic between the United States and Moscow during World War II, proved a sensation. Thanks to luck (recovering a partly destroyed code book and the Soviets' risky reuse of pages from one-time code pads) and their codebreakers' skill, the Army's Signal Intelligence Service, forerunner of the National Security Agency, managed in 1946 to begin decoding part of the Soviets' wartime diplomatic cable traffic. The contents of this trove have rekindled remnants of the bitter Cold War era debate over charges of Communist influences in the U.S. government.

This book offers illuminating analysis, the most exhaustive to date, of these decryptions. It profits, too, from Haynes and Klehr's efforts to cross-check Venona with archives of the U.S. Communist Party (CPUSA). Originally smuggled to the Comintern for safekeeping, these records became, after the USSR's collapse, partially available at the Russian Center for the Preservation and Study of Documents of Recent History (RTsKhIDNI).

The result is a startling picture of Soviet influence and espionage in wartime agencies and mainline departments—one that is closer to the maximalist than minimalist position staked out in Cold War debates over McCarthyism. Alger Hiss and Julius Rosenberg, toward whose guilt the scholarly pendulum has tilted in recent years, are the least of it. Venona reveals other Manhattan Project espionage agents (three besides the Greenglass-Rosenberg coterie and Klaus Fuchs). It shows that many in Hiss's circle or other groups of federal jobholders charged with doing Soviet bidding in the 1930s and 1940s did indeed have contact with and serve the ends of Soviet intelligence agencies. Arcane disputes about the roles and loyalties of Assistant Treasury Secretary Harry Dexter White; Lauchlin Currie, a top aide to FDR; and Laurence Duggan, an influential State Department official, seem resolved. KGB dispatches detail how they—and others—exerted influence on behalf of and passed privileged data to the USSR.

The authors reserve sternest judgment for the CPUSA. Not every spy was a Communist, nor every Red a spy, but surprising numbers of Party members were, and many Party leaders (including Earl Browder) abetted these schemes: "It became clear that espionage was a regular activity of the American Communist party." Klehr and Haynes count code names of 349 people listed in Venona as having had links with Soviet intelligence, less than 200 of whom have been successfully identified by their real names.

The results confirm the validity of most revelations of Elizabeth Bentley, Whittaker Chambers, and several other pilgrims from communism and of the soberer findings of the House Un-American Activities Committee and Senate Internal Security Subcommittee. Haynes and Klehr do not attempt a general assessment of these committees, but their findings from Venona suggest that knee-jerk criticism may need some rethinking. They distance themselves from Senator Joseph R. McCarthy, whose charges against the likes of Secretary of State Dean Acheson and General George S. Marshall they deem reckless. (It is telling that only two names on the "108 list," the basis of some of McCarthy's earliest charges, show up in Venona. Though many names discussed here were bandied about in the anti-Communist scrimmages of the 1950s, the latecomer McCarthy amassed such weak material that he is largely marginal to the events treated in this book.)

Haynes and Klehr suggest that earlier revelation of Venona would have saved historians from misconceptions about communism and anti-Comunism in the postwar years. They are right, but less so, perhaps, then they imply. It is remarkable how close Earl Latham came in *The Communist Controversy in Washington* (1966) by careful analysis of testimony in that benighted pre-Venona age—a view skeptical of the contentions of either extreme. With Haynes and Klehr's book, those who never succumbed to the totalist position that "all anticommunism was McCarthyism" now have ample reason to know how right they were.

RICHARD M. FRIED

University of Illinois
Chicago

HIRSCHHORN, BERNARD. 1997. *Democracy Reformed: Richard Spencer Childs and His Fight for Better Government*. Pp. xxiv, 233. Westport, CT: Greenwood Press. $59.95.

Richard Childs's remarkable reform career spanned seven decades of the twentieth century. Heir to the Bon Ami cleansing powder fortune and to a family legacy of civic activism, Childs left an indelible mark on American politics through his leadership in such organizations as the National Municipal League. His lifelong dedication to the short ballot and the council-manager form of government deserves the thoughtful analysis that Bernard Hirschhorn gives it. Tracing Childs's activism from the Progressive Era through the Vietnam years, Hirschhorn shows that Childs remained convinced that democracy could be perfected by limiting the number of elected officials. If voters chose only the most visible and important public servants, Childs argued, not only would they choose more responsibly, but, more important, they would be better able to express their political will and control their representatives.

Hirschhorn's book is topically arranged, covering Childs's advocacy of the short ballot, the council-manager system, proportional representation, the appointive judiciary, political party reform, unicameral legislatures, and an end to the election of coroners. He dramatizes how, throughout his extraordinarily long life, Childs was always ready to rethink state, county, and municipal political structures in a quest to make representation effective. This study quickly puts to rest any contention that the Progressive impulse ended with World War I, although the author does note a marked break between structural political reformers of the Progressive Era and the advocates of New Deal governmental activism.

Hirschhorn makes the important point that the Progressives' commitment to efficiency was not simply a smokescreen for economy in government; that "business values" were not necessarily a weapon against the interests of "the people." Instead, by "efficiency," Progressives like Childs meant the ability to discern the popular will and to translate it into practice. According to Childs, the Jacksonian impulse to elect everyone from governor to coroner diminished popular power by overburdening voters and, more important, by encouraging blind partisanship that left the most important political decisions to party bosses.

In many ways, Childs embodied the ideals of Progressive structural reform, with his critique of political parties, his faith in expertise and efficiency, and his belief in the need to separate politics and administration. However, Hirschhorn's portrait is more complex. He shows, for example, that Childs never believed that city managers—a profession that he invented—could actually abstain from creating policy, merely that they could remain aloof from partisan bickering. Despite his call for nonpartisan elections, Childs also believed that political parties should be reformed, not eliminated. Likewise, the stereotype of the "goo goo" who valued good government over democracy is discarded; Hirschhorn argues that Childs focused on the need to make democracy work in practice and not just in theory, portraying him as alert to the pitfalls of elitism and to the needs of minorities. His account also stresses the sometimes overlooked but important differences between the council-manager system and its predecessor, the commission form of government.

If it is sometimes hard to distinguish Hirschhorn's beliefs from Childs's own, the source of this sympathy is not hard to locate. Hirschhorn is certain that,

although Childs was a self-proclaimed "mugwump," he avoided the elitism that is often attributed to good-government activists. This certainty may have been partly influenced by Hirschhorn's personal acquaintance with Childs (the book is dedicated to his memory), but it is also true that Childs's enthusiasm for his schemes is contagious. His striking confidence that he knew what "the people" wanted may have an element of hubris, but that was probably a necessary ingredient in a reform career as single-minded and as long-lived as his proved to be.

SARAH M. HENRY

Union College
Schenectady
New York

NINKOVICH, FRANK. 1999. *The Wilsonian Century: U.S. Foreign Policy Since 1900*. Pp. ix, 320. Chicago: University of Chicago Press. $27.50.

In *The Wilsonian Century*, Frank Ninkovich presents a breathtaking review of twentieth-century American foreign policy. Since international commitment characterized that policy, Ninkovich's book is an equally impressive summary of twentieth-century international affairs, from wars—hot and cold—to an emerging "liberal world order" based on great power cooperation. Ninkovich's central theme is the preponderant influence of Woodrow Wilson's internationalism on the course of U.S. foreign policy. But Ninkovich's Wilsonianism is not the giddy idealism so often criticized by so-called realists. Rather, Ninkovich focuses on what he calls the "bleak side" of Wilson's thoughts, which assumed "that world history had stumbled onto new, dangerous, and radically uncertain terrain that obliged American policy-makers to abandon traditional diplomacy."

Wilson's bleakness, according to Ninkovich, superseded the "normal internationalism" that emerged early in the century as the United States forsook its isolation and took the world stage. For Ninkovich, normality means a "kind of benign but hazy global vision" that aspires "for a world of liberal capitalism, democracy, and great-power cooperation, undergirded by commercial and cultural cooperation." In effect, Ninkovich has turned much of the scholarship about Wilson on its head: the idealist's dreams are actually nightmares; realists pine for a "liberal world order." To further twist the gymnastics, Ninkovich argues that Wilsonianism guided U.S. policymakers through the crises of World War II and the Cold War. Once those crises passed, normal internationalism flowered. "Far from being the centerpiece of American utopianism, then, Wilsonianism was a self-liquidating creed because, as Warren Harding had long ago recognized, it was not an ideology suited to 'normalcy.'" Ninkovich's Wilson is the prophet of gloom and doom ever scorned in happy times.

Ninkovich's Wilsonianism consists of five fundamental assumptions that ultimately became "axiomatic for American statesmen" who feared first German and Japanese tries at world hegemony, then the Soviet Union's. First, Wilson recognized that "total war" meant that wars had become so destructive they could no longer be used to advance foreign policy interests. Second, total war threatened the destruction of liberal democracy. Third, the balance-of-power system was now obsolete. Fourth, the United States could no longer hide within its isolationism—modern international relations were global relations. Finally, all of these assumptions led inexorably to the most fundamental Wilsonian assumption: "*any* conflict anywhere, unless nipped in the bud, threatened to escalate into

another world war more calamitous than the first" (emphasis in original).

Nipping conflicts in the bud, of course, resulted in U.S. involvement in World War II, Korea, Vietnam, Grenada, Iraq, and—currently—the Balkans. Consequently, the Wilsonianism that defined the twentieth century was spawned and sustained by crises. It endured, Ninkovich argues persuasively, "because the alternatives always seemed worse and because, despite its shortcomings, it worked."

Ironically, what one misses in Ninkovich's definition of Wilsonianism are the giddy ideals. Ninkovich does not seem to accept that his definition of normal internationalism seems strikingly Wilsonian—capitalism, democracy, and international cooperation. Rather than some Hegelian dialectic between normal and Wilsonian internationalism, Wilson was very much a proponent of Ninkovich's normal internationalism. If crises diverted his attention, they did not shake his commitment.

As one expects to find in anything Ninkovich writes, he emphasizes not only events but also the images and imaginings that policymakers carried in their collective heads and relied upon in formulating their responses to those events. Indeed, he proposes early on to explore what happens when the traditional frameworks of historical understanding within U.S. society "lose their scriptural status and the stories have to be revised or new narrative frameworks altogether have to be adopted." This slant always produces fascinating insights.

Ninkovich succeeds in showing us the dark, depressing side of Wilson's historical understanding, but it costs him sight of Wilson's grander ideals. Both Wilsonianism and normal internationalism clung on so tenaciously throughout the twentieth century because each derived from the same image of

America's place in the world. Both ideas—and ideals—were deeply ingrained in the foreign policy psyche of generations of American leaders. Ninkovich has spotlighted the crisis orientation of Wilsonianism and illuminated it as the shining thread running throughout twentieth-century U.S. foreign policy.

FREDERICK S. CALHOUN

United States Marshals Service
Arlington
Virginia

PEGRAM, THOMAS R. 1998. *Battling Demon Rum: The Struggle for a Dry America, 1800-1933.* Pp. xv, 207. Chicago: Ivan R. Dee. $24.95.

To learn about the American temperance movement, general readers and scholars alike should begin with *Battling Demon Rum*. Thomas Pegram of Loyola College, Baltimore, has written the most accessible and the most up-to-date synthesis. Although short and unfootnoted, his book incorporates the extensive new research published since the early 1960s. Pegram displays a knack for lively anecdotes and telling statistics. For instance, a jury in a liquor case was indicted for "drinking the evidence"; at the turn of the century, Chicago had more saloons than the fifteen states that composed the South. Statistics for national per capita consumption of alcoholic beverages help readers understand the changing nature of the drink problem and the effectiveness of temperance propaganda and coercive laws.

Instead of presenting temperance in antiquarian isolation, Pegram firmly places the movement in the context of the social and political history of nineteenth- and early-twentieth-century America. He identifies two periods of prohibitionist success: statewide prohibition in the North and Midwest inspired by the 1851 Maine law and the victories of the Anti-Saloon League, beginning in 1907, which culminated in the ratification of the Eighteenth Amendment to the U.S. Constitution. Pegram focuses on "the relationship between American political institutions and temperance reform." His book relates the failures and successes of the campaigns for prohibition to changes and continuities in political culture, especially those of political parties. He emphasizes that, except in times of crisis, partisan endorsement of a policy as divisive as prohibition lacked appeal to party politicians.

Pegram is particularly strong on the period from the aftermath of the Civil War until the repeal of national prohibition, the era of the Women's Christian Temperance Union, the National Prohibition Party, and the Anti-Saloon League. In his account, national prohibition appears to have been the unlikely result of unusual circumstances and of masterful lobbying by the Anti-Saloon League. But pressure groups could do only so much. The lack of commitment of the political parties to prohibition explains, in turn, its failure to satisfy public opinion and repeal.

Pegram is a political historian who previously wrote articles about the Anti-Saloon League. He draws on social history to explain political history but is understandably brief on the nonpolitical aspects of the temperance story, such as the creation of a subculture in which millions of people found meaning and identity. The strength of his book as general U.S. history and the book's brevity help explain another limitation. Presenting temperance and prohibition as an instance of American exceptionalism, Pegram reports the battle for sobriety elsewhere in only a half-dozen brief passages. Otherwise, he ignores the fact that people in other countries worried about alcoholic drink, sometimes organized themselves into temperance societies, and even agitated for prohibition. An international perspective could have enriched the analysis of *Battling Demon Rum* by helping distinguish between what was peculiar to the United States and what was widespread in English-speaking and Scandinavian countries. This is a minor criticism of a very good book.

DAVID M. FAHEY

Miami University
Oxford
Ohio

RATCLIFFE, DONALD J. 1998. *Party Spirit in a Frontier Republic: Democratic Politics in Ohio 1793-1821.* Pp. xii, 336. Columbus: Ohio State University Press. No price.

Donald J. Ratcliffe's fine history of political parties in Ohio in a period when parties supposedly did not yet exist is a refreshingly old-fashioned challenge to recent historiographical trends. Partisan loyalties ran deep in the new state notwithstanding the Republicans' domination of electoral politics and the apparent weakness of the Federalist opposition. Previous writers (including this one) have too hastily concluded that true political parties would develop only in the Jacksonian era, when friends and foes of Old Hickory competed for the favor of an expanding electorate on more even terms. The political formations of the previous decades, they have argued, were ephemeral and personalistic, loose alliances of local big men and their clients. But Ratcliffe demolishes the "myth of gentry control," thus turning the conventional narrative of party development and political modernization on its head. Under their extraordinarily democratic state constitution, Ohio voters were powerfully engaged by fundamental issues

affecting the very survival of the American republic. Political crises and conflicts sustained the urgency of partisan identities, durable enough to survive more apathetic periods, including the "era of good feelings" after the War of 1812. The electorate exercised its power over would-be oligarchs or "aristocrats" from the onset of statehood. Party spirit flourished. Indeed, "the language and symbols and ideas learned during the conflicts of Jefferson and Madison's day" played a crucial role in rationalizing and legitimating the new dispensation of parties that emerged in the late 1820s and 1830s. If techniques of electoral mobilization became more sophisticated and systematic in these later years, voters did not have to be taught the importance of partisan loyalties.

Republicans and Federalists were not evenly matched in early Ohio, but Ratcliffe shows that both parties played critical roles in the development of the new state's vigorous partisan political culture. Taking their cues from the national party—and from their own experiences in their states of origin—Ohio Republicans identified with the patriot heroes who had secured American independence. Republican statehood proponents saw their campaign against the "despotic" regime of Federalist territorial governor Arthur St. Clair as a local version of Jefferson's "Revolution of 1800," itself yet another episode in the global conflict between republicanism and monarchism. The ease with which Ohio Republicans could conflate local, national, and global developments helps explain why they organized so effectively and quickly, binding "a heterogeneous society together" by mobilizing ideological tendencies and partisan loyalties that "already existed among the electorate." Because of their national orientation, Ohio Republicans were never satisfied with local ascendancy, for when the next great crisis came, Federalists could provide critical support for counterrevolutionary forces elsewhere in the union and beyond. To secure the Revolution, Republicans felt compelled to institutionalize a permanent mobilization of patriotic voters, thus leading to the precocious development of "organizational techniques"—including popular nominating conventions—"that became the staple of the Second Party System."

Because the Federalists had little hope of statewide success, they were forced to cultivate alliances with dissident Republicans who chafed at party discipline. In a political culture still imbued with the anti-party values of the revolutionary generation, Republican efforts to institutionalize popular power often proved counterproductive: a suspicious electorate resisted popular electoral mobilization and manipulation. But faithful Republicans did not therefore lay down their electoral weapons. Convinced that recalcitrant voters were the dupes of counterrevolutionary reaction, party loyalists redoubled their efforts to mobilize the electorate. This dialectical process, driven by divisions between Republicans and by popular resistance to party direction, ultimately served to strengthen party loyalties.

Ratcliffe's important book will be recognized as the definitive study of Ohio politics in the frontier era. It also offers a more generally useful account of what parties meant to early American voters and of how party loyalties persisted in the long interval between the first party "system" of the 1790s and the rise of a second party system in the Jacksonian era. Well written and richly documented, *Party Spirit in a Frontier Republic* deserves a wide readership.

PETER S. ONUF

University of Virginia
Charlottesville

STEPHENSON, DONALD GRIER, JR. 1999. *Campaigns and the Court: The U.S. Supreme Court in Presidential Elections.* Pp. xiv, 363. New York: Columbia University Press. $49.50. Paperbound, $19.50.

This valuable study focuses on "the [Supreme] Court's susceptibility to entanglement" in presidential election campaigns, which "has *necessarily* been a characteristic of American politics because of the constitutional role that the justices have assumed for themselves" (emphasis in original). Donald Grier Stephenson, Jr., explores the consequences of such entanglement for the Court, the electoral process, public policy, and constitutional government in general.

Stephenson finds the Court to have been a major campaign issue in (or four years after) those critical elections that established or redefined a governing coalition that would dominate for a generation, as well as in a few noncritical elections. Looking at 10 campaigns in all, he describes the prevailing party systems and contemporary Supreme Court, recounts the politically relevant judicial decisions and the campaign arguments about the Court, and analyzes the effects of the campaigns on the Court, the political process, and public policy. Stephenson has thoroughly canvassed the extensive body of primary and secondary sources to trace the relationship between judicial decision making and electoral politics over the past two centuries, and he enlivens his narrative with many apt quotations. Specialists will find that he has reordered familiar materials in an important way; general readers will be rewarded with a focused and judicious survey of American political and legal history.

The analytical framework of the study tests five propositions about the Court's involvement in the political process. Three of them prove to be generally valid: that the Court is more likely to become embroiled in politics when it has negated acts of other agencies than when it has upheld them; that Court actions help to define and clarify the issues in a campaign; and that the emergence of judicial issues in a campaign tends to provoke a more fundamental debate about the role of the Court and the legitimacy of judicial review in a democratic political process. Two other propositions, both relating to Court behavior after being supported by the losing side in an election, appear more problematic. Stephenson finds that, contrary to the received wisdom among judicial scholars, the Court in the following decade may not come generally into line with the policies of the new regime. Moreover, only in the period of dealignment after 1968 has the Court, immediately following the chastening election, made decisions that provoked the new regime (although new regimes have attempted to curb the Court anyway, in anticipation rather than reaction). In the most notable instance, the Court did not oppose the New Deal after being an issue in the 1936 campaign, but the experience of the 1930s should remind us that the Court may have much at stake in an election even though its decisions and role are not issues in the campaign. The Court was not an issue in the realigning election of 1932, but it really lost in that election, and its subsequent opposition to the new regime made it a campaign issue in 1936 and provoked the most daring Court-curbing proposal in our history, Roosevelt's Court-packing plan.

In asking finally whether or not judicial entanglement in political campaigns is healthy, Stephenson concludes that a Court "routinely the target of partisan attack and the focus of presidential campaigns" would jeopardize the rule of law, whereas a Court "thoroughly and consistently insulated from partisan attack" would undermine popular sovereignty. The virtue of moderation thus suggests to Stephenson that entanglement once a generation is enough. Jefferson thought that each future generation deserved its own revolution. If judicial review is the device by which the American constitutional system has made revolution unnecessary, then Stephenson's formula moderates Jefferson's in corresponding fashion.

JOHN B. TAYLOR

Washington College
Chestertown
Maryland

THURBER, TIMOTHY N. 1999. *The Politics of Equality: Hubert H. Humphrey and the African American Freedom Struggle.* Pp. ix, 352. New York: Columbia University Press. $40.00. Paperbound, $18.50.

There have been a number of books about the life and work of Hubert H. Humphrey, and many books about the civil rights movement, but here is a book exclusively about Hubert H. Humphrey and his unique role in the struggle of African Americans to achieve freedom and equality.

In *The Politics of Equality*, Timothy N. Thurber, of the History Department at the State University of New York at Oswego, traces Humphrey's life from its beginnings in South Dakota, through the long years of service as a U.S. senator from Minnesota, to his four years as vice president of the United States under President Lyndon B. Johnson. But throughout this highly readable and informative book, the focus is completely on Humphrey's many efforts to extend the fullest measure of civil rights protection to African Americans.

It is an exciting tale, quite worth the telling. Humphrey first emerged as a champion of African American civil rights when, as mayor of Minneapolis, Minnesota, he insisted that a civil rights plank be inserted in the 1948 Democratic Party platform. For years, while serving in the U.S. Senate, Humphrey introduced and actively supported numerous civil rights bills.

Humphrey's efforts bore their most conspicuous fruit when the Senate passed the Civil Rights Act of 1964. This landmark legislation, which outlawed racial segregation in places of public accommodation throughout the United States, was enacted only after Humphrey, as the Democratic floor leader for the bill in the U.S. Senate, successfully overcame a determined Southern filibuster of the proposed civil rights law.

Thurber brings a new perspective to Humphrey's efforts on behalf of African American civil rights. Humphrey was mainly interested in economic reforms, Thurber argues, rather than civil rights reforms. Humphrey believed that civil rights for African Americans would be meaningless if African Americans did not simultaneously get the good jobs and adequate incomes that would make civil rights worth having. Thurber leaves the impression that Humphrey was distracted by civil rights issues from working toward his most cherished goal: greater economic opportunity for all Americans of whatever race, creed, or ethnic origin.

With scholarly care and fairness, Thurber chronicles Humphrey's failures as well as successes in the civil rights arena. In fact, after the triumph of helping to pass the Civil Rights Act of 1964, Humphrey lost much of his effectiveness as a civil rights advocate. At the 1964 Democratic National Convention in Atlantic City, New Jersey, Humphrey had the unpleasant assignment of quieting down the strident civil rights demands of an outspoken group of African Americans from the state of Mississippi (the Mississippi Freedom Democratic Party). When Humphrey ran unsuccessfully for president of the United States in 1968, his strong pro–civil rights identity cost him the support of blue-collar white Democrats in major U.S. cities in the North and the East—and those lost blue-collar white votes were a major part of the reason Humphrey lost the 1968 presidential election to Richard Nixon.

This book is a must read for those interested in either Hubert Humphrey or the American civil rights movement. The book is also recommended for those who want to take a thought-provoking look at the way in which race and economic class became strangely intertwined in the American politics of the 1960s and 1970s. According to Thurber, by accomplishing so much for African American civil rights, Humphrey put the emphasis in Democratic Party politics on social concerns rather than economic concerns. The irony, Thurber concludes, is that, in his heart, Humphrey cared much more about his economic agenda (full employment) than his social agenda (African American civil rights).

ROBERT D. LOEVY

Colorado College
Colorado Springs

SOCIOLOGY

ACUÑA, RODOLFO F. 1998. *Sometimes There Is No Other Side: Chicanos and the Myth of Equality.* Pp. xiii, 292. Notre Dame, IN: University of Notre Dame Press. No price.

This is an important book. It lays out the paradigmatic, historical, and case-study materials to support the underlying proposition that truth and objectivity, especially in the humanities and social sciences, are constructed, and it outlines the crucial roles that juridical, educational, and legislative institutions play in that creation.

Strongly influenced by Thomas Kuhn's *Structure of Scientific Revolutions* in formulating his underlying intellectual template (while simultaneously rejecting its positivistic formulations), Acuña provides the major outlines of American university paradigms and values and simultaneously highlights the need for intense agitation to move these paradigmatic outlines beyond their stasis. Acuña admits that Kuhn's concentration on the scientific paradigm is less clear when applied to social phenomena, but neoliberalism is the prevailing mode of discourse for American culture and its associated positivistic orientation as especially promulgated by Comte. This overriding paradigm arranges many other embedded phenomena, such as law, the politics of history, and the prevailing ideology that comforts and guides institutions and especially those in higher education.

For Acuña, the American intellectual paradigm generally is in the hands of the history makers, who reflect the existing paradigm and create not only the outlines of history but also its substance. Behind this paradigm is the often unstated premise that the authority of substance and truth is in the hands of those most able to provide "objective" explanations and are indisputably fair in the treatment of materials and peoples. Thus, Chicano studies and ethnic studies in general seek to counter both exclusion and authoritative definition, and these fields of study have the unenviable task of developing optional paradigms as well as setting the record straight. Acuña would agree that such a process has been both uneven and intermittent, and in the present, both fields of study are becoming more and more like that which they opposed.

Yet, as is the case for most processes of creation, new oppositions arise to counter such semiparadigmatic oppositions as Chicano and ethnic studies. Acuña sets out a detailed account of the basis of the "culture war ideology" in the United States, which is led by a fascinating group of often internally variable proponents and organizations. This analysis is particularly interesting because it includes those who would seem to be liberal critics of the far Right such as Arthur Schlesinger, whose Committee of Scholars in Defense of History arose in response to Afrocentrism and ethnic studies.

Acuña would generally suggest that most American universities are heavily invested in the traditional paradigm and supported by an array of ideological commitments from Left to Right but all of which underscore a neoliberal and very conservative undemocratic process of inclusion, acceptance, and evaluation. "Objectivity" and "truth," from this point of view, are the coin words used by the academy to rationalize its own existence and support the hierarchical structures of evaluation and reward. Nowhere does this become more apparent than in the case study that Acuña presents concerning an attempt to appoint him as a professor of Chicano studies to the University of California, Santa Barbara, and the ensuing lawsuit of *Acuña* v. *The Regents of the University of California*. However, what is most instructive regarding other than just the procedural questions involved in this case is the manner in which elaborated convictions concerning objectivity and truth become intertwined with ideologies held by those involved in the evaluation process, the manner in which Acuña was attacked for his political beliefs rather than his scholarship, and, finally, the manner in which many levels of the university colluded both unintentionally and intentionally to deny him appointment as a senior professor at the university.

In truth, Acuña empirically validates the lack of real evaluation in the assessment process in which the upper administrators of the University of California, Santa Barbara, were engaged. For the most part, Acuña supports the argument that the very structure within the university precludes the possibility of the actual evaluation of a scholar's work (there are, however, chancellors and deans who do read everything). Nevertheless, Acuña won the case when the jury found that the University of California, Santa Barbara, had discriminated against him because of age and used the pretext that his work was not scholarly.

If I were to find fault with this important book, it would be to suggest strongly that institutions of whatever ilk are seldom total either ideologically or structurally. In fact, the decision in Acuña's favor points in that direction: regardless of institutional misrepresentation, legal interference from the court, and the power of a university system, the men and women of a jury were simply not taken in by all of the machinations of the court or university. This points to the need for paradigmatic change that calls for an enhancement of opportunities for "common folk" to participate democratically in all aspects of juridical, legislative, and educational institutions. In the final analysis, greater democracy is called for; otherwise, elaborated institutions with all of their attending systematic faults will continue to uphold an evaluation process in which decision makers do not even read the contents of what they are assessing to make terminal decisions.

CARLOS G. VÉLEZ-IBÁÑEZ

University of California
Riverside

FRIEDMAN, LAWRENCE M. 1999. *The Horizontal Society*. Pp. x, 310. New Haven, CT: Yale University Press. $29.95.

Lawrence M. Friedman's purpose is to explore why personal identity is intensifying in a world of homogenizing modernity. His answer is found in his conception of a horizontal society, by which he means the end of traditional status distinctions such as between nobles and serfs or males and females. Whereas, before the onset of modernity, one's life was very much predetermined by one's status within one's family and community, now the individual is free to choose his or her identity, roles, place of residence, and affiliations, whether to fellow bird-watchers or to a nation-state. This is also a society in which everyone expects to have individual rights. Two such rights are the right to migrate and citizenship rights, both of which Friedman explores in some detail.

The philosophies of individualism, rights, and personal choice are aspects of modernity that are spreading worldwide. Yet modernity simultaneously introduces personal strains that encourage the individual to look for connection with others. Thus horizontal society paradoxically fosters a sense of ethnic identity: nationalism is a social movement of expressive individualism, which is in itself an aspect of modernity. "Homeless minds" build new "nations," forming new identities through choice as substitutes for the caste and role security of earlier times.

Friedman writes largely by analogy. Thus, having investigated the rise of nationalism, he labels all those different groups in contemporary American society engaged in various forms of identity politics as nations: the feminist, gay, and deaf "nations" and even the "nations" of Gray Panthers and cancer patients. But the meaning of nationalism is specific and highly political, implying a search for sovereignty and the reordering of domestic and international political relations. Social movements, status groups, and interest groups are not nations, and their impact on domestic politics is far less radical than the impact of nationalism. By way of example, it is not true, as Friedman claims (p. 111), that "no blood has been shed" in the search for sovereignty in Quebec. In the high period of terrorism (1963-70), at least 3 people were killed and another 27 injured. Nationalism poses a serious threat to Canada as a political entity; by contrast, feminism, multiculturalism, and other such social movements can be easily absorbed in Canada's liberal democracy.

Friedman also exaggerates the extent to which vertical divisions in society have given way to horizontal individualism and choice. That society is now more horizontal does not mean it is without power relationships. The global spread of modernity is also the global spread of capitalism. As traditional roles and family and community supports erode under capitalism's onslaught, class takes on a greater, not a lesser, significance. The rolelessness that unemployment engenders in newly urbanizing societies is an important underlying cause of the identity politics of, for example, Muslim fundamentalism, which attracts relatively educated young men who cannot find jobs. And in the United States, class position continues to be the most important determinant of one's life chances. The apparent declining significance of class is an artifact both of politics and of fashionable postmodern academic analysis: it does not reflect individuals' real social situations.

This is a book that will receive a good deal of attention; it is very well written, uses interesting examples, and interprets rather heavy academic concepts in a lively way. One can question Friedman's sociology and his use of a single term to encapsulate a variety of social changes, but his discussion of two apparently conflicting social trends, the rise of individualism and the rise of nationalism, is convincing and compelling.

RHODA E. HOWARD-HASSMANN

McMaster University
Hamilton
Ontario
Canada

GREGORY, STEPHEN. 1998. *Black Corona: Race and the Politics of Place in an Urban Community*. Pp. xii, 282. Princeton, NJ: Princeton University Press. $29.95.

In *Black Corona*, Stephen Gregory explores the way the African American residents of Corona and East Elmhurst, in the borough of Queens, New York, have constructed for themselves—across time and within the physical spaces of their community—historical memories, collective meanings, and social identities. While, for Gregory, class position and class consciousness remain essential elements in social movement formation and practice, he works from the understanding that activism is shaped by the informal networks that structure everyday life. These networks he sees as an inherent part of the process through which people name and create cultural identities for themselves and organize resistance against the intrusions of political and economic power.

Given this paradigm, Gregory wants to overturn what he calls "power-evasive discourses," which assume poverty and social pathology to be the key categories in the study of urban African American communities. Such discourses tend to overlook the complexity and creative energy of the social and political activity that informs the neighborhood spaces of black life. Gregory's subject, therefore, is precisely the way the cultural networks and political activism within these communities vitally produce and reinforce each other. With its re-creation of the individuality of local activists, its painstaking retelling of Corona's social history since the late nineteenth century, its record of how that history informs and shapes current social practice, and its discussion of the continually revised meanings and content of that practice, Gregory's study makes an invaluable contribution to both the literature on black community life and the literature on the character of local political activism generally.

Specifically, the first part of the book examines the history of black community activism in Corona from the late nineteenth century, when upwardly mobile African American families began seeking refuge from growing racial violence in Manhattan, through the rise of a social infrastructure of churches, fraternal organizations, and mutual benefit societies in the interwar years, to the involvement of Corona and East Elmhurst in the civil rights movement and the war on poverty. The work then moves to contemporary activism. It looks first at efforts of black residents of Lefrak City to organize their young people and to challenge perceptions of the apartment complex as a site of crime, welfare dependency, and family disorganization. The next chapter looks at the character of the leading block associations in East Elmhurst and their impact on both local and citywide politics. The final section of the book traces the attempt of the block associations to work with their white Jackson Heights neighbors to take on the Port Authority with respect to its decision to build an automated guided train to LaGuardia Airport. Here, Gregory focuses on the ability of the state, in the guise of the Port Authority, to divide communities and co-opt neighborhoods by setting up agendas that get people to focus on local concerns and short-term interests.

Through persuasive and engaging ethnographic detail, Gregory brings to life the individuals who, drawing upon both organizational and personal commitment, give leadership to the community and wage a constant struggle to enhance its independence and autonomy. A weakness of the book, however, is its tendency to force the cultural and political activities of the Corona residents into a procrustean bed of postmodern theorizing. Too often Gregory relies upon a jargon that, in its efforts to name and convey the meaning of the community's social practices and networks, lacks clarity. A more accessible language would have strengthened the analysis.

Through a close, ethnographic examination of both the history and contemporary strivings of activism in the contiguous middle- and working-class black neighborhoods of East Elmhurst and Corona, Gregory has painstakingly documented the process of identity construction as it occurs in the racialized spaces of the postindustrial city. The identities that emerge are complex and heterogeneous. The residents, on the one hand, bring multiple histories, conflicting class positions, and a variety of political perspectives to their common spatial situation. On the other hand, they face a set of state actors ready to construct stereotypical and demeaning images of who they are and of the sources of the problems they face. The residents, therefore, must constantly reconstruct and renegotiate their sense of how they are related to one another as a community. These are complexities that Gregory's study captures well.

JOSEPH KLING

St. Lawrence University
Canton
New York

HERMAN, ANDREW. 1999. *The "Better Angels" of Capitalism: Rhetoric, Narrative, and Moral Identity Among Men of the American Upper Class.* Pp. ix, 287. Boulder, CO: Westview Press. $55.00.

Ours is a language that works in terms of things and substances that can be seen as occupying certain places within a space. In speaking of ourselves and our surroundings in this way, however, we often speak metaphorically—we understand what is not immediately perceptible in terms of what is. Although we all inhabit a similar basic space of practical bodily activities in which five chairs are five chairs for everyone, when it comes to those aspects of our lives that do not have an immediately perceptible structure, we must, like a good novelist, create them. Nowhere is this more crucial to us than in our moral lives. Indeed, if we are to take control of our lives, to be masters of our own fates, the words we use to talk to ourselves about ourselves and our relations to our surroundings are crucial. They work to draw our attention to the opportunities for action available to us and to how we should orient ourselves toward such openings.

This is Andrew Herman's aim in this richly textured book. Through interviews with a sample of 18 men drawn from the top 1-2 percent of the population in terms of wealth and income distribution, he wants to come to an understanding of the symbolic realms in terms of which such men make sense of their wealth to themselves. How do they create an imaginary social reality around themselves within which their financial wealth can be transformed into moral worth? What allows them to experience their actions not just as intelligible and legitimate but as noble and honorable?

They do it by constructing themselves as " 'better angels' of capitalism," Herman suggests, as people who see themselves as doing good works in the community. Herman takes this term and the central theme of his book from the following passage in George Bush's presidential nomination acceptance speech at the 1988 Republican National Convention: "Prosperity has a purpose. It is to allow us to pursue 'the better angels' [of capitalism]. . . . Prosperity . . . means taking your idealism and making it concrete by certain acts of goodness."

But one cannot transform oneself into a "better angel" all alone. Talking solely to oneself cannot make it so unless one can draw on symbolic resources widely available, historically, to all in one's cultural surroundings. Herman traces the crucial symbolic resources back to two major, creative narratives in Western social theory: to Machiavelli's writing in fifteenth- and sixteenth-century Italy on the relations between fortune and virtue and to Adam Smith's writing in eighteenth-century Scotland on the marketplace. Together, these narratives provide the symbolic resources in terms of which it is possible for wealthy men justifiably to develop around themselves a "principality," a sovereign realm of autonomy, freedom, and control, within which they can experience themselves as having overcome fortune by the strength of their personal virtues.

Such a sovereign realm, however, is defined solely in terms of things procured in the marketplace—money, wealth, commodities—and one's virtues, in terms of one's abilities to master "abject" others, that is, those who are defined as being weak and corrupt and lacking the virtues of the sovereign subject. Thus, in such a realm, as Herman points out, good citizenship and the doing of concrete acts of goodness is a luxury that only the rich can afford—rather than being a necessary and intrinsic part of everyone's place in daily life. "Shouldn't we all have the privilege of pursuing and being 'better angels'?" is Herman's concluding question.

JOHN SHOTTER

University of New Hampshire
Durham

NUSSBAUM, MARTHA C. 1999. *Sex and Social Justice*. Pp. ix, 476. New York: Oxford University Press. $35.00.

This collection of 15 essays articulates and defends Nussbaum's conception of liberal feminism. The essays provide a compelling answer to the question, What could sex and sexuality have to do with justice? Traditionally, liberalism has considered sexuality to be a private matter, and a person's sex to be relatively unimportant. Nussbaum, a feminist and advocate of gay rights, takes issue with both contentions. Moreover, many feminists consider the framework of liberalism, with its male emphasis on individual freedom and choice, to be inadequate to the experience of women. In addition, many feminists are also suspicious of universalist theories of justice. Hence, Nussbaum's liberal feminism is distinctive both in relation to liberalism and in relation to feminism.

Nussbaum's perspective is internationalist. Several of the finest essays in the book address the economic plight of women in developing countries, and they argue that conventional approaches in development economics are inadequate to the problem. While Nussbaum's internationalist perspective is a needed antidote to the narrow parochialism of much academic feminism, its universal reach must encounter the issue of cultural relativism. Nussbaum argues effectively against relativism in "Judging Other Cultures: The Case of Genital Mutilation." Her argument is impressive because it does not simply rely upon the

self-refuting character of relativistic arguments, but it points to specific problems with the relativist's monolithic notion of a culture, and it insists on sticking very close to the facts surrounding the cultural practice of genital mutilation.

Nussbaum, unlike many liberals and liberal feminists, argues for the social and cultural shaping of our preferences and desires. Rather than positing desire or preference as an unanalyzed given unique to each person, Nussbaum, influenced by the feminist thought of Catharine MacKinnon and Andrea Dworkin, argues that culture and law play an important role in forming our desires. Sexual desire, for example, is shaped by cultural institutions like pornography; it is a historical and cultural formation and not a natural force. Like MacKinnon, Dworkin, and Foucault, Nussbaum considers sexual desire, and the cultural institutions that form sexual desire, to be historical and contingent and open to criticism. Like MacKinnon and Dworkin, she finds much to criticize in some pornography, although she considers the legal remedy they endorse to be deeply problematic. With her views on the cultural shaping of sexual desire and her criticism of pornography, Nussbaum's liberalism parts company from classical liberalism, which considers the realm of sexuality to be private and pornography to be free speech.

In other essays, however, Nussbaum is closer to the traditional liberal position on sexuality. Her essay advocating the legalization of prostitution, for example, emphasizes the importance of individual choice and downplays the idea that our desires, as well as our choices, might be socially formed in ways that are deeply damaging to us. While advocating more options for employment for impoverished women who choose prostitution, Nussbaum does not connect prostitution with pornography and heterosexuality as one might expect given her sympathetic reading of MacKinnon and Dworkin.

One of the more fascinating essays in the volume, "Platonic Love and Colorado Law: The Relevance of Ancient Greek Norms to Modern Sexual Controversies," describes Nussbaum's testimony concerning an amendment intended to nullify civil rights ordinances protecting homosexuals, which had been passed in Aspen, Boulder, and Denver. In a complex argument, Nussbaum maintains both that the mores of Greek sexuality were importantly different from ours (sexuality is a historical, cultural institution) and that one difference was an acceptance of certain behaviors that we would label "homosexual."

With this collection, Nussbaum has defined a powerful and original feminist position. It is essential reading for feminists, political theorists, and legal scholars.

CHARLOTTE WITT

University of New Hampshire
Durham

SINGER, SIMON I. 1996. *Recriminalizing Delinquency: Violent Juvenile Crime and Juvenile Justice Reform.* Pp. xiii, 230. New York: Cambridge University Press. $54.95. Paperbound, $19.95.

Sociologist Simon Singer draws upon the experiences of a single jurisdiction (New York State) to examine the most prominent trend in contemporary juvenile crime policy—the transfer of young offenders to criminal court, where they can be tried as adults. Nearly every state legislature, the U.S. Congress, and virtually all candidates for elected office now embrace criminal-court transfer as a necessary keystone of juvenile crime policy. Thousands of young people are handed over to adult courts every year based upon the presumption that criminal courts deliver more severe and more certain justice and thus reduce crime.

Several researchers have ably examined this presumption (see works by Charles Frazier, Donna Bishop, Jeffrey Fagan, Barry Field, and Franklin Zimring). Most of the previous work on criminal-court transfer, however, is atheoretical and descriptive and is often set within a legal or justice-system framework rather than being grounded in social science. Singer attempts to do the latter and largely succeeds.

Drawing upon an array of material, including media accounts, interviews, and administrative data, Singer reviews the origins of juvenile justice, describes its decision-making culture, and explores the enduring political appeal of transfer laws. The book includes a brisk analysis of crime trends in New York, before and after the reforms that essentially removed from the juvenile court all 15- year-olds and 14-year-olds (and even some 13-year-olds) charged with serious crimes.

In the end, Singer finds no consistent differences in serious juvenile crime following New York's policy reform. In most instances where crime appears to fall, rates dropped in upstate New York but not in New York City (or vice versa), raising doubts about the influence of statewide polices. When rates did drop in New York City, there were often comparable declines in nearby jurisdictions (for example, Philadelphia) that had not expanded criminal-court transfer laws.

The book suggests several explanations for the lack of a deterrent effect. Among these is Singer's central thesis, namely, that there are so many players in juvenile justice systems that the decisions of one group are never totally accepted by other groups. Prosecutors never charge every young offender arrested by police. Judges never impose harsh sentences on every offender charged by prosecutors. This "loose coupling" creates a justice system that is a "negotiated order" and reduces the chances that a single policy initiative will have a consistent effect on crime. Ironically, loose coupling also increases the system's need for potent symbols of uniformity such as punitive criminal-court transfer laws.

Singer's use of organizational perspective is a welcome addition to the literature on juvenile justice reform, and loose coupling is a useful device for tracing the impact of justice policies. This approach will be even more valuable, however, when loose coupling becomes more than a device. For instance, Singer mentions that jurisdictions often have measurable differences in the extent to which they are loosely coupled. A detailed analysis of these differences and their impact on policy should be revealing.

The final chapter of the book may be disquieting for ardent opponents of criminal-court transfer. After thoroughly discrediting transfer as a crime-control policy, Singer allows that juvenile justice proponents should learn to accept transfer because it expresses the public's genuine desire for punishment. Moreover, he suggests that writing transfer policies into law may be beneficial because it encourages the justice system to focus on the severity of the offenses rather than on the nature of offenders (the traditional juvenile court philosophy). Singer anticipates that such a shift in focus will prevent criminal-court transfer from being used against nonviolent juveniles. Some readers may find it hard to share Singer's faith in the good sense of American justice, especially considering the passion displayed by state and federal lawmakers as they continue to escalate mandatory sentences for drug offenders.

JEFFREY A. BUTTS

Urban Institute
Washington, D.C.

ECONOMICS

GRISWOLD, CHARLES L., JR. 1999. *Adam Smith and the Virtues of Enlightenment.* Pp. xiv, 412. New York: Cambridge University Press. $59.95. Paperbound, $21.95.

Adam Smith was not a prolific writer. He published only two books in his lifetime. *An Inquiry into the Nature and Causes of the Wealth of Nations* (1776) more or less quickly established his reputation as a brilliant political economist. Indeed, in time, this work so eclipsed the writings of his predecessors on this subject that Smith, arguably erroneously, became known as the founder of the discipline of political economy.

Smith's only other book published in his lifetime was *The Theory of Moral Sentiments.* It was first published in 1759; the sixth edition, which contains extensive revisions and changes, was published shortly before Smith's death in 1790. Not long after Smith's death, this work nearly disappeared from the philosophical canon. Griswold seeks to restore this latter work as "a resource for our reflections on modernity"; he presents *The Theory of Moral Sentiments* as an overlooked, misunderstood resource that may be used to justify and defend the ideals of Enlightenment thought.

As an explanation and commentary on *The Theory of Moral Sentiments,* Griswold's book succeeds admirably. Griswold explains how Smith bases his theory on the fundamental role of the sentiment or emotion sympathy, which Smith uses to mean fellow feeling with any passion whatever. This sympathy is worked on by the imagination, to imagine how we would be in the actor's situation. We then imagine how other people view the appropriateness of our behavior, and we use that feedback to modify our beings. In time, we imagine how an impartial spectator would view us, thus internalizing conscience and our sense of duty. Hence, for Smith, morals arise in society as various actors and spectators, both real and imagined, interact.

Yet Griswold does more than just elaborate upon Smith's *Theory of Moral Sentiments*. Griswold's Smith will surprise most readers. Drawing upon Smith's posthumously published *Essays on Philosophical Subjects*, particularly the essay "The Principles Which Lead and Direct Philosophical Enquiries; Illustrated by the History of Astronomy," Griswold argues that Smith was actually a Humean theological and epistemological skeptic. Essentially, Smith may be viewed as Hume's greatest follower, who carried out and enacted Hume's skepticism. Moreover, Griswold's Smith is an exceptionally clever fellow, who is not above quoting selectively, as when, for example, he uses Plato against himself. Smith strives to remain in the domain of appearances. Nature for Smith is unfeeling and indifferent to us; God, if such exists, is not a source of rational governance; Platonic ideals, essences, or substances are to be scrupulously avoided. Instead, like Goffman's *Presentation of Self in Everyday Life*, Smith views us as critics and players in the theater of the world. Indeed, Griswold views the theater metaphor as a guiding principle of Smith's skeptical thought; we are not allowed backstage or anywhere else from which we can see the true meaning of life, morals, or reality.

Hence, by Griswold's reading, for Smith (as for Marx), it is human production that drives theory and practice forward. Morals, as well as religious, scientific, and economic thought, are essentially productions of the imagination. These productions are not mere fantasies, but they are the results of feelings, sentiments, emotions, some reasoning, as well as a large aesthetic component that induces humans to strive to create order, harmony, symmetry, beauty, and

intellectual tranquillity. Griswold fears that if Smith's Humean skepticism becomes the common intellectual property of society, it could easily degenerate into a crude subjective, narcissistic expressivism, giving destructive priority to the subjective feelings of the actor, hence severely undermining morality.

The economic upshot of Griswold's reading is this: the pursuit of wealth is fueled by a deception; nature is not, after all, a harmonious whole; there is no miraculous spontaneous harmony that will take care of everything if only we let the natural course be; nature cannot ultimately be our guide; and the invisible hand is merely a sophisticated expression of the imagination. Hence, for Griswold, most people, most of the time, have fundamentally, seriously, misread *The Wealth of Nations*.

Adam Smith and the Virtues of Enlightenment is written by and largely for philosophers; it is not an easy read. Yet it should be studied by all who are interested in Adam Smith; it may fundamentally change the way they view Smith. Moreover, given the importance of its subject matter, Griswold's work merits a careful, deep reading by a large part of the contemporary literati.

SPENCER J. PACK

Connecticut College
New London

RAYNAULD, ANDRE and JEAN-PIERRE VIDAL. 1998. *Labour Standards and International Com- petitiveness: A Comparative Analysis of Developing and Industrialized Countries*. Pp. ix, 117. Cheltenham, U.K.: Edward Elgar. $70.00.

The establishment of uniform standards regulating working conditions has recently resurfaced on the agenda of international trade negotiations and in the broader public policy debate. The issue is a difficult one both from a humanitarian perspective and from the point of view of rigorous analytics. Though much work has been done, little can be said conclusively concerning the desirability of labor standards or which standards should be uniformly adopted. In this slim volume, Raynauld and Vidal weigh in on several aspects of the issue with thoughtful microeconomic arguments and empirical evidence.

Raynauld and Vidal begin with a detailed and interesting discussion of the history of labor standards in the United States and Europe. The historical events are embedded in a presentation of the broader political debate surrounding the establishment of labor standards within each country and in various international agencies. In the view of the authors, the fundamental tension underlying the labor standards debate turns on whether the proponents of labor standards are pursuing humanitarian goals or whether their objective is simply to protect domestic industry.

The authors themselves try to walk a very thin line. They search for rigorous arguments supporting the imposition of labor standards solidly grounded in microeconomic theory while arguing that such standards do not have implications for international trade. That is, there are strong arguments for labor standards, but we do not have to fear that these standards will affect our international competitiveness.

Several points made in the analytical chapter are well taken and worth emphasizing. For example, the notion that labor standards undermine competitiveness by eating into firm profits is quite nicely handled. Raynauld and Vidal point out that a business cannot survive if the total compensation package for each worker exceeds the worker's contribution to the firm's value. A firm that offers improved working conditions necessarily must pay

lower money wages, leaving the competitiveness of the firm unaffected.

However, the discussion avoids the critical issue concerning competitiveness: what happens to a firm that is forced by law or international agreement to improve working conditions that are not as highly valued by workers as their money wages? These firms will certainly find themselves disadvantaged in the marketplace.

The central analytical point of the book also suffers from incomplete treatment. Raynauld and Vidal's most forceful argument in favor of labor standards in developing countries turns on the possibility that the labor market has two potential equilibrium wages: a low equilibrium, characterized by inhumanely long working hours and a subsistence wage, and a high equilibrium, characterized by a tolerable workweek and a living wage. The argument is made that social policy can be used to outlaw the low-wage equilibrium, thereby forcing the market to the high-wage equilibrium.

Raynauld and Vidal are not the first to suggest that the labor market might have two equilibria. That is, the demand and supply of labor intersect twice: once at a low wage and again at a high wage. Virtually all of the arguments of this type suffer from some analytical weakness, and Raynauld and Vidal's is no exception. Even if one accepts the labor supply curve as derived by the authors and the analysis as presented, the low-wage equilibrium turns out to be unstable. That is, the normal dynamics of the labor market will lead the economy toward the high-wage equilibrium. No intervention is required.

The empirical analysis suffers from a similar weakness. The authors present evidence that high-standard countries have enjoyed an increase in their share of international trade, leading to the conclusion that labor standards have not undermined international competitiveness. However, their evidence, in fact, points to the opposite conclusion. Consider, for example, how we would expect labor standards to affect a labor-scarce country that imports labor-intensive goods and exports capital-intensive goods. Labor standards are very likely to further contract the production of labor-intensive goods, requiring greater imports. Such a country will experience a rise in its share of world trade. Do we want to say that the increase in trade has made this country more internationally competitive? No, of course not. In fact, the labor standards have made the import-competing industry less competitive, necessitating the increase in trade.

Raynauld and Vidal have made an interesting and thought-provoking contribution to the debate on labor standards. Much work remains to be done, however, to fully evaluate their analytical points and empirical evidence.

DRUSILLA K. BROWN

Tufts University
Medford
Massachusetts

OTHER BOOKS

AARON, HENRY J. and JOHN B. SHOVEN. 1999. *Should the United States Privatize Social Security?* Pp. xii, 178. Cambridge: MIT Press. $24.95.

ALBROW, MARTIN. 1999. *Sociology: The Basics.* Pp. xiv, 203. New York: Routledge. $60.00. Paperbound, $16.99.

ANDERSON, JEFFREY J., ed. 1999. *Regional Integration and Democracy: Expanding on the European Experience.* Pp. viii, 334. Lanham, MD: Rowman & Littlefield. $65.00. Paperbound, $24.95.

BECKER, DAVID G. and RICHARD L. SKLAR, eds. 1999. *Postimperialism and World Politics.* Pp. x, 397. Westport, CT: Greenwood Press. $69.50.

BENNETT, WILLIAM J. 1999. *The Death of Outrage: Bill Clinton and the Assault on American Ideals.* Pp. 170. New York: Touchstone. Paperbound, $30.00.

BENOIT, WILLIAM L. 1999. *Seeing Spots: A Functional Analysis of Presidential Television Advertisements, 1952-1996.* Pp. xii, 238. Westport, CT: Praeger. $59.95.

BENSON, DELWIN E., ROSS "SKIP" SHELTON, and DON W. STEINBACH. 1999. *Wildlife Stewardship and Recreation on Private Lands.* Pp. xiii, 170. College Station: Texas A&M University Press. $29.95.

BERTSCH, GARY K., SEEMA GAHLAUT, and ANUPAM SRIVASTAVA, eds. 1999. *Engaging India: United States Strategic Relations with the World's Largest Democracy.* Pp. xix, 284. New York: Routledge. $75.00. Paperbound, $24.99.

BLASSINGAME, JOHN W., JOHN R. McKIVIGAN, and PETER P. HINKS, eds. 1999. *The Frederick Douglass Papers.* Vol. 1. Pp. lvi, 222. New Haven, CT: Yale University Press. $45.00.

BOGDANOR, VERNON. 1999. *Devolution in the United Kingdom.* Pp. viii, 329. New York: Oxford University Press. Paperbound, $14.95.

BRUSTEIN, ROBERT. 1998. *Cultural Calisthenics: Writings on Race, Politics, and Theatre.* Pp. 291. Chicago: Ivan R. Dee. Paperbound, no price.

CAMPBELL, DAVID and MICHAEL J. SHAPIRO, eds. 1999. *Moral Spaces: Rethinking Ethics and World Politics.* Pp. xx, 268. Minneapolis: University of Minnesota Press. Paperbound, $19.95.

CARR, DAVID W. 1999. *The Significance of Gorbachev's Economic Reforms.* Pp. 98. Danbury, CT: Routledge. Paperbound, $13.95.

COLUMBUS, FRANK, ed. 1999. *Central and Eastern Europe in Transition.* Vol. 3. Pp. vi, 293. Commack, NY: Nova Science. $59.00.

COOK, LINDA J., MITCHELL A. ORENSTEIN, and MARILYN RUESCHEMEYER, eds. 1999. *Left Parties and Social Policy in Post-Communist Europe.* Pp. vii, 270. Boulder, CO: Westview Press. $69.00. Paperbound, $25.00.

CREESE, GILLIAN. 1999. *Contracting Masculinity: Gender, Class, and Race in a White-Collar Union.* Pp. vii, 278. New York: Oxford University Press. Paperbound, $21.95.

CUNNINGHAM, ROBERT, III and ROBERT M. CUNNINGHAM, JR. 1997. *The Blues: A History of the Blue Cross and Blue Shield System.* Pp. xii, 311. DeKalb: Northern Illinois University Press. No price.

DIAMOND, PETER A., ed. 1999. *Issues in Privatizing Social Security: Report of an Expert Panel of the National Academy of Social Insurance.* Pp. xvii, 168. Cambridge: MIT Press. $25.00.

FAWCETT, LOUISE and YEZID SAYIGH, eds. 1999. *The Third World Beyond the Cold War: Continuity and Change.* Pp. viii, 294. New York: Oxford University Press. $78.00.

FISHMAN, JOSHUA A., ed. 1999. *Handbook of Language and Ethnic Identity.* Pp. xii, 468. New York: Oxford University Press. $65.00.

FLEMING, THOMAS. 1999. *Duel: Alexander Hamilton, Aaron Burr and the Future of America.* Pp. xiii, 466. New York: Basic Books. $30.00.

GANGULY, RAJAT. 1998. *Kin State Intervention in Ethnic Conflicts: Lessons from South Asia.* Pp. 266. New Delhi: Sage. No price.

GIRLING, JOHN. 1998. *France: Political and Social Change.* Pp. vi, 182. New York: Routledge. $75.00. Paperbound, $24.99.

GOFF, BRIAN and ARTHUR A. FLEISHER III. 1999. *Spoiled Rotten: Affluence, Anxiety, and Social Decay in America.* Pp. xii, 254. Boulder, CO: Westview Press. $25.00.

GONSALVES, ERIC and NANCY JETLY, eds. 1999. *The Dynamics of South Asia: Regional Cooperation and SAARC.* Pp. 277. New Delhi: Sage. $45.00.

GORDON, HAIM, ed. 1999. *Looking Back at the June 1967 War.* Pp. xiii, 203. Westport, CT: Praeger. $59.95.

GRAHAM-BROWN, SARAH. 1999. *Sanctioning Saddam: The Politics of Intervention in Iraq.* Pp. xvii, 380. New York: St. Martin's Press. $35.00.

GRASSO, CHRISTOPHER. 1999. *A Speaking Aristocracy: Transforming Public Discourse in Eighteenth-Century Connecticut.* Pp. viii, 511. Chapel Hill: University of North Carolina Press. $59.95. Paperbound, $24.95.

HARRIS, J. R. 1998. *Industrial Espionage and Technology Transfer: Britain and France in the Eighteenth Century.* Pp. xviii, 655. Brookfield, VT: Ashgate. $113.95.

HARRISS-WHITE, BARBARA and S. SUBRAMANIAN, eds. 1999. *Illfare in India: Essays on India's Social Sector in Honour of S. Guhan.* Pp. 411. New Delhi: Sage. No price.

HASAN, ZOYA. 1998. *Quest for Power: Oppositional Movements and Post-Congress Politics in Uttar Pradesh.* Pp. viii, 280. New York: Oxford University Press. $24.95.

HEARN, ROGER. 1999. *U.N. Peacekeeping in Action: The Namibian Experience.* Pp. xiv, 272. Commack, NY: Nova Science. $59.00.

HERRMANN, PETER, ed. 1999. *Challenges for a Global Welfare System.* Pp. 180. Commack, NY: Nova Science. $59.00.

HOPMANN, P. TERRENCE. 1998. *The Negotiation Process and the Resolution of International Conflicts.* Pp. xi, 353. Columbia: University of South Carolina Press. $24.95.

HUNTER, HELEN-LOUISE. 1999. *Kim Il-Song's North Korea.* Pp. xviii, 262. Westport, CT: Praeger. $45.00.

JUDGE, DAVID. 1999. *Representation: Theory and Practice in Britain.* Pp. ix, 230. New York: Routledge. $100.00. Paperbound, $25.99.

KRIEGER, JOEL. 1999. *British Politics in the Global Age: Can Social Democracy Survive?* Pp. xv, 213. New York: Oxford University Press. $49.95. Paperbound, $19.95.

LASATER, MARTIN L. 1999. *The Taiwan Conundrum in United States China Policy.* Pp. xiv, 329. Boulder, CO: Westview Press. $69.00.

LIEVEN, ANATOL. 1998. *Chechnya: Tombstone of Russian Power.* Pp. xii, 436. New Haven, CT: Yale University Press. $35.00.

LISTER, MARJORIE, ed. 1999. *New Perspectives on European Union Develop-*

ment Cooperation. Pp. viii, 175. Boulder, CO: Westview Press. $60.00.

MALIZIA, EMIL E. and EDWARD J. FESER. 1999. *Understanding Local Economic Development.* Pp. xvi, 298. New Brunswick, NJ: CUPR Press. $24.95.

MOSSE, GEORGE L. 1999. *The Fascist Revolution: Toward a General Theory of Fascism.* Pp. xviii, 230. New York: Howard Fertig. $35.00.

PACHAURI, SAROJ, ed. 1999. *Implementing a Reproductive Health Agenda in India: The Beginning.* Pp. xlvii, 608. New York: Population Council. $15.00.

PEREZ, LOUIS A., JR. 1999. *On Becoming Cuban: Identity, Nationality, and Culture.* Pp. xiv, 579. Chapel Hill: University of Northern Carolina Press. $39.95.

PETERSON, DALE. 1999. *Storyville, USA.* Pp. viii, 299. Athens: University of Georgia Press. $25.95.

PRAKASH, GYAN. 1999. *Another Reason: Science and the Imagination of Modern India.* Pp. viii, 511. Princeton, NJ: Princeton University Press. $49.50. Paperbound, $17.95.

ROUNTREE, HELEN C. and THOMAS E. DAVIDSON. 1997. *Eastern Shore Indians of Virginia and Maryland.* Pp. xv, 329. Charlottesville: University Press of Virginia. Paperbound, no price.

RUBIN, MIRI. 1999. *Gentile Tales: The Narrative Assault on Late Medieval Jews.* Pp. xiii, 266. New Haven, CT: Yale University Press. $30.00.

SAMADDAR, RANABIR. 1999. *The Marginal Nation: Transborder Migration from Bangladesh to West Bengal.* Pp. 227. New Delhi: Sage. No price.

SCHERER, JENNIFER M. and RITA J. SIMON. 1999. *Euthanasia and the Right to Die: A Comparative View.* Pp. viii, 151. Lanham, MD: Rowman &

Littlefield. $59.00. Paperbound, $22.95.

SMITH, THOMAS T. 1999. *The United States Army and the Texas Frontier Economy, 1845-1900.* Pp. xi, 307. College Station: Texas A&M University Press. $34.95.

STACK, JOHN F., JR. and LUI HEBRON, eds. 1999. *The Ethnic Entanglement: Conflict and Intervention in World Politics.* Pp. viii, 174. Westport, CT: Praeger. $59.95.

STEANS, JILL. 1998. *Gender and International Relations.* Pp. vi, 224. New Brunswick, NJ: Rutgers University Press. $49.00. Paperbound, $19.00.

STIMSON, RICHARD A. 1999. *Playing with the Numbers: How So-called Experts Mislead Us About the Economy.* Pp. 284. High Point, NC: Westchester Press. Paperbound, $12.00.

STROUTHOUS, ANDREW. 1999. *United States Labor and Political Action, 1918-24.* Pp. xi, 208. New York: St. Martin's Press. $64.00.

STRUYK, RAYMOND J. 1999. *Reconstructive Critics: Think Tanks in Post-Soviet Bloc Democracies.* Pp. xiv, 267. Washington, DC: Urban Institute Press. $49.50. Paperbound, $23.50.

TIMMERMANS, STEFAN. 1999. *Sudden Death and the Myth of CPR.* Pp. xvii, 256. Philadelphia: Temple University Press. $54.95. Paperbound, $22.95.

TUCKER, SPENCER C. 1999. *Vietnam.* Pp. ix, 244. Lexington: University Press of Kentucky. $42.00. Paperbound, $19.00.

WAYNE, STEPHEN J. 2000. *The Road to the White House, 2000: The Politics of Presidential Elections.* Pp. xv, 345. New York: St. Martin's Press. $35.00.

WEBER, RONALD E. and PAUL BRACE, eds. 1999. *American State and Local Politics: Directions for the 21st Century.* Pp. xiv, 361. New York: Chatham House. Paperbound, $29.95.

INDEX

Reliable

Confidence in knowing. It's important to feel secure about your insurance coverage. Now you can. AAPSS carefully selects experienced providers with the financial stability to ensure competitive insurance options for its members.

Take advantage of one of your best member-ship benefits. Affordable coverage. Reliable providers. Portable benefits. **Call 800 424-9883** to speak to a customer service representative. Because you want an insurance plan you can count on.

GROUP INSURANCE FOR AAPSS MEMBERS
Cancer Expense • Catastrophe Major Medical Dental Plan • High Limit Accident • Medicare Supplement • Member Assistance • Term Life

Rated among the *top ten** journals in both Political and Social Science.
*Source: ISI®'s Journal Citation Reports®

Politics & Society

Edited by
The Politics Society Editorial Board

. . . an alternative, critical voice of the social sciences that raises questions about the way the world is organized politically, economically, and socially. Presents engaged as well as rational discourse and reconstructs social inquiry through scholarship addressed to fundamental questions of theory, policy, and politics.

Recent Article Highlights

Aristide R. Zolberg and Long Litt Woon
Why Islam Is Like Spanish:Cultural Incorporation in Europe and the United States

Sanford Schram and Joe Soss
The Real Value of Welfare:Why Poor Families Do Not Migrate

Marc Schneiberg
Political and Institutional Conditions for Governance by Association: Private Order and Price Controls in American Fire Insurance

Claire Jean Kim
The Racial Triangulation of Asian Americans

Heather L. Williams
Mobile Capital and Transborder Labor Rights Mobilization

Quarterly:
March, June, September, December
Yearly rates:
Individual $64
Institution $267
576 pages
ISSN: 0032-3292

SAGE CONTENTS ALERT

STAY CURRENT ON THE LATEST RESEARCH...

FREE.

Sage Publications is pleased to announce **SAGE CONTENTS ALERT** a pre-publication alerting service **FREE** to all subscribers. If you have e-mail, you can now receive the table of contents for any journal you choose, delivered by e-mail directly to your PC.

You can automatically receive:

- Future Article Titles and Author(s)
- Volume and Issue Number
- Journal Title and Publication Date

Plus:

- Calls for Papers
- Special Issue Announcements
- News from the Editor

Registration is simple – just give us your name, the journal title(s) you want to receive, and your e-mail address.

E-mail: <u>contents.alert@sagepub.com</u>
Visit Website: <u>www.sagepub.com</u>
Or mail to: Sage Contents Alert
Sage Publications
2455 Teller Road
Thousand Oaks, CA 91320

VISIT SAGE ONLINE AT: WWW.SAGEPUB.COM

Find what you are looking for faster!

Our advanced search engine allows you to find what you are looking for quickly and easily. Searches can be conducted by:

- Author/Editor
- Keyword/Discipline
- Product Type
- ISSN/ISBN
- Title

Payment online is secure and confidential!

Rest assured that all Web site transactions are completed on a secured server. Only you and Sage Customer Service have access to ordering information. Using your Visa, MasterCard, Discover, or American Express card, you can complete your order in just minutes.

Placing your order is easier than ever before!

Ordering online is simple using the Sage shopping cart feature. Just click on the "Buy Now!" logo next to the product, and it is automatically added to your shopping cart. When you are ready to check out, a listing of all selected products appears for confirmation before your order is completed.

WE'RE ONLINE!
www.sagepub.com